ON A SAILOR'S GRAVE
(NO ROSES GROW)

First published in 2005 by

WOODFIELD PUBLISHING
Bognor Regis, West Sussex, England
www.woodfieldpublishing.com

© Mike Kemble, 2005

The right of Mike Kemble
to be identified as Author of this work
has been asserted in accordance with
the Copyright, Designs and Patents Act 1988

ISBN 1-873203-99-3

On a Sailor's Grave (No Roses Grow)

Maritime Disasters of the Second World War

MIKE KEMBLE

Woodfield

To Sue, my wife – a computer widow!

CONTENTS

Foreword

As part of the generation that was born just after the end of the Second World War, and having recently completed 36 years service in the Royal Navy myself, I have always had the greatest respect for the men and women who defended this country so selflessly throughout those very difficult, testing and often frightening years. Even today, I feel humble in the company of surviving veterans because they shared an experience that today's generation can barely begin to imagine. If we, their descendants, are to heed the hard-won lessons of the past and avoid the horrors of another global conflict, then there can never be too much history written. That is why I welcome Mike Kemble's absorbing contribution.

The author has compiled this anthology through a self-professed fascination with the Second World War and its maritime aspects in particular. He has clearly committed many hours of painstaking research to this project, a fact made evident by the detail included in the key events that he describes. Whilst some events are well known to history enthusiasts, I particularly like his inclusion of other, less well-documented, subjects. This provides a nice balance to his work for which he should be congratulated.

Finally, it is very fitting that this book should be published in the year that has marked the sixtieth anniversary of the end of the Second World War. As the numbers of those who experienced these events sadly decline, it is important that this generation's knowledge continues to be refreshed by collections such as this.

Captain P.J. Walker CBE, Royal Navy (Retd.)
July 2005

Introduction

I am neither a historian nor a Master of Something (or other) from Oxbridge, but I do have an insatiable curiosity to find things out. My life has been in the main, Army. I served for 17 years, most of which was with the 1st Royal Tank Regiment. I left the Army in November 1994, having taken up residence in Sutton Coldfield, the scene of my last posting to the, now gone, St George's Barracks. I served in Germany, Dorset and Northern Ireland throughout my career. If I have any regrets at all it is the realisation that for most of my life I have lived alongside history and failed to see it. Oh if only I had been the owner of a decent camera when a youth!

Ever since my childhood I have been interested in World War 2. Then it was mainly the intrepid "adventures" of Douglas Bader and Guy Gibson, but always there was an admiration for the mechanical splendour of Germany's beautiful battleship the *Bismarck*. I had a model of her for a very long time. I also had an admiration for the bravery of the sailors who went to sea in that most invisible of vessels, the submarine, and in particular, the U-Boats.

Time passed, the years rolled along and marriage and an Army career put my interests on the back burner, so to speak (raising a family and moving about on never-ending postings tends to keep the mind focussed). Then, around about the year 2000 I got my first "proper" computer and eventually found my way into cyberspace and the internet. The next major leap in my research hobby was my introduction, via Telewest, to broadband; no more dial-up connections and broken links – my universe was now complete!

A "freebie" website started it off followed by my purchasing my own domain for the princely sum of $9 per year. Then I got the bug for which there is no known cure, research and investigations followed. I took my site to a company in the USA (realwebhost.net) and asked them to 'host' it (place it on their servers). The cost very much depends upon the site size x broadband access x cost per gigabit – currently $216 per year. At the time of writing this I have just received my very first ever donation to help me run the site. I get e-mails from all over the world asking for help (which I always try to give) including two e-mails from "high up" foreign military head-quarters, asking for permission to use articles from my site in Military publications! I was delighted and, of course, said yes.

Eventually my site grew and grew and a friend in America once remarked that when she had six months to spare she might read it all! *Bismarck* and U-Boats duly arrived on my site, followed by Captain Walker and, thanks to the bait thrown my way by Ray Holden, HMS *Kite*. Other pages have followed on, such as *Scharnhorst* and other tales of the sea. All of them, I noted, involved a large loss of life or a large percentage of the crews were lost.

By this time I was working 60 hours a week with a security company, the hours on night shifts allowing me time to read books and check details. An HGV lorry driver friend of mine in Coventry who I call "Stay" Sharp suggested that I write a book connecting them all together. I laughed, but, oh dear, another piece of bait had been thrown my way!

My knowledge of the written word (or lack of it!) allows for some readability, but if you should find a grammatical error or two, please allow me some license – it's only a hobby after all!

In a manner of speaking, the following two quotes are by way of a disclaimer. Whilst I have tried my utmost to present fact, there are naturally grey areas where even eyewitness recollections become confused. What I present to you in this book is what I believe to be fact, as does any "proper" historian of any conscience.

> *A man is his own easiest dupe, for what he wishes to be true he generally believes to be true.* **Demosthenes** *(c. 384-322 BC)*

> *I struggled in the beginning, I said I was going to write the truth so help me god. And I thought I was. I found I couldn't. Nobody can write the absolute truth.* **Henry Miller**

Finally, my thanks to Captain Johnny Walker's grandson, Capt Patrick Walker RN (Retd), for agreeing to write a foreword to this book. I am honoured.

Mike Kemble
Sutton Coldfield, Summer 2005
60 years after the end of the conflict

1. The Sinking of the *Athenia*

On September 3rd 1939 the German U-Boat U-30 had been at sea for several days, under strict orders to avoid contact or discovery, when she received notification that Germany was now at war with Great Britain. U-30's commander was Lieutenant Fritz-Julius Lemp, who had been in command for almost a year. Before sailing, all German U-Boats had been issued with strict orders to operate within the Prize Rules – international laws governing the conduct of war at sea. This was known as the Hague Convention. Merchant ships were to be stopped and searched and if they were found to be carrying enemy cargo, they could be sunk, but only after the crew had been seen safely into lifeboats. U-30 had received this signal.

According to the testimony of Admiral Doenitz at his trial at Nuremberg, when notified of the outbreak of hostilities Lemp had been under orders to keep a lookout for armed merchant cruisers. Doenitz was not specific as to why this should be a priority at the outbreak of war.

Germany had invaded Poland on 1st September 1939 and on 3rd September 1939 at 11:15 hrs Britain declared war on Germany. The *Athenia* had left Glasgow on 1st September and was heading for Montreal with 1,100 passengers, more than 300 of whom were American. Many were women and children. On the evening of September 3rd she was sighted by the U-30 about 250 miles northwest of Inishtrahull, Northern Ireland. She was running without lights.

Upon sighting the ship Lemp decided that she was an 'armed merchant cruiser' and shadowed her, watching her zig-zig course and speed. Lemp then attacked *Athenia* without warning. He fired two torpedoes, one of which exploded amidships, ripping open the bulkhead between the engine room and the boiler room. As soon as he had fired the two torpedoes he dived in case a torpedo should come back at him. One did misfire. As he came back up to the surface he saw the *Athenia* starting to list and fired a third torpedo. This too missed. Perhaps this torpedo being fired caused some of the survivors, in their panic, to imagine that they had been "fired upon", as was stated at the enquiry. Lemp was, by now, close enough to see *Athenia*'s silhouette, but something troubled him, as radio operator Hogel later recalled:

> "I realized it could not be a troop transport but had passengers on board. I knew her name from the call sign – Athenia. Then the commander came to the radio room and asked for the Lloyds Register, which listed all sea vessels and the various types. His fingers came to rest on the Athenia. He was, of course, shocked".

This gives a clear insight into what had gone through Lemp's mind and his reaction. Soon afterwards the U-30 intercepted a plain language transmission from the ship identifying itself as the *Athenia*. Now that *Athenia* had been transmitting there was little need for Lemp to conceal his location, but he failed to radio back to base with his report, instead choosing to remain silent.

Lemp remained silent for 11 more days, finally calling in on September 14th, but he still he failed to mention the *Athenia*; instead he reported damage received in a confrontation with two destroyers after he had sunk the freighter *Fanad Head*, and to request permission to offload a wounded man in Iceland for urgent medical attention. In fact, the Germans would not learn the facts until September 27 when the U-30 returned to Kiel Harbour.

The *Athenia* sank with the loss of 112 passengers and crew. Most of the dead (figures vary by half dozen, according to different sources) had been trapped below deck in the 3rd and tourist dining rooms when the U-30 struck (a familiar story when reading about loss of life at sea in passenger ships; the 'lower classes' always suffer the worst). One eyewitness described the decks as 'strewn with bodies' and another told of trapped children in cabins below. Amongst the dead were 28 Americans, all civilian[1].

Lemp did not give any assistance to the survivors, contrary to the rules of engagement, and a few days layer when he sank the *Blairlogie*

---

[1] Despite the fact that Lemp had murdered 28 US citizens, within hours Roosevelt announced that his Government was preparing "*a declaration of American neutrality*".

he did nothing there for survivors either (although it is possible that he knew the Norwegian freighter *Knut Nelson* was in the vicinity and assumed they would come to the stricken ship's aid). Going by his track record I somehow do not think so, it seems more likely that he just wanted to flee the scene as quickly as possible.

Within 24 hours news of the Nazi outrage echoed around the world. On the first day of the war Germany had broken all the rules. It was described as an act of total war against civilians. This was a propaganda gift to the British, who used it to its full extent. Foreign newspapers gave it front page reports.

When the first British reports were received, the German government did not believe them. The Propaganda Ministry asked if the Kriegsmarine was responsible and was told by naval authorities that no U-Boats were in the area. On September 7th Grand Admiral Raeder stated that all U-Boats had been contacted and none was responsible for the disaster. This was also conveyed to the American ambassador. This statement was not entirely true, for several boats had not reported in, including the U-30.

The significance was not lost on Hitler. The first thing was to deny everything. According to Josef Goebbels, the Nazi Minister of Propaganda, it was, in fact, a torpedo from a British submarine that had hit the *Athenia*. Later he added that it was a dirty trick by Winston Churchill to discredit Germany and pull the United States into the war. Hitler was furious and imposed severe restrictions on all U-Boat operations. Admiral Doenitz, commander of the U-Boat arm, was to be frustrated by these restrictions for many months.

The next step which Hitler undertook was to send out an immediate order to the Kriegsmarine:

> "The Fuhrer has forbidden attacks on passenger ships sailing independently or in convoy".

No amount of official denials could convince the outside world that the loss of SS *Athenia* was anything but a return to "German barbarism", as the unrestricted submarine warfare of the First World War had been termed. Such moral limitations on submarine operations were not entirely logical. For a submarine, stealth is its most effective weapon. The Hague Convention agreements requiring submarines to surface and warn surface vessels, allowing crews to launch boats before attacking, were unrealistic. The British reaction was to immediately implement the convoy system and ordered all shipping to comply.

When the U-30 returned to Kiel, Lemp and his crew were given strict orders and sworn to absolute secrecy. They were not to mention anything at all to do with the incident at any time. But the U-30 had arrived in post with victory pennants displayed on her conning tower, one of which showed 14,000 tons, the tonnage of the *Athenia*. The official U-Boat Command War Diary makes no mention of the incident and Lemp was ordered to falsify his War Diary by rewriting two complete pages. An entry for any vessel of 14,000 tons does not appear. Lemp was later killed when the U-110 was captured and secret papers were found on the enigma code machine.

The website navalhistory.net states that:

> "Battle of the Atlantic – The six year long battle starts on the 3*rd* September with the sinking of the liner Athenia by U-30 (Lt Lemp) northwest of Ireland. She was mistaken for an armed merchant cruiser, and her destruction leads the Admiralty to believe unrestricted submarine warfare has been launched. Full convoy plans are put into operation, but in fact Hitler has ordered the U-Boats to adhere to international law and after the Athenia incident, tightens controls for a while"

Athenia's sister ship *Leticia* did in fact later serve as an Armed Merchant Cruiser but was later converted back and eventually ended the war as a Hospital Ship.

The following information was found on an *Athenia*-related website belonging to Mackenzie J Gregory. These are the names of the 19 crewmembers lost from the *Athenia* sinking. The first 18 are on the Tower Hill Memorial. The last one is Canadian and is commemorated in Halifax Nova, Scotia. I have not been able to find a list of the passengers.

CARLIN, Assistant Steward, JAMES, S.S. *Athenia* (Glasgow). Merchant Navy. 3rd - 4th September 1939. Age 56. Panel 12.

DONNELLY, Assistant Steward, IAN, S.S. *Athenia* (Glasgow). Merchant Navy. 3rd - 4th September 1939. Age 26. Panel 12.

DONNELLY, Assistant Steward, JOHN, S.S. *Athenia* (Glasgow). Merchant Navy. 3rd - 4th September 1939. Age 23. Panel 12.

ELDER, Donkeyman, JAMES, S.S. *Athenia* (Glasgow). Merchant Navy. 3rd - 4th September 1939. Age 45. Husband of Mary Elder, of Cambuslang, Lanarkshire. Panel 12.

FORDYCE, Watchman, CHARLES, S.S. *Athenia* (Glasgow). Merchant Navy. 3rd - 4th September 1939. Age 65. Son of George and Jessie Fordyce; husband of Mary Penelope Fordyce. Panel 12.

GALLAGHER, Greaser, HUGH, S.S. *Athenia* (Glasgow). Merchant Navy. 3rd - 4th September 1939. Age 23. Son of Thomas Gallagher, and of Isabel Gallagher, of Glasgow. Panel 12.

HARROWER, Stewardess, ALISON, S.S. *Athenia* (Glasgow). Merchant Navy. 3rd - 4th September 1939. Age 41. Daughter of William and Hannah Foster Denny Harrower. Panel 12.

HOGG, Assistant Steward, JOHN, S.S. *Athenia* (Glasgow). Merchant Navy. 3rd - 4th September 1939. Age 51. Husband of Sarah A. Hogg, of Brantford, Ontario, Canada. Panel 12.

JOHNSTON, Stewardess, MARGARET, S.S. *Athenia* (Glasgow). Merchant Navy. 3rd - 4th September 1939. Age 41. Daughter of James and Christina Johnston, of Glasgow. Panel 12.

KENT, Assistant Steward, JOHN, S.S. *Athenia* (Glasgow). Merchant Navy. 3rd - 4th September 1939. Age 50. Husband of Jessie Darroch Kent, of Bridgeton, Glasgow. Panel 12.

LAWLER, Stewardess, JESSIE, S.S. *Athenia* (Glasgow). Merchant Navy. 3rd - 4th September 1939. Age 60. Wife of Patrick Lawler, of Sholing, Southampton. Panel 12.

MARSHALL, Bellboy, JAMES, S.S. *Athenia* (Glasgow). Merchant Navy. 3rd - 4th September 1939. Age 15. Panel 12.

MORRISON, Steward, DAVID, S.S. *Athenia* (Glasgow). Merchant Navy. 3rd - 4th September 1939. Age 32. Panel 12.

McDERMOTT, Assistant Steward, MICHAEL J., S.S. *Athenia* (Glasgow). Merchant Navy. 3rd - 4th September 1939. Age 33. Panel 12.

McJARROW, Printer, JOHN, S.S. *Athenia* (Glasgow). Merchant Navy. 3rd - 4th September 1939. Age 39. Panel 12.

McKEOWN, Steward, JOHN, S.S. *Athenia* (Glasgow). Merchant Navy. 3rd - 4th September 1939. Age 47. Husband of M. E. McKeown, of Dunoon, Argyllshire. Panel 12.

PROVAN, Barber, DAVID, S.S. *Athenia* (Glasgow). Merchant Navy. 3rd - 4th September 1939. Age 65. Son of Alec and Margaret Provan; husband of Martha Provan, of Glasgow. Panel 12.

THOMSON, Assistant Steward, SAMUEL, S.S. *Athenia* (Glasgow). Merchant Navy. 3rd - 4th September 1939. Age 45. Husband of Julia McCafferty Thomson. of Glasgow. Panel 12.

BAIRD, Stewardess, HANNAH S.S. *Athenia* (Glasgow). Merchant Navy. 3rd - 4th September 1939 Canadian Merchant Navy HALIFAX MEMORIAL Nova Scotia, Canada Panel 17.

For those wishing to search the records: Registers and Indexes of Birth, Marriages & Deaths of Passengers & Seamen at Sea. The records are held in what is known as BT files and it is very important you remember the file No. The file you need to access is "BT334" This will give you the following information: Name of ship, official No. port of registry, date of death, place of death, name of deceased, sex, age, rating/rank, nationality and birthplace, last place of abode, cause of death and remarks.

Outward Bound Passenger Lists 1890 -1960 are held in BT27 and gives information on passenger lists of people leaving the United Kingdom by sea kept by the Board of Trade's Commercial and Statistical Department and its successors. There is also BT32 covering 1906 -1951 Registers of passenger lists kept by the Board of Trade's Commercial, Labour and Statistical Department and its successors.

Please note the PRO will not search their files for you, if you are unable to attend in person, they will give the names of independent researchers who will do it for an hourly fee (very expensive). Public Records Office, Kew, Richmond, Surrey TW9 4DU.

The Athenia.

Athenia sinking.

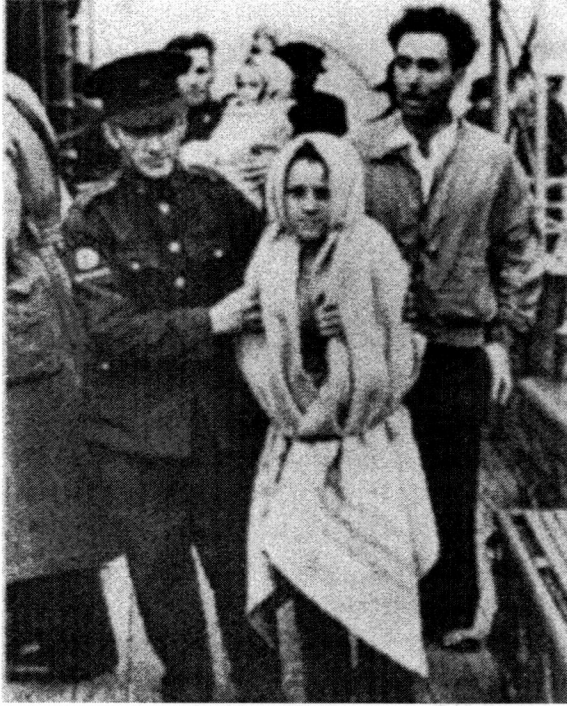

Athenia survivors.

U-30

Lieutenant Fritz-Julius Lemp – commander of U-30.

2. The Battle of the Atlantic

Number of ships in the merchant fleets of the world in 1939

British Empire	2,965
USA	1,409
Japan	1,054
Norway	816
Germany	713
Italy	571
France	502
Holland	477
Greece	389
Russia	299
Sweden	259

At the outbreak of war Britain had many ships mothballed or awaiting scrapping, due to the depression of the 1930s; these were quickly recovered. Then, during the opening few months of the war, the number of ships available to the UK increased as ships from neutral or occupied nations headed for the safety of British waters. Sweden and Norway were the main contributors, along with France, Belgium and, later, Greece.

Casualties

The numbers of casualties on both sides were greater than the combined deaths in all the naval battles over the previous 500 years! With so many nationalities involved in several theatres of war, it is hard to give accurate figures but it is certain that over 50,000 allied and neutral merchant seamen and gunners lost their lives, approximately two thirds of these being victims of the U-Boats. 5,150 allied merchant ships were lost during the war, and 2,828 of these were sunk by submarines, mostly by U-Boats (but to put it in perspective, this was less than 1% of the ships that sailed the Atlantic during the war years). In addition, 148 warships were lost to U-Boats, including two battleships and three aircraft carriers.

Merchant Seamen killed:

United Kingdom	22490
Neutral	6500 (approx)
Indian Lascars (UK)	6093
USA	5662
Norway	4795
Greece	2000 (approx)
Chinese (UK)	2023
Holland	1914
Denmark	1886
Canada	1437
Belgium	893
South Africa	182
Australia	109
New Zealand	72

Gunners on Merchant Ships:

UK	3935
Of which RN	2713
Of which RAMR[2]	1222
USA	1640[3]

U-Boats

Total commissioned	1,170
– of which sunk	785
Sailed on operational patrols	863
– of which sunk	754
Sailors who went to sea	39,000
– of whom were killed	27,491
– of whom were captured	5,000

---

[2] RAMR = Royal Artillery Maritime Regiment.
[3] to end of 1944 only.

Headquarters Western Approaches

Western Approaches originally had its HQ in Plymouth, but when London was virtually closed as a major port in 1940 and south coast ports were under attack, a new HQ was chosen and prepared in Liverpool and the move was made early in 1941. The Royal Navy set up was in Derby House and the Merchant Navy part was in the nearby Royal Liver Building. There were other shore establishments as far afield as Greenock and Milford Haven and in Northern Ireland. It is said that Western Approaches eventually became responsible for more personnel than had been administered by the entire Admiralty before the war. The Royal Naval HQ can be seen today in its "original 1942" layout, underneath Derby House, entrance in Rumford Street, off Chapel Street & Water Street. If you can find India Buildings on Water Street, Rumford Street is behind you opposite. Fear not, it is not commercialised. Unfortunately, it is not open all the year round. March – October is the normal routine.

Admiral Sir Max Horton

Shore establishments had the job of maintaining the ships whereas HQ Western Approaches was "to ensure the safe and timely arrival" of the convoys. Admiral Sir Percy Noble commanded Western Approaches from early 1941 to November 1942 and built much of the basis for later success. He also built it up during its difficult, formative, months. Sir Max Horton replaced him. Although Noble was as good a Commander as Horton, most experts agree that Western Approaches really began to "hum" when Horton took over. It was Horton who despatched Captain Johnnie Walker with his Black Swan Class Sloops to hunt and destroy U-Boats wherever they may be found. This was a far cry from the previous tactics of escorts waiting with convoys to be attacked. The idea of a Hunter/Killer group was almost certainly Walker's, who studied the "unfashionable" anti-submarine warfare before the war. It was widely believed at the time that Captain Walker could "smell" a U-Boat for miles, but nowadays, with the knowledge that we have of Bletchley Park and Enigma, this probably was not quite accurate! Nevertheless, once Walker found a

U-Boat, it did not get away! Walker's ships were based in Gladstone Dock, Liverpool.

Admiral Horton had been a successful WWI submarine commander (just like his opposite number Admiral Doenitz) and his sinking of the German cruiser *Hela* on 13 September 1914 was actually the first ever sinking of an enemy ship by a British submarine. Before Western Approaches Horton had been Flag Officer Submarines, and his deep knowledge of submarines undoubtedly helped him to counter U-Boats. Of Jewish extraction, Horton was described as "absolutely ruthless and so astute he could see through a brick wall" by a member of his staff.

Horton spent all morning, every morning at Derby House. He lived there. But on afternoons he could usually be found playing golf at Hoylake, across the Mersey on the Wirral. He would then dine, play some bridge and reappear in the Operations Room each evening. In the event of a convoy battle developing or taking place, Horton would usually stay up all night, in pyjamas and dressing gown, supervising the events. However, whereas Sir Percy Noble had known all the Wrens by their first names, Max Horton would only address the senior officer present and if he did address the girls it would be "WREN!"[4] Horton died in 1951.

U-Boats

A U-Boat is the term popularly used when referring to the German *Unterzeeboot*. It was not really a submerged fighting machine but a ship that could submerge. Most U-Boats, where practical, would surface in order to engage the enemy. German U-Boats in 1916 and 1917 had virtually starved Britain, nearly cutting the supply to British ports. The situation was saved only by the Admiralty introducing the convoy system, albeit reluctantly. The losses fell dramatically. The lesson had been well learnt and when Britain found herself at war in 1939, the convoy was reintroduced at once. U-Boats had put to sea before war was declared and many British ships were on the high seas alone. The convoy system had one major drawback

---

[4] The work done by these girls and their counterparts in the WAAF was astounding and is mentioned here with pride and gratitude.

though, it effectively cut any cargo ship's load-bearing capacity by one third over the period convoys were in use, multiplied by the number of ships used.[5] This was, in its own way, a minor victory for the Germans.

The propaganda machine of the Allies transformed the crews of the U-Boats into Nazi monsters and vicious murdering bullies but in Germany their courage and skill was recognised as deserving public adulation and this they received, being regarded on a par with the Luftwaffe. As WW2 progressed the adulation afforded to the Luftwaffe waned, but the U-Boat crews remained popular to the end.

Were they callous bullies? I think not. The vast majority were simply the counterparts of their Allied enemy – sailors doing a job. It took a very special kind of person to can go down deep beneath the waves in an iron 'coffin'; I do not think I could have done it... But propaganda is an extremely useful tool in war and the U-Boats were demonised to maintain a thirst for revenge and the will to win among allied seamen. In fact, some U-Boat Commanders were known to have surfaced alongside lifeboats to provision them and give them a course for safety.[6]

U-Boat Production

Thanks to an Anglo-German agreement, Germany began to build U-Boats in 1934 and in 1935 a flotilla was formed at Kiel under the command of Kapitan Karl Doenitz. By 1939, there were six flotillas operational. Early successes of these U-Boats in WW2 included the sinking of the *Royal Oak* in Scapa Flow. Other "successes" were seized upon by Allied propaganda and events such as the sinking of the liner *Athenia* (Lemp, U-30) serving to turn the public into hating these German sailors. So much so that when prisoners were later being put ashore from one of Captain Walker's hunter-killer ships, HMS *Wild Goose*, members of the public attacked them on the

---

[5] The loss was accounted for in the time it took convoys to assemble and the fact that a convoy could only travel as fast as its slowest ship.

[6] One of these, Otto Kretschmer, survived the war as a POW in Canada. He was lucky he did not get shot for espionage because he conducted a successful spy ring there.

streets of Liverpool, the escorting servicemen having to protect the Germans from the crowd.

The *Athenia* was sunk in direct contravention of International Law under the 1935 London Submarine Agreement in which all parties undertook to observe the Hague Convention. In 1939 Hitler had ordered that these rules be observed but in the case of the *Athenia* no warnings were given and 110 of her passengers and 18 members of her crew died. Germany eventually officially dropped all pretext to the "rules" three months later.

It should be noted, however, that several U-Boat commanders helped survivors when it was safe to do so.

Werner Hess (U-530):

> *"Admiral Doenitz never ordered us to shoot survivors. We had a clear order, which we always complied with as far as conditions allowed, to help survivors, but they must not be brought on board. We ourselves certainly met English survivors in the North Atlantic and gave them food and cans of water. We even sent a signal giving their position. There was always the chance that our own boat would be sunk one day".*

The merchant cruiser *Laurentic* was torpedoed one night in Nov 1940. The crew took to the boats and a voice called out in the dark asking if they had enough food. Fearing a trap, they kept quiet and a voice shouted "Goodnight British" and the U-Boat sailed away. It was the legendary Otto Kretschmer. It is very difficult to prove, or disprove stories of survivors being machine gunned in the water, it is also difficult to judge if this was purely a propaganda ploy or actual events. I suspect the former.

The Beginning

The Battle of the Atlantic was the longest continuous battle ever. It began with the sinking of the SS *Athenia* by U-30 on the evening of 3rd September 1939 and continued until Germany finally surrendered in May 1945.

At the beginning of the war and into the first two years, the U-Boat was not the only danger to British ships. Mines, surface ships, aircraft and armed raiders all had to be overcome. The *Graf Zeppelin*, Germany's only aircraft carrier, never saw service and the Royal

Navy soon took care of the surface raiders. Britain's island status meant that all her oil, most of her raw materials and a lot of her food had to be imported. The U-Boats waged a war of attrition. Every ship sunk was a ship that would never again carry cargo. Crew losses could be quickly overcome, but replacing a ship took time. In the period pre Dec 1941, if the U-Boats had succeeded, Britain, no matter how valiant her people were, could not have survived. By the end of 1940 the Germans had sunk 1,281 ships, mostly British, totalling 4,747,033 tons. This was about one fifth of her pre-1939 merchant fleet.

It is now freely admitted that the threat of the submarine had been severely underestimated between the wars. This is usually referred to as the "Jutland Syndrome" amongst naval personnel. Captain Walker was one of only a few officers who attended this "unfashionable" Anti Submarine Warfare training, as did the Staff Officer (Anti Submarines) HQ Western Approaches. No specific anti submarine vessels were available to the Royal Navy, the specialist convoy escort enjoying an extremely low priority! Indeed such things as aircraft carrying escort carriers did not even exist, although later were to prove highly advantageous in the battle against the U-Boat.

Anti Submarine Warfare

The Royal Navy's main anti submarine weapon was the 1917-vintage depth charge and a very secret ASDIC (sound detection equipment) now known as 'sonar'.

ASDIC was a submarine detection device housed in a dome beneath the ship. It sent out a narrow beam of sound in a series of pulses, which would reflect back from a submerged object within a max range of 3000 yards. The echo produced an accurate range and bearing to the target. Differences in the temperatures at differing levels beneath the sea confused the ASDIC somewhat and if the ship was travelling too fast.

A depth charge was a 250lb drum of explosive preset to explode at a given depth. WW2 U-Boats could dive deeper than the Royal Navy anticipated, certainly a lot deeper that their British or American counterparts. To sink a U-Boat a depth charge had to detonate within 20 feet of the submerged hull. Not an easy task when the submarine can move in all three dimensions.

One tactic used by Walker was to sit on top of it and wait for its air to run out. As he roamed independent of convoys he could afford this relative "luxury" and used it to great effect. In one such attack he even predicted (correctly) exactly when the U-Boat would surface.

Exercises in anti-submarine warfare had been restricted to the scenario of one or two destroyers attacking a single submarine and consequently the introduction of the U-Boat 'wolf pack' in 1940 came as a complete shock to the Royal Navy. Commander C.D. Howard-Johnson. Staff Officer Anti Submarines Western Approaches HQ wrote:

> "*I was serving in gunboats in China in 1930 when I decided to specialise in anti submarine warfare because I reckoned that we had nearly been brought to our knees in WW1 by the sub and this would be an interesting line for the future. To qualify in A/S was looked upon rather poorly in those days and many friends raised eyebrows that such a keen and bright officer should head for such a "backwater" full of lazy, hard drinkers! I was Staff A/S Officer of the 6th Destroyer Flotilla at the time of the Spanish Civil War and I found that amongst the four ASDIC operators in each of the 9 destroyers half only managed to get 4 hours operating their ASDIC sets in the year!*"

The Gap

Up to 1941 there had been a significant gap in the centre of the Atlantic where no aircraft could reach and escorts had to return to base for refuelling in most cases. Then Britain occupied Iceland and the gap shrank a little. Later the Americans were to join the British in Iceland. The Canadian Navy stretched its cover eastwards and the Royal Navy westwards, until, in May 1941, the two Navies met. In July 1941 the first westbound convoy joined the first eastbound convoy, receiving full protection right across the Atlantic. The U-Boat "happy time" was coming to an end.

The only problem now was that the "air gap" had yet to be closed. Infighting between the RAF's Coastal Command and Bomber Command meant that planes with the range to cover this gap were kept for bombing raids over Germany. We had to await the arrival of the American long-range Liberator before we could close the gap. In September of the same year, the US Navy took responsibility to escort convoys in the Western Atlantic that contained US shipping. Two destroyers were sunk by U-Boat as an inevitable consequence, the *Kearney* and the *Reuben James*.[7]

The arrival of radar on board the escorts added another factor in favour of the Allies, along with the introduction of star-shell and snowflake flares to illuminate U-Boats. The U-Boats were still small targets though!

Wolf Pack Tactics

For the wolf pack tactics of the U-Boats to work effectively they had to use radio but when a surfaced U-Boat transmitted a convoy or weather report it revealed its own location to the Allies. It was detected by HF/DF[8] on board escorting warships, as well as shore-based stations. The result was that the position of a transmitting U-Boat could be fixed and an attack usually ensued. Somehow, German knowledge of HF/DF had been transmitted to U-Boat bases, but was contained within a routine report, which did not cause any concerns and was overlooked, no action being taken. Captain Walker and his Hunter Killers used HF/DF to great effect. A few U-Boat commanders refused to answer High Command until the third day, if they didn't they would be reported missing. Some naval officers believe that their greatest mistake in the Battle of The Atlantic was Admiralty's reluctance to divert shipping from other theatres to take care of the U-Boats once and for all, in 1940-41, when there were not so many of them. In the first 12 months of the war only 37 U-Boats were actually built. It was 1941 before building progressed, but a valuable chance had been lost. In April 230 boats had been built but of these, only 32 became "online" for operations. 1941 ended in somewhat of a stalemate, the U-Boat had sunk 432 ships and in turn 32 U-Boats had been sunk, 27 of these by Royal Naval escort vessels.

---

[7] It should be noted that these were actually nearer the UK than the United States at the time.
[8] High Frequency Direction Finding or 'Huff Duff' as the sailors called it.

If the U-Boat offensive in the Atlantic had succeeded in the period 1942-44, the invasion of Europe would never have taken place, as the Allies would not have been able to transport so many thousands of troops to Britain in preparation for June 1944. Either way, if the U-Boat had succeeded, history would have been dramatically rewritten and I would not be writing this. It was a very close run thing. It was to be a fight to the finish, no quarter asked, or given. An actual surrender of a U-Boat was an extremely rare occurrence. Bearing in mind that a U-Boat always dived when discovered, survival chances were necessarily greatly reduced. Records of the vast majority of U-Boat losses all relate with "no survivors".

December 1941 into 1942

The sneak attack upon Pearl Harbour by the Japanese in December 1941 surprised even the Germans but a few days later they declared war on the United States and Doenitz sent some long-range U-Boats to America's east coast in January 1942. The US coast was not blacked out and the U-Boats enjoyed a "happy time" where their targets were silhouetted against the brightly lit coastline. One U-Boat recorded that he sat, on the surface, and watched the funfair on Coney Island, listening to the noise. Eyewitnesses on the beaches of America clearly remember watching U-Boats sailing past them, or watching as a passing tanker would suddenly erupt into flame scarcely yards from the shores. People out walking their dogs recalled seeing U-Boats shelling passing steamers and ships that "suddenly burst into flame".

With the help of "milch cows" or U-Boat tenders, Doenitz was able to maintain a force averaging eight U-Boats at a time, operating some 3,500 miles from German held ports. The American reaction appears to be nothing short of criminal. Despite the persistent flow of information from Bletchley Park and the Admiralty, they appeared to do nothing, nor learn from British lessons. Convoys were not adopted and it was not until April, three months later, that a coastal blackout was ordered. During this time not a single German submarine was sunk. Britain was not at all pleased; many of the ships being sunk were British that had been escorted through U-Boats packs and heavy seas almost to the very entrances to harbours only to see them torpedoed whilst sailing unprotected in American coastal waters.

Up to May 1942 the Germans sank 362 ships in American waters. In fairness it must be mentioned that at the same time American troops were being hard pressed in the Pacific by the advancing Japanese, but the Commander in Chief of The Eastern Seaboard, Admiral King, has to shoulder the vast majority of the blame for simply failing to do anything for so long. Eventually the Americans gathered together their anti submarine ships, including some borrowed from Britain, and at long last set up a convoy system. Immediately the sinking of ships tailed off and U-Boats began to be sunk. As a result, Doenitz pulled his U-Boats out of US coastal waters, but by October 1942 he had 192 operational U-Boats, compared with just 100 at the beginning of the year.

German Pride

By the end of 1942 German shipyards were producing five new U-Boats per week. The average cost of a Type 7C U-Boat was 3 million Reichmarks (£300,000) and the larger Type 9c, 4 million Reichmarks. There were often discussions amongst U-Boat crews as to which yard built the better boat! Hamburg's shipyards came out as the most soundly built but even here opinion was divided as to whether Blohm & Voss or Deutsche Werft were the best of these. Apparently, Blohm & Voss gave some finishing touches missing in other boats. The same pride displayed by the crews of the U-Boats was displayed by the yards that built the boats. Leutnant von Egan-Krieger of the U-615 recalled:

"One day while we were at Kiel two men suddenly appeared from Blohm & Voss and insisted on stripping down the exhaust. One of the workers admitted that he may have accidentally left a screwdriver in it whilst the boat was being built and his conscience had troubled him ever since in case the rattling of the loose screwdriver might one day endanger the boat whilst we were making a quiet underwater escape from a British escort. They found the screwdriver, reassembled the exhaust and returned to Hamburg. We were full of admiration for the man who had admitted his mistake and for Blohm & Voss for following it up so thoroughly."

On the 18th May when the escort ship HMS *Anemone* attacked the U-615, the Anemone was an escort with convoy HX229. Not long after U-615 had been forced to dive, she was depth charged by *Anemone*, dropping about 10 depth charges set to 150 feet and 385 feet. U-615 was part of an attacking wolfpack and escaped, silent, unharmed.

In the last six months of 1942 U-Boats accounted for another 575 ships, totalling 3 million tons. The total for 1942 was a staggering 1,160 ships – a tonnage of over 6 million. Another 1.6 million tons had been sunk elsewhere, making the total for the year more than 1939, 1940 and 1941 combined. It was not all one-sided, however. U-Boat losses were 66 in the last six months of the year.

One very significant factor can be realised when these figures are analysed. For the first time U-Boats sunk by aircraft exceeded the numbers sunk by ships. A handful of very long range Liberators were now operating out of Iceland and Northern Ireland – the air gap was narrowing…

Turning the Tide

By the time 1943 came along, Captain Walker was beginning to achieve phenomenal success with his new custom built Black Swan class anti-submarine hunter-killer sloops, in both the Atlantic and the Bay of Biscay. All the early U-Boat commanders and sailors had either perished with their U-Boats or been captured, mostly the former. The Aces, the real "experts" had all gone. Most U-Boat commanders by 1943 had been only junior officers at the outbreak of the war. Most were only in their 20s, were tremendously loyal both to Hitler and to Doenitz, felt it was a great honour to be in U-Boats and wore the white-covered cap with pride, affording themselves a status not given to many, more senior, officers. U-Boat captains at this time were the "elite" of the German Navy.

The average U-Boat had a crew of about 50, 39 of which were ratings. The concept of the "all volunteer" crew put about by Germany was not quite accurate; officers did not "volunteer" and were expected to do whatever their superiors deemed necessary. An example of this was Kapitanleutnant Bahr, of the U-305, who had previously served aboard the Cruiser *Prinz Eugen*. The move from Cruiser to U-boat was to cost him his life in January 1944 when U-305 was sunk with all hands.

Werner Hess of the U-530, volunteering for the U-Boats, had a different reason than most:

> *"My father was a well known Social Democrat and was having a difficult time under Hitler. Life on a U-Boat was hard but after I became a U-Boat man my father was left in peace."*

U-Boat Manning

As the Allies began turning the tables and U-Boat loses began to mount, and shipping losses began to fall, volunteers for the U-Boat Arm began to slacken off dramatically. An observer at the time noted that very few U-Boat crewmen were married and that even fewer volunteers were married. Technical men were in short supply and men were "invited" to volunteer. For a German, there was no question but to comply. All in all, the vast majority were volunteers and served with absolute loyalty and devotion. But to say that all U-Boats were manned only by volunteers is a myth. It will have been approximately 80% in favour of the volunteer. A few of these sailors would also have been Nazi's but most were just sailors fighting for their country. The scene's in the superbly made German film production *Das Boot* in which the 'politically correct' officer is treated with some contempt and wry humour (knowing smirks behind his back, etc) are probably quite accurate. The Battle of The Atlantic was to continue to the final day of the war, and in one or two cases, beyond...

Rerouted Convoys

By May 1943 shipping losses were reducing rapidly and U-Boats were finding targets harder to come by. As the war was coming to a close, Doenitz had the foresight to order that all German records were to be moved to Flensburg, near Denmark, and in the event, to be handed over to the British and Americans. As a result of the Western allies having access to those, it was determined that the Germans did not have a clue why shipping was able to divert around their U-

Boat packs. They wrongly assumed massive advances in radar technology as well as intelligence from both French Resistance and British Intelligence. They also assumed that HF/DF was now so good the British were able to "sense" their U-Boats in waiting. They refused to believe that it was their enigma naval codes that had been broken and that the British were reading orders to the U-Boats as quickly as the U-Boat commanders themselves. Post war books occasionally hinted that German codes were being broken but as Churchill had insisted, members of the Intelligence fraternity had all signed a "black book" to swear that they would never talk about their part in the war and for nearly 30 years historians had the impression that HF/DF and Naval Officer skills were responsible.

In a bizarre coincidence in May 1943 a Halifax of 58 Squadron Royal Air Force, commanded by Wing Commander W. Oulton, sank the U-463. The same aircraft sank two other U-Boats the same month, the U-563 and the U-663 – each exactly 100 'up' from the previous one!

The spring and summer of 1943 saw the swing in favour of the Allies in the Battle of The Atlantic. The combination of the support groups, the anti-submarine ships, the closing of the air gap and the changes to Allied codes (which the Germans had known) all combined to defeat the U-Boats.

In May 1943 Doenitz lost 41 U-Boats. The Allies lost 50 ships. Doenitz removed his remaining U-Boats from the Atlantic for the time being. In July 1943 the turnover of new shipping finally overtook the tonnage sunk since 1939 and thereafter the issue was never in doubt. This was mainly due to the prefabricated Liberty Ships being thrown off American slipways at the rate of one every 4 or 5 days. During this time Doenitz lost one of his sons when U-954, on its first patrol, was lost – sunk by a Liberator from 120 Squadron.

Enigma

In 1974 a publication called "The Ultra Secret" by F.W. Winterbotham partially lifted the veil of secrecy that surrounded Bletchley Park. Known on the U-Boats as Schlussel-M, (Key Machine) the Enigma machine had been in our hands since before WW2 broke out. It was to be quite a while before names such as Alan Turing, Colossus, bombe, and the work really carried out at Bletchley Park, Station X, was to become common knowledge. Nowadays, Bletchley Park has its own web site for all to see (see referrals) and an excellent publication by Hugo Sebag-Montefiore entitled *Enigma, The Battle for the Code* is available on the bookshelves on this very subject.

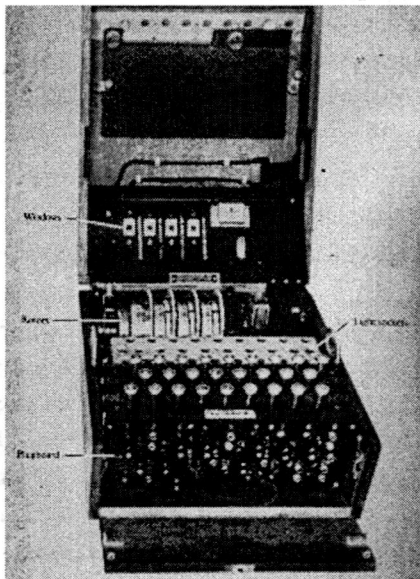

Enigma code machine.

Final Touches

History shows that Doenitz never really recovered from the 1943 losses. Technological advances such as acoustic torpedoes, schnorkels, etc came too late to make any significant difference and he was running out of suitable men to crew his boats. It was remarked that farmhands from Bavaria, after only a few months training, were taking out boats. Morale in the U-Boat arm held up to the end, but was never to go back to the initial euphoria of the early years. After this time, wolf pack tactics were abandoned and U-Boats were sent out singly. Attacks against convoys continued but never with anything like the intensity of the wolf pack days. The life expectancy of a U-Boat was slashed to only one and a half patrols.

In August 1944, with the introduction of the massive "tallboy" bombs, the RAF finally had the power to destroy the heavily protected U-Boat pens and duly despatched them with a raid by the Lancasters of 617 Squadron (The Dam Busters) and soon after this the advancing Allies put paid to any ideas the Germans had in France. As soon as any U-Boat had left these bunkers, it was at the mercy of marauding aircraft and in the final year of the war, 57 U-Boats were destroyed by bombs, compared with only five in the previous five years. It just goes to show what might have been achieved if the Coastal Command and Bomber Command had resolved their differences early on.

From March 1943 to the end of the war, mainly due to air power, a staggering 590 U-Boats were destroyed, 290 of these by aircraft alone, 174 by ships alone and the remainder by a combination of the two.

Doenitz succeeded Hitler at the end and spent the final days frantically trying to rescue people from the clutches of the advancing Red Army. On the final day of the war 49 U-Boats were at sea and were ordered to surrender to Allied ports. But U-Boat officers at Kiel disobeyed their Commander and "Fuhrer" and scuttled every remaining U-Boat in German waters whilst Doenitz was asleep. One or two U-Boats even sank ships after the end of the war, claiming they had not received the surrender signals!

A few U-Boats survived the war to become tourist attractions: U-505 rests in Chicago, USA and U-534 was lifted from the sea off Aarhus in Denmark[9] and now resides in the Historic Warships Museum, Birkenhead, Merseyside, opposite HQ Western Approaches and a statue of Walker looking out over the River Mersey from the Pier Head, Liverpool, next to the Merchant Naval Memorial.

Most of the remaining U-Boats captured were eventually used as target practice and sunk.

---

[9] An RAF Liberator sank U-534 on the last day of the war, but her crew managed to escape, so she was not designated a "war grave".

An Atlantic convoy.

The result of a U-Boat attack.

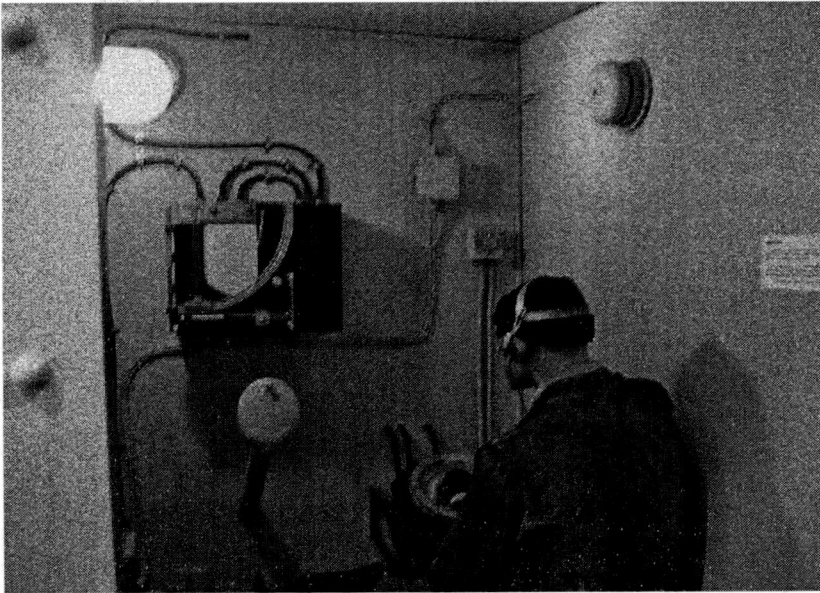

ASDIC Operator.

Captain F. Johnnie Walker RN.

3. The Loss of the Mighty *Hood*

HMS *Hood*, 'The Mighty *Hood*' as she was popularly known in the Royal Navy, was the largest warship in the world when she was commissioned in 1920 and became a symbol of British Naval strength in the inter-war years. Although she was classified as a battle cruiser, *Hood* was more than that but less than a battleship, an improved version of the *Queen Elizabeth* Class. A bit of a hybrid really, with the same main armament of 8 x 381mm guns, a higher position for the secondary armament, sloped armour belt and improved torpedo protection, she included the latest ideas of naval construction in 1915. Speed requirements meant a very long hull was essential – HMS *Hood* was the longest ship built for the Royal Navy ... ever.

Admiral Jellicoe, Commander-in-Chief of the Grand Fleet, stated that new battle cruisers, rather than battleships, were needed to combat the latest German ships, so the *Hood*'s design was altered with less armour, but incorporating the latest technology, small tube boilers, providing more power with much lighter machinery. As a result of lessons learnt from the Battle of Jutland, a considerable amount of armour was added, giving *Hood* a level of protection similar to the *Queen Elizabeth* Class, but even with this extra weight and a final displacement of over 42,000 tons, she was still seven knots faster.

Hood's career in the inter-war period included the famous world cruise with fellow battle cruiser *Repulse* in 1923-24, which took them to the Far East, the Pacific and the United States. She served with the Home and Atlantic Fleets until 1936, when she was transferred to the Mediterranean.

Hood had been due a for major refit in 1939, including the removal of her 600-ton conning tower and improvements to her deck armour, but with too few capital ships available she could not be spared. Sadly, this was to be the reason why she was sunk later on...

On the outbreak of war HMS *Hood* was at Scapa Flow with the Home Fleet. In June 1940 she was allocated to Force H, in the Mediterranean. Force H's first task was its most distasteful, to neutralise the French squadron at Oran in Algeria. At 1755hrs on 3rd July 1940 *Hood* and her compatriots opened fire; the battleship *Bretagne* was blown up and the *Provence* and *Dunkerque* badly damaged. *Hood* returned to the Home Fleet and on 19th May 1941 she sailed with the brand new battleship *Prince of Wales* to intercept the German battleship *Bismarck* which was attempting to break out into the North Atlantic.

Bismarck, accompanied by the heavy cruiser *Prinz Eugen*, was shadowed on radar by the *Norfolk* and *Suffolk,* which reported their position to HMS *Hood*. In the Denmark Strait on the morning of 24th May Admiral Holland ordered his ships to close the range and shortly before 0600hrs both sides opened fire. The *Bismarck*'s fifth salvo hit the *Hood* amidships, penetrating the secondary armament magazine. The detonation spread to the main magazine, resulting in a catastrophic explosion which tore the ship in half. Only three of her 1,418 crew survived.

The sinking of the *Hood* and the appalling loss of life were greeted with deepest shock in Britain. Prime Minister Winston Churchill famously signalled to the fleet: *'The Bismarck must be sunk at all costs.'* Crippled by Fleet Air Arm aircraft, *Bismarck* was engaged by the battleships *King George V* and *Rodney* on the morning of 27 May, before being sunk with torpedoes, although it is now widely believed, and possibly correctly, that *Bismarck* actually went down as a result of scuttling. Perhaps it can best be described as a combination of the two. The destruction of the Mighty *Hood* had been avenged after one of the most dramatic chases in naval history.

The website of the HMS *Hood* Association states that:

"In the second week of May 1941 there was a marked increase in German air reconnaissance flights between Greenland and Jan Mayen Island. It seemed likely that the reconnaissance was to check on the current range of the pack ice in the region, but why this was vital to the Germans the British were unsure. It was possible that the Germans were planning raids on Jan Mayen Island or Iceland itself. Another possibility

was that this was a precursor to a breakout into the Atlantic by German surface warships – possibly even their newly worked-up battleship Bismarck. On 14 May, Admiral John Tovey, Commander-in-Chief of the British Home Fleet, asked the British Flag Officer in Iceland for a report on the prevailing ice conditions as well as an assessment on the motive behind the German reconnaissance. The Flag Officer's opinion was that the Germans were most likely planning for an Atlantic breakout by Bismarck."

When the *Bismarck* was launched on 14 February 1939, she was the first of the new breed of ships that Hitler and Grand Admiral Raeder hoped would herald the rebirth of the German surface battle fleet. Although listed as 35,000 tons to ensure that she fell within the limits of the London Naval Treaty, *Bismarck* did, in fact, displace well over that. She was actually of comparable size and main armament to the largest British warship of that time, HMS *Hood*. Despite the similarities, there were differences between the two ships: *Bismarck* was a modern battleship in the truest sense. Her critical spaces were well protected by excellent internal compartments and high quality heavy armour. She also boasted the latest electronics plus very accurate and rapid firing gunnery systems. She and her sister *Tirpitz* were arguably among the best ships at that time. By comparison *Hood* was well-built for her day (1920), but by 1941 was arguably an aged battle cruiser. She had adequate protection in some key areas, but not all. Because of her machinery, she was filled with large, somewhat open spaces. Though her speed had been reduced over the years, at 29 knots, she was still fast for her size. Her guns were deadly, but she had outdated gunnery systems. She did boast advanced radar, but her crew had hardly enough time to become proficient in its use.

To fight each other, *Bismarck* could absorb more damage while firing faster and more accurately than *Hood*. *Bismarck* could take and give more in battle. Each ship had the ability to sink or severely damage the other, but the advantage clearly was with *Bismarck*. This is not a negative reflection on *Hood*, but simply an observance that *Bismarck* was 20 years more modern than *Hood*. *Bismarck's* design reflected all that had been learned between the times the two ships were built.

Hood, *Prince of Wales* and destroyers, weighed anchor at 2356 hrs. They departed Scapa Flow at midnight, 22nd May, heading for Hvalsfjord. Shortly thereafter, the destroyers were divided into two divisions – one to screen *Hood* and the other to screen *Prince of Wales*. The vessels then commenced zigzagging and steered 310°. This continued until 1855 hours, when the course was altered to 283°. By noon, 23 May, the vessels were at 62° 55' N 02° 14.8' W and on a heading of 270°. Shortly thereafter, another successful RIX was conducted. At 1400 hours, the destroyers *Anthony* and *Antelope*, short on fuel, parted company with the force and headed for Iceland. As the day wore on for the remaining vessels, the weather grew cloudy and the sea swells became heavier.

Back at Scapa Flow, Tovey was now faced with a decision about whether to sail himself so when Tovey at last found out for certain that the German ships were no longer at Bergen, he still had the uncertainty about enemy intentions remaining. Lütjens's force had in fact sailed from Bergen during the early evening of 21st May. The poor weather conditions had been perfect for an undetected departure.

At roughly 1915 hrs 23rd May, Able Seaman Newell on board the cruiser HMS *Suffolk*, in the Denmark Straits, was on duty as the starboard after look out. He was there to cover the 'blind' zone in *Suffolk's* radar coverage astern. As he scanned the horizon he saw *Bismarck*, and then *Prinz Eugen* roughly 7 miles away. He immediately called out 'Ship bearing green one four oh', followed seconds later by 'two ships bearing green one four oh'. *Suffolk* heeled over to port to seek the cover of the fog bank. It was also probable that *Bismarck* had not spotted *Suffolk* as she did not open fire. Signals were sent out to say that contact with the enemy had at last been made.

By 2000 hrs, *Hood's* force was at 63°20N' 27°00'W. Shortly before this, at 1939 hrs, Vice-Admiral Holland ordered his vessels to raise steam for full speed and to change course to 295°. Shortly thereafter, at 2004 hrs, he had the news he had been waiting for: *Suffolk* had positively sighted *Bismarck* and its consort in the Denmark Strait. This was followed-up by a report from *Norfolk* at 2040 hrs. Plots put the Germans approximately 300 miles to the north of Holland's force. Vice Admiral Holland had possibly tow choices. The first option was to cut across their bows on a westward course whilst they headed south. This would allow all the British guns to bear on the German ships whilst the enemy would only be able to fire at the British squadron with their forward guns. Of course, such a move could be easily countered. The second choice was for Holland's ships to cross the German squadrons path well ahead, then swing around and approach from the west. This would silhouette the Germans against the morning sky and considerably ease range finding for the British.

By 2054 hrs, HMS *Hood* was steaming at 27 knots on a heading of 295°. As the speed increased, the destroyers were struggling to maintain station in the heavy seas. Vice-Admiral Holland signalled to the destroyers 'If you are unable to maintain this speed, I will have to go on without you. You should follow at your best speed'. The four tiny destroyers did their best to keep up with the old battle cruiser fairly but took a horrendous buffeting in doing so. At 2200 hrs, the crews of *Hood*, *Prince of Wales* and their accompanying destroyers were officially notified of the Germans presence in the Denmark Strait. Interception and anticipated action would take place between 0140 and 0200 hours that morning. All hands were ordered to be prepared to change into clean undergarments (to help prevent infection should they be wounded) and to don battle gear (life vests, flash gear, gas masks, helmets and, where necessary, cold weather gear). At 2230 hrs, 'darken ship' was ordered. By 0015 hours, 24 May, crews aboard both ships had been called to action stations and the battle ensigns were raised. They were then an estimated 120 miles south of the German ships.

So it was that shortly after midnight HMS *Suffolk* reported that she had lost radar contact with the German vessels. Aboard HMS *Hood*, Vice-Admiral Holland calmly received the news. With no definite position for the German warships, he ordered that the crews to go to relaxed action stations (permission to sleep or at least relax at action stations) and a reduction in the ships' speed to 25 knots. The heading changed to the north (340°) in order to cover any possible reversal of course by the Germans.

And so by now it was a guessing game for the British forces. Loss of contact by *Suffolk* was a blow and suggested that the German squadron may well have altered course. This being the case, he had to decide what that course alteration might be. They may have decided that having been tracked it was likely that British forces would be concentrated to intercept them, and that it would be better to reverse course and disappear into the Arctic Ocean. Alternatively, they may have altered course to the south-east or the south-west. In any case, it seemed to Holland that the best course of action was to close the distance between his ships and the last known position of the German squadron as quickly as possible at this point. He signalled to his force at 0030 hrs that 'If enemy is not in sight by 0210, I will probably alter course 180° until cruisers regain touch'. He then once again signalled his battle plan: 'Intend both ships to engage *Bismarck* and to leave *Prinz Eugen* to *Norfolk* and Suffolk'. Of course, due to the ban on radio usage, this message was not transmitted to either *Suffolk* or *Norfolk*. At 0147 hrs, Holland signalled 'If battle cruisers turn 200° at 0205 destroyers continue to search to the northward'.

Due to the poor weather and restricted visibility, it is not known if all four destroyers received the order. This order shows the extent to which, just a few hours before the engagement took place, the British forces were 'searching in the dark'. At 0203 hrs, just after dawn (approximately 0200 hrs in those latitudes at that time of year), *Hood* and *Prince of Wales* assumed a more southerly course of 200° at a speed of 25 knots. The destroyers then parted with the large ships to screen at 15 mile intervals to the north. This was to better the chances of locating the Germans should they successfully elude the *Suffolk* and *Norfolk*. Holland also ordered *Prince of Wales* to use her Type 284 gunnery radar to search 020 - 140°. Unfortunately, *Prince of Wales's* Type 284 radar was experiencing troubles, which rendered it more or less defective. Captain Leach therefore requested permission to use the somewhat more powerful Type 281 radar, but his request was refused, as the transmissions/emissions would have caused great interference to *Hood's* own Type 284 radar.

At 0247 hrs, *Suffolk* regained radar contact with the fleeing German vessels. Her reports placed the Germans approximately 35 miles/64.8 km north-west of *Hood* and *Prince of Wales*. Holland ordered another heading change, this time to 220°. Speed was gradually increased to 28 knots. By 0341 hrs, both vessels were on a course of 240°. At 0450 hrs, *Prince of Wales* took over guide of the fleet, positioning herself ahead of *Hood*. Why this temporary switching of position took place is not clear. It is recorded in *Prince of Wales's* log as well as in the narrative of the operation written afterwards by Captain Leach but neither document explains the reason behind the move.

Hood resumed guide at 0505 hrs. Between 0500 and 0510 hrs, Holland quietly ordered, 'Prepare for instant action'. The crews then went to the first level of readiness. The command crew trained their binoculars and strained their eyes to the north, as they silently waited for contact to be made. Over the past few hours the sky had grown lighter and visibility gradually increased, so that at roughly 0535 - 0536 hrs, lookouts in *Prince of Wales* visually sighted smoke and mast tops of the enemy vessels at a range of at least 38,000 yards (18.75 nm). By 0537 hrs enough of the ships could be seen to confirm they were the Germans. *Prince of Wales* transmitted an enemy report at 0537 hrs. Translated from code, it read: '*Emergency to Admiralty and C-in-C Home Fleet. One battleship and one heavy cruiser, bearing 335, distance 17 miles. My position 63-20 North, 31-50 West. My course 240. Speed 28 knots*'. *Hood* sighted the Germans shortly thereafter, but did not transmit her enemy report until 0543 hours.

The Germans were well aware of the approach of the British warships, hydrophones aboard *Prinz Eugen* had detected the sounds of fast moving turbine-driven vessels some time earlier in the hour. The initial assumption was that they were cruisers. Spotters in *Prinz Eugen* and *Bismarck* first sighted the smoke plumes of the approaching British vessels around 0535 hrs. At 0537 hrs, they intercepted *Prince of Wales's* enemy report. Despite this, they apparently were not yet aware that they were being intercepted by major warships. An intercept of any kind was not apparent until 0543, when *Hood* was sighted and her enemy report intercepted. Though the foes were still thought to be cruisers, the alarm was ordered in both German ships.

After the alarm at 0545hrs, the German crews, like their British counterparts, prepared themselves and anxiously awaited orders. These, however, were not soon to come, Admiral Lütjens was in somewhat of a quandary, as he had strict orders not to engage enemy warships unless absolutely necessary. His main priority was to get out into the Atlantic unscathed. If he took the time to engage the approaching vessels, it may delay him sufficiently to allow other British warships to join the fray. Worse, he could sustain damage or lose one or even both of his ships. He took no apparent action other than to order a possible increase in speed by *Bismarck*. At 0537 hrs, Vice-Admiral Holland had ordered his vessels to turn 40° to starboard together. This put the vessels on a heading of 280°, and placed the enemy fine off *Hood* and *Prince of Wales*'s bows. The British ships were steaming at nearly 29 knots, with *Prince of Wales* roughly 800 yards off *Hood*'s starboard quarter. Unfortunately, rather than come out ahead of the Germans, Holland's force had actually been on a diverging course. Now that his original intentions were no longer possible, Holland's plan was to make a head-on dash at the enemy, then turn at short range to bring his full guns to bear.

Holland had a possible reason for doing this: First, he may have been considering *Hood*'s susceptibility to long range, high velocity, plunging shells: her weak deck armour and some areas of her side armour could easily be penetrated with disastrous results. It was critical that HMS *Hood* closed the range as quickly as possible but without allowing the Germans to slip ahead of his ships. Once the range had been closed, *Hood* would still be susceptible to enemy fire, but fire at such ranges would come at flatter trajectories. *Hood*'s main side armour during such an engagement should hopefully stand up to enemy gunfire. He may have merely been trying to present an end-on and smaller target until he was within ranges more suited to accurate gunnery for *Hood*. There were still some risks and major disadvantages to the approach he had in mind however, by approaching virtually head-on, the British ships would not be able to bring their full compliment of main guns (8 x 15" for *Hood* and 10 x 14" for *Prince of Wales*) to bear. The ships would also be charging into the wind, the spray would make using their optical range finders difficult. Holland also had his ships in close formation. If the enemy did find the range, it would be fairly easy to shift fire from one ship to the other. Lastly, as the ships raced towards each other, the Germans would still have the advantage of bringing full guns (8 x 15" for *Bismarck* and 8 x 8" for *Prinz Eugen*) to bear. Their optical equipment (already far superior to the British types) would also suffer less from the effects of the wind and spray, as the wind would be on their other sides. Lastly, if the ship were not perfectly end-on, it would actually present the German gunners with a large target.

Action commenced at 0552 1/2 hours, as *Hood*'s two forward turrets fired the first salvoes. Half a minute later, *Prince of Wales*'s forward turrets followed suit. *Hood*'s first salvo fell near *Prinz Eugen* but did not actually hit. *Prince of Wales*'s opening salvo was observed to be at least 1,500 yards over and to the right of *Bismarck*. The Germans were shocked to learn that the approaching vessels were not cruisers – they were in fact major combatants – a King George V class battleship and even worse, the famed and feared battle cruiser HMS *Hood*. At 0555 hrs, after about two minutes of British shelling, Captain Lindemann then gave permission to open fire. *Bismarck*, firing four gun salvoes, shot first followed shortly by *Prinz Eugen*. Both vessels concentrated their fire on the lead British vessel, *Hood*. *Bismarck*'s first salvo fell in front and slightly to starboard of *Hood*. *Bismarck*'s second, fell directly between *Hood* and *Prince of Wales*. Its third salvo appeared to straddle *Hood*. Meanwhile, *Prinz Eugen* had loosed between 2 and 3 salvoes herself. One of these salvoes straddled *Hood* at roughly the same time that *Bismarck*'s third salvo fell. A hit on *Hood* from *Prinz Eugen* started a bright fire that proceeded to spread across a portion of the shelter deck to port of the main mast and aft superstructure. Though it apparently did not reach the motor launches/boats, it did reach various ready-use ammunition lockers and began 'cooking off' the munitions inside.

Vice-Admiral Holland realised that the situation was getting desperate: The Germans had already found the range and HMS *Hood* was taking hits. He was also suffering casualties on the burning shelter deck. Neither of his own ships appeared to be scoring any decisive hits on the enemy. *Hood*, having made the error of opening fire against the wrong ship was only now getting the correct range for *Bismarck*. At 0555 hours both ships turned to port to open up firing from their rear turrets. Sometime during the first moments of the execution of this turn, *Hood* was dealt her death blow, *Bismarck*'s 5th salvo had straddled, with one or two shells likely striking *Hood* somewhere around the main mast, or possibly through a narrow weak zone in her side. Aboard *Prince of Wales*, Captain Leach happened to be looking at *Hood*:

> *"...at the moment when a salvo arrived and it appeared to be across the ship somewhere about the mainmast. In that salvo there were, I think, two shots short and one over, but it may have been the other way round. But I formed the impression at the time that something had arrived on board Hood in a position just before the mainmast and slightly starboard. It was not a very definite impression that I had, but it was sufficiently definite to make me look at Hood for a further period. In fact I wondered what the result was going to be, and between one and two seconds after I formed that impression, an explosion took place in the Hood, which appeared to me to come from very much the same position in the ship. There was a very fierce upward rush of flame the shape of a funnel, rather a thin funnel, and almost instantaneously the ship was enveloped in smoke from one end to the other."*

Although there was naturally some variation in the reports that witnesses gave, most agree that a tall, slim geyser of flame, similar in appearance to a welding torch, shot up from the area around the main mast (possibly venting flame/gas shooting up from the engine room vents). At the same time, a gigantic, strangely quiet, explosion or conflagration wracked the entire aft end of the ship. Large pieces of debris were observed in the air. As the flames turned into a mushroom cloud, the entire ship became wreathed in heavy smoke. She slowed to a stop and heeled heavily to starboard."

On *Hood*, a bright flash was seen to sweep round outside and everyone was thrown to the floor. The ship momentarily righted herself, then she began an roll to port, a roll from which she never recovered. As she rolled to port, she began to go down by the stern. The bow began to swing sharply upwards, HMS *Hood* was going down and doing so quickly. In his book Flagship *Hood*, survivor Ted Briggs records that Vice-Admiral Holland, sat dejectedly in his seat, with Captain Kerr attempting to stand at his side, and that no order was given to abandon ship, it really was not necessary. Everyone seemed to realise what was happening. Those that could do so, very calmly left their stations in an attempt to clear the foundering ship. The 'Mighty *Hood*', most famous of all warships, had just been devastated by a massive explosion. It truly was unfathomable if not nightmarish to all who watched. This spectacle resulted in a momentary lull in the battle. The section of the ship from just before the main mast aft to "Y" turret was laid waste – a mass of largely unrecognisable steel and twisted framework. Witnesses watched in horror as the remains of the stern, twisted, swung vertical and quickly sank. The front section swung high into the air at an angle between 45° and vertical and began to pivot about as it rapidly sank. According to the Germans, as the bow rose into the air, *Hood*'s forward turrets were seen to fire one last salvo. If this is true, it is likely due to a short or a mechanical failure. Another possibility is that they were venting flames from an internal fire or smaller scale explosion.

Hood was gone. Out of her crew of 1,418 men, only three, Midshipman William Dundas, Able Seaman Robert Tilburn and Signalman Ted Briggs remained. Dundas had escaped the Compass Platform by kicking out one of the starboard windows. He squeezed through to safety just as the sea reached him. Moments earlier, Ted Briggs had exited the Compass Platform by the starboard side door. As Ted reached the door, the Squadron Navigator, Commander Warrand, smiled and selflessly moved aside and gestured for him to leave first. Though he was sure that Commanders Warrand and Gregson had also made it outside, he was never to see either of them again. As Ted climbed down the ladderways, the sea overtook him. He came to the surface a short time later. Meanwhile, on *Hood*'s port forward shelter deck, Able Seaman Bob Tilburn escaped by climbing down onto the fo'c'sle deck and diving into the sea. He narrowly missed being fatally trapped by *Hood*'s plunging superstructure. After being dragged down some distance, he freed himself and reached the surface. There was no trace of the other 1,415 crewmen. Of HMS *Hood* herself, all that remained on the surface was a morass of floating debris and an oil slick 4" deep. Fire flickered here and there among the debris. They were eventually rescued by HMS Electra and landed in Iceland on May 24th then flown home to the United Kingdom.

The first enquiry was convened in early June. They quickly reached the conclusion that one or more shells from *Bismarck* had managed to penetrate *Hood*'s armour/protective plating and detonate her aft magazines. Although it was a logical conclusion, the proceedings came under scrutiny. As it turned out, very few witnesses were called, and of the *Hood* survivors, only Dundas gave evidence. Verbatim records of the evidence were not made and to make matters worse, the appropriate experts had not been called. It was not long before the Admiralty decided that a second board would have to be convened.

The second Board convened on 27th August 1941 under the Chairmanship of Rear-Admiral H.T.C. Walker, a former Captain of the *Hood*. This board called two of the three survivors (Ted Briggs and Bob Tilburn), numerous eyewitnesses from *Prince of Wales*, *Suffolk* and *Norfolk*. It also called experts in the fields of construction and armament/explosives. Although far more thorough than the first enquiry, the second Board ultimately reached much the same conclusions as the first Board – A salvo from *Bismarck* penetrated *Hood*'s vitals and detonated the aft magazines. Other possibilities exist, but a shell from *Bismarck* was the most likely cause.

The nineteen page report concluded:

"(1) That the sinking of the HOOD was due to a hit from BISMARCK's 15-in shell in or adjacent to HOOD's 4-in or 15-in magazines, causing them all to explode and wreck the after part of the ship. The probability is that the 4-in magazines exploded first.

(2) There is no conclusive evidence that one or two torpedo warheads detonated or exploded simultaneously with the magazines, or at any other time, but the possibility cannot be entirely excluded. We consider that if they had done so their effect would not have been so disastrous as to cause the immediate destruction of the ship, and on the whole we are of the opinion that they did not.

(3) That the fire which was seen on HOOD's boat deck, and in which U.P. and/or 4-in ammunition was certainly involved, was not the cause of her loss.

A writer to the Times of London, in a letter entitled "DESIGN OF THE HOOD NO MISCALCULATION -The Handicap of Age" stated the *Hood* had not been destroyed by a "lucky hit" but because:

"*...she had to fight a ship 22 years more modern than herself. This was not the fault of the British seamen. It was the direct responsibility of* *those who opposed the rebuilding of the British Battle Fleet until 1937, two years before the second great war started. It is fair to her gallant crew that this should be written."*

In a letter to the Controller and the First Lord, Sir Dudley Pound wrote on 28th May:

"The loss of HOOD from internal explosion after a few minutes' action at 23,000 yards is disturbing, as we thought that the defects in construction which led to the similar loss of three capital ships at Jutland had been eliminated. . . . Now, after the lapse of 25 years, we have the first close action between one of our capital ships and that of the Germans since the Battle of Jutland and the HOOD has been destroyed in what appears to the onlooker to be in exactly the same manner as the QUEEN MARY, INDEFATIGABLE and INVINCIBLE, in spite of the action which was taken subsequent to Jutland to prevent further ships being destroyed as a result of 'flash'. . . . In the light of this experience, will you please have the whole matter re-opened, going back to the records of the last war and see whether any theory can be evolved that would explain the loss of all four ships from some cause other than 'flash'."

The original construction cost was £6,025,000 (of which John Brown and Company Ltd reportedly made £214,108).

HMS *Hood* contained 380 telephones at the time of her loss and had 3,874 electric light fittings. She had nearly 200 miles of permanent electric cable, which weighed approximately 100 tons. General provisions for 4 months amounted to 320 tons, including one month's fresh meat. Breakfast consisted of 100 gallons of tea, four sides of bacon, 300 lbs of tomatoes, 600 lbs bread, 75 lbs of butter. Fuel consumption at full speed was 3 yards to the gallon and the crew were paid a total of £6,000 per month.

Information contained on the official HMS *Hood* Web site is reproduced by kind permission of Frank Allen.

HMS Hood.

Rare image of the Hood blowing up.

The Bismarck fires upon HMS Hood – as seen from Prinz Eugen.

The last moments of the Mighty Hood as seen from Bismarck 14 miles away.

4. The Hunt for the *Bismarck*

The Battleship *Bismarck*, pride of Hitler's Kriegsmarine and marvel of marine engineering, was built for only one purpose – to destroy allied shipping and to rule the waves. How close she came to that purpose is already well documented and was the subject of the well known film, *Sink the Bismarck*.

The shot which sank the *Hood* may have been a bit fortuitous (see previous chapter) but then the Royal Navy was to have some luck also – when a Fairey Swordfish aircraft from HMS *Ark Royal* fired a torpedo which caught the rudder of *Bismarck*, causing her steering to lock her into a circular course, thus enabling the Royal Navy to close in and finish her off.

Although she was an 'enemy' ship, I have always marvelled at the sleek superstructure and exquisite lines of this beautiful ship. Alas, the Atlantic Ocean has her now and forever, lying broken and humiliated on the seabed.[10]

On 1 July 1936 her keel was laid at the Blohm & Voss Shipyard in Hamburg (Yard No. BV509, slipway 9). On 14 February 1939 she was launched by Dorothea von Loewenfeld, granddaughter of the German Chancellor Otto von Bismarck. *Bismarck* had a displacement of 45,950 metric tons and a full load displacement of 50,955.7 metric tons.[11] Her overall length was 251 metres and her beam 36 metres. More than 90% of *Bismarck*'s steel hull was welded. As added protection against an underwater hit, her double bottom extended over about 80% of her length. Her upper deck ran from bow to stern, beneath which was the battery deck, the armoured deck and the upper and middle platform decks. A lower platform deck ran parallel with

---

[10] It has become apparent in recent years, following the discovery of the *Bismarck* on the seabed, in a secret location, that she was in fact scuttled before the Royal Navy could sink her.

[11] According to some US sources from a Technical Mission to Europe, her full load displacement was 53,546 metric tons.

the stowage spaces, which formed the overhead of the double bottom, almost throughout.

Longitudinally, the ship was divided into 22 compartments, numbered in sequence, stern forward. Forty percent of her weight was in armour. The propulsion unit comprised 9% of the ships weight and consisted of three turbines, for which twelve high-pressure boilers provided steam. It was designed to provide a top speed of 29 knots, but modifications increased this to more than 30 knots and 150,000 HP. *Bismarck* was one of the fastest battleships built up to that time although her range was 1000 nautical miles less than that of the *Scharnhorst* class ships.

From October through November 1940 she conducted sea trials in the Baltic Sea. On 9th December 1940 she returned to Hamburg for completion of her refitting and to prepare for sea and by 24th January 1941 she was ready to sail.

On 7th and 8th March she passed through the Kiel Canal for the last time and took on supplies at Scheerhafen (Kiel) of ammunition, fuel, water and two Arado 196 Seaplanes. Striped camouflage paint was added and the ship was now fully equipped.

On 5th May 1941, after more sea trials in the Baltic, Hitler visited the ship and spent a total of five hours on board. On 12th May 1941 Admiral Lutjens and his staff arrived on board and on 18th May 1941 "Operation Rheinübung" began. At 1200hrs on 19th May her position is written as 54° 45' north, 13° 20' east in her War Diary. *Bismarck* joined *Prinz Eugen* and destroyers Z-16 *Friedrich Eckoldt* and Z-23 off Rügen Island. Later on destroyer Z-10 *Hans Lody* joined the formation. At 1300 hrs on the 20th May, the Swedish Cruiser *Gotland* sighted the passage of these ships and the "secret" was out. On 21st May, at 1315 hrs, a lone Spitfire from Coastal Command spotted and photographed *Bismarck* lying in the Grimstadfjord, Norway.

Not many know that *Bismarck* was discovered by a PR pilot called Michael 'Babe' Suckling, who landed at Wick from the Norway fjords with his photos, where *Bismarck* was identified. The film was required in London and his was the only transport available with limited fuel. He flew to Nottingham where he ran out of fuel, but fortunately where he had a friend who owned a garage and car so they drove all the way in the black out to London with the film arriving there at 2pm. The film about *Bismarck* shows a PR pilot discovering the ship but he looks rather old. 'Babe' Suckling was so named because of his youthful appearance. He later lost his life, as did many PR pilots (the losses were 50% at one stage).

Bismarck sailed at 2000 hrs the same day for the Atlantic.

Also on the 21st May Bletchley Park managed to decode signals from the month of April. One of these stated that *Bismarck* had taken on prize crews and charts. This led the Admiralty to the conclusion that the *Bismarck* was intended to carry out a raid on allied shipping routes. That was Bletchley Park's sole contribution to the battle against the *Bismarck*. Baron Burkard von Mullenheim-Rechberg states on this subject in his book printed in 1982:

> *"British intelligence learned in March or April 1941 that Bismarck was going to take on a new supply of charts at Gotenhafen. This news confirmed the suspicion that she was about to undertake an operation in the Atlantic, and the Home fleet was alerted accordingly. British intelligence got that information either from an agent in Gotenhafen or by decoding German administrative radio signals – it is still not clear which.*
>
> *Evaluation of this risk raises questions concerning such matters as who served in the Gotenhafen chart centre and why orders like the one to take on new charts were transmitted by radio rather than telephone or teletype. I do not have any personal knowledge in these areas nor is it possible for me to reconstruct what happened. The handling of administrative details of that nature could I hardly have entered into Lutjens's calculations at all, let alone as risks to be averted."*

Even in the early 1980s the Baron had obviously never heard of the fact that we had cracked the Enigma codes!

Hugo-Sebag Montefiorre, in his book *Enigma - The Battle for the Code* states:

> *'Nevertheless, there was jubilation in Bletchley Park's Hut 6, the Air Force Enigma code breaking unit, when the news of the sinking came through. The code breakers there believed that without their contribution Germany's giant battleship would never have been found. Code breakers did not normally real messages once they had worked out the Enigma settings for the day. But on 25 May, Keith Batey, the man who was to*

marry Mavis Lever (Dilly Knox's helper during the Battle of Matapan) happened to pay a visit to the machine room. That was where secretaries, using British Typex cipher machines, set up so as to act like replica Enigmas with the correct settings for the day in question, typed out the coded messages to produce the true plain-language texts. One of the typists turned to Batey and, pointing to a piece of paper containing the message she had just deciphered, said, 'This one looks interesting.' A German Air Force officer in Athens in connection with the invasion of Crete, had wanted to find out Bismarck's whereabouts, since a close relation was on the ship. A signal was sent requesting this information. The reply stated that Bismarck was making for the west coast of France. This information appears to have reached Admiral Tovey on his flagship shortly after he had already decided that Bismarck's destination must be Brest. So unknown to the celebrating Batey, and the codebreakers in Hut 6, their work, which could, in different circumstances, have been decisive, may not in fact have influenced the search for Bismarck after all.'

Baron Burkard von Mullenheim-Rechberg, in his own story of being a survivor of the *Bismarck* confirms this:

'I have often been asked whether the British success in breaking the German naval code at the beginning of the Second World War had anything to do with the pursuit and destruction of the Bismarck. Such questions have been inspired by new publications describing this breakthrough, which was discreetly handled for many years after the war, in a sometimes sensational manner.'

British experts succeeded in decoding some of the German operational radio transmissions so rapidly that the Admiralty was able to take timely countermeasures and, at times, to frustrate the intentions of the Seekriegsleitung. But in May 1941 they could not read the secret radio traffic between the *Bismarck* and headquarters ashore. It is true that in the second week of May they were able to decode the radio signals of German reconnaissance planes – which, because of the limited coding facilities of an aircraft, were not in the most secure code – and through them to anticipate an imminent sortie of German naval forces into the Atlantic. Likewise, during Exercise Rhine they were able to read the Luftwaffe's lightly encoded radio signals regarding preparations to provide the *Bismarck* with air cover from France on 26 May. But it was mainly by using conventional methods of reconnaissance that the British gained their success against Exercise Rhine.

At 1922 hrs on 23rd May *Bismarck* sighted the cruiser *Suffolk* off Iceland and just over an hour later the cruiser *Norfolk*, at which she fired five salvos. No hits were recorded but *Bismarck*'s forward facing radar (FuMo23) was damaged. On the 24th May two ships were sighted and The Battle of Iceland commenced: one of these ships was the *Prince of Wales*, the other HMS *Hood*. *Hood* opened fire first at 0553 hrs and three shells from the *Prince of Wales* registered hits on the *Bismarck*. At 0601hrs the entry in Bismarck's war diary reads simply "Hood Blows Up" and then shortly after, "obtain four hits on the *Prince of Wales*".

0632hrs. *Bismarck* reports: "Battle cruiser, probably Hood, sunk. Another capital ship, *King George V* or *Renown*, damaged. Two heavy cruisers keeping contact." And at 0705hrs *Bismarck* reports: "We have sunk a battleship at about 63° 10' north, 32° 00' west." The next entry appears five hours later at 1200, giving position 60° 50' north, 37° 50' west.

The *Hood* had gone down in a single blow, 1,400 men gone virtually in an instant. Only three men were found alive and rescued from the Atlantic. The Hood's upper deck was not as armoured as it should have been, enabling a shell from the *Bismarck* to pass through the decking and explode inside a magazine, which blew up the whole ship.

Bismarck sailed on and in the evening parted company with the *Prinz Eugen*. *Bismarck* fired some salvos at the shadowing *Suffolk* and *Norfolk* but recorded no hits. That evening she set course for St Nazaire, for refuelling, and reported that due to enemy radar she was unable to shake off her pursuers. At 2300hrs she was sighted by US Coastguard vessel *Madoc* and at midnight eight Swordfish suddenly attacked; one torpedo hit was recorded, starboard amidships. These aircraft were from the carrier *Victorious* and had attacked at almost extreme range. Mark E. Horan gives the following account of the raid:

On 18 May 1942, Grand Admiral Erich Raeder set in motion the most dramatic test of the Royal Navy's ability to defend the North

Atlantic shipping lanes to date. Operation "Rheinübung" would see the first use of the Kriegsmarine newest warships, the schlachtschiffe KMS *Bismarck* (Kapitän zur See Ernst Lindemann), and the schwere kreuzer KMS *Prinz Eugen* (Kapitän zur See Helmuth Brinkmann). Command was vested in the Vice-Admiral Gunther Lütjens, recently returned from commanding the highly successful Atlantic sortie by the battleships *Scharnhorst* and *Gneisenau*. Based on his earlier experience, as well as the separate operations of panzerschiffe Admiral Scheer and schwere kreuzer Admiral Hipper, great things were expected. Raeder's timing would appear to have been impeccable, for the strength of the Royal Navy's Home Fleet, under Admiral Sir John Tovey, KCB, DSO, RN, was at a low ebb. Though Admiral Tovey theoretically controlled the Royal Navy's three most effective battleships, the venerable HMS *Hood*, the largest warship afloat, HMS King *George V* the new fleet flagship, and HMS *Prince of Wales*, still fitting out, the fleet currently contained not a single aircraft carrier.

The newest edition to the Royal Navy's carrier force, HMS *Victorious*, having been commissioned on 15 May 1941 under Captain H.C. Bovell, RN, was currently at Liverpool preparing for her shakedown cruise. There being a war on even shakedowns involved a mission. Plans had already been set in motion for *Victorious* to deliver 48 RAF Hurricane IIs to Gibraltar and hence to the beleaguered island of Malta. At the same time *Victorious* embarked two Fleet Air Arm organizations to handle fighter and anti-submarine defence of the ship en-route: 800Z flight with six Fulmar II fighters, and 825 Squadron with of nine brand new Swordfish 1s, three of which were equipped with the newest in strike technology, Anti-Surface-Vessel (ASV) radar. Bigger things were on tap in the Mediterranean for 825 Squadron, which was slated to replace the long serving 820 Squadron as one of HMS *Ark Royal*'s torpedo-spotter-reconnaissance squadrons. For 800Z Flight, the job was much more mundane; they were simply ferrying new replacement fighters for *Ark Royal*'s two fighter squadrons, after which the pilots were scheduled to lead the RAF fighters on to Malta.

HMS *Victorious* actually embarked 800Z Flight on 11 May. Eight days later, as she moved into the Clyde, 825 Squadron flew aboard.

On the 20th the final preparations seemed to be in place when she embarked the 48 RAF fighters. Then fate intervened. Early on the 21st, RAF reconnaissance aircraft had placed the two German warships at Korsfjord near Bergen, Norway, and all indications were that they intended to break out shortly. As such, Captain Bovell was ordered to disembark the RAF fighters and proceed to Scapa Flow forthwith to join the Home Fleet. On arrival, Admiral Tovey personally interviewed the commander of 825 Squadron, Lieutenant-Commander (A) Eugene Kingsmill Esmonde, RN, as to his squadron's ability to deliver a torpedo attack. Only after Esmonde satisfied him that the squadron's training level was satisfactory did Tovey consent to add *Victorious* to his force, which consisted of BB HMS *King George V* (F), Rear Admiral A.T.B. Curteis, CB, RN's 2nd Cruiser Squadron (CLs HMS *Galatea* (F), HMS *Aurora*, HMS *Kenya*, HMS *Hermione*) and DDs HMS *Active*, HMS *Punjabi*, HMS *Nestor*, HMS *Inglefield*, HMS *Intrepid* and HMS *Lance*. Along the way he would be joined by BC HMS *Repulse* as well.

The spectacular events of the next 72 hours were to prove to be a nadir for the Royal Navy. The RAF confirmed the breakout on 22 May, followed, less than 24 hours later by the dramatic discovery of the force in the Denmark Strait by HMS *Suffolk* and later HMS *Norfolk*, flying the flag of the commander of the 1st Cruiser Squadron, Rear-Admiral W. Frederick Wake-Walker, CB, OBE, RN. On the morning of 24th, Vice-Admiral Lancelot E. Holland, CB, RN's Squadron, consisting of BC HMS *Hood* (F), BB HMS *Prince of Wales*, as well as the DDs HMS *Electra*, HMS *Anthony*, HMS *Echo*, HMS *Icarus*, HMS *Achates* and HMS *Antelope* managed to "corner the fox", but soon found that the this fox had teeth. At 0600, only minutes into the fight, the great flagship blew up. Minutes later, at 0613, Captain J.C. Leach, MVO, RN was forced to withdraw *Prince of Wales* under the cover of smoke.

Throughout the remainder of the morning and afternoon, while Rear-Admiral Wake-Walker shadowed *Bismarck* with his own cruisers and *Prince of Wales*, Admiral Tovey strove to cut off the German squadron with the remainder of the Home Fleet. As the morning turned into afternoon, he decided to hold Esmonde to his word and, at 1509, detached *Victorious*, escorted by Rear-Admiral Curteis's four

cruisers, to forge ahead, close on *Bismarck* and deliver a torpedo attack in a further effort to slow the quarry down. Although *Victorious'*
Commander Flying, Commander H.C. Ranald, RN, desired the
distance closed to 100 miles before launch, *Victorious* could not get
inside 120 miles in the high seas and finally, at 2210, all nine Swordfish of 825 Squadron set off on the mission assigned, organized in
three sub-flights thus:

1st Sub-Flight:

(5)A+ L-Cdr. (A) E.K. Esmonde, RN, Lt. C.C. Ennever, RN, PO(A)
S.E. Parker - port beam

(5)C S-Lt.(A) J.C. Thompson, RN; A/S-Lt. R.L. Parkinson, RN;
PO(A) A.L. Johnson, RN - port bow

(5)B Lt. T.N.G. MacLean, RNVR; Mid.(A) L. Bailey, RNVR ; NA
D.A. Bruce - port

2nd Sub-Flight:

(5)F+ Lt. P.D. Gick, RN; A/S-Lt.(A) V.K. *Norfolk*, RN; PO(A) L.D.
Sayer - port side; bow

(5)G Lt.(A) F.W.C. Garthwaite, RNVR; S-Lt.(A) W.A. Gillingham,
RNVR; LA H.T A. Wheeler, RN - starboard bow

(5)H/V4337 S-Lt.(A) P.B. Jackson, RN; A/S-Lt. D.A. Berrill, RN; LA
F.G. Sparkes - starboard quarter

3rd Sub-Flight:

(5)K Lt.(A) H.C.M. Pollard, RN; S-Lt.(A) D.M. Beattie, RNVR; LA
P.W. Clitheroe - port quarter

(5)L S-Lt.(A) R. G. Lawson, RNVR; A/S-Lt. F.L. Robinson, RN; LA
I.L. Owen - port quarter

(5)M Sub-Lt.(A) A.J. Houston, RNVR; S-Lt.(A) J.R. Geater, RNVR;
PO(A) W.J. Clinton, RN - did not find *Bismarck*

As soon as they were airborne the Swordfish disappeared into a rain
squall and were lost to view, but the squadron was able to form up
without too much difficulty and set off on a course of 225o. Meanwhile, at 2300, three Fulmars of 800Z Squadron followed with
orders to observe the attack and then maintain contact at all costs so

that, if necessary, another strike could be flown off the next day at dawn. The faster Fulmars soon overtook the lumbering Swordfish, and the combined force continued towards *Bismarck* at 85 knots.

Realistically, the prospects for the attack were not good. The squadron was ill-prepared for its assignment, several of the pilots having only made their first carrier landing on the 19th, and they had not made even a single squadron attack in training. Under the prevailing weather conditions, eight-tenths cloud cover at 1,500 feet with intermittent rain squalls, a visual search was like looking for the proverbial 'needle in a haystack', but the squadron's new ASV radar was expected to make the difference. At 2327 ASV contact was established on a contact some 16 miles ahead of the formation and *Bismarck* was sighted briefly through a gap in the clouds only to be lost again seconds later. Descending below the clouds with his squadron, Esmonde located the cruisers still shadowing, and HMS *Norfolk* directed the aircraft towards their target some fourteen miles ahead on the starboard bow.

At 2350 hours a further ASV contact was made and Esmonde again led his squadron below the cloud cover to begin his attack. Unexpectedly, the contact proved to be the United States Coast Guard cutter *Madoc*, peacefully pitching and rolling in the heavy Atlantic swell. Unfortunately *Bismarck*, then only six miles to the south, spotted the aircraft and the vital element of surprise was lost. When the Swordfish finally closed to deliver their torpedo attack, they were met by a 'very vigorous and accurate' barrage of heavy and light AA, which tagged Esmonde's Swordfish (5A) at a range of four miles. Though Swordfish 5M lost contact in the dense cloud covering the area, the remaining eight aircraft pressed home their attack with élan.

At exactly midnight Esmonde led the first sub-flight into a simultaneous attack. His starboard lower aileron was hit almost immediately, and he abandoned his original intention to attack from starboard, deciding to drop there and then, whilst he was still in a good position on the target's port beam and *Bismarck* was nicely silhouetted against the glow of the setting sun. Both he, and Sub-Lieutenant(A) Thompson, in 5C, released on *Bismarck*'s port bow from an altitude of 100'. The third member of the flight, Lieutenant(A) MacLean, in 5B, got separated in the descent through the clouds and attacked separately, but also on the port side. Proving that his ship handling skills were superb, Kapitän Lindemann artfully dodged all three "fish".

The three Swordfish of the second sub-flight were led in by Lieutenant Gick. Approaching from starboard, he was not satisfied with the approach angle, and elected to pull back into the clouds and work his way round to a better position. The remainder of his flight continued on however, Lieutenant (A) Garthwaite in 5G dropping on *Bismarck*'s starboard bow and Sub-Lieutenant Jackson, in 5H/V4337 from her starboard quarter, but again Lindemann avoided the deadly missiles.

Moments later, the two Swordfish remaining in the third sub-flight appeared on the *Bismarck*'s port quarter, and amid a hail of AA fire, Lieutenant Pollard, in 5J, and Sub-Lieutenant Lawson, in 5K released form a good angle but, again, to no avail. Meanwhile, Percy Gick, in 5F, now appeared low down on the water on the enemy's port bow. His sudden appearance caught the Germans by surprise, and there was no avoiding his torpedo, which ploughed into *Bismarck* amidships, exploding on her armour belt.

As the aircraft turned away, the air gunners sprayed *Bismarck*'s superstructure and gun positions with .303 machine gun fire at almost point blank range. As one of the air gunners remarked later: "It didn't sink the *Bismarck*, but it certainly kept their heads down and in any case, it relieved our feelings." As the Swordfish departed, Petty Officer Airman Parker, Esmonde's TAG, signalled "Have attacked with torpedoes. Only one observed."

A German account of the attack is summarized from an eyewitness report and states:

> "They came in flying low over the water, launched their torpedoes and zoomed away. Flak was pouring from every gun barrel but didn't seem to hit them. The first torpedo hissed past 150 yards in front of the Bismarck's bow. The second did the same and the third. Helmsman Hansen was operating the press buttons of the steering gear as, time and time again, the Bismarck manoeuvred out of danger. She evaded a fifth and then a sixth, when yet another torpedo darted straight towards the ship. A

*few seconds later a tremendous shudder ran through the hull and a tower-
ing column of water rose at Bismarck's side. The nickel-chrome-steel
armour plate of her ship's side survived the attack ..."*

The single hit was confirmed by a shadowing Fulmar pilot who,
just after midnight, reported a "great, black column of dense smoke
rising from the starboard side" and also that "the battleship's speed
was reduced." At this point, relief was in order for the three Fulmars
over *Bismarck*, 0100, *Victorious* launched a further pair to relieve those
on duty and continue shadowing *Bismarck* until dawn. The crews of
these two aircraft were:

Squadron	Pilot	Observer
800Z	Lt.(A) Brian Donald Campbell, RN	S-Lt (A) Mathew Gordon Goodger, RNVR (age 22) - FTR
800Z	Lt. F.C. Furlong	S-Lt. (A) J.E.M. Hoare - Rescued

This mission proved to be beyond the rookie crews of 800Z
Flight. Operating at night, in horrific weather, without radar, the aircraft soon found themselves separated; neither was able to locate
their target. Lost at sea, with little hope of survival short of a miracle,
both aircraft eventually were forced to settle into the Atlantic. Lieu-
tenant(A) Cambell, RN and Sub-Lieutenant Goodger were slated to
join the vast number of Naval personnel missing and presumed lost.
Lieutenant Furlong and Sub-Lieutenant Hoare proved much luckier.
Left bobbing in the stormy North Atlantic in their small raft for 36
hours, the forlorn pair were ultimately rescued by the SS *Braverhill*.

Sunset was at 0052 hours, and the returning strike force had to
make most of their journey back to HMS *Victorious* in the dark. With
the homing beacon aboard the carrier unserviceable, Captain Bovell,
risking the danger from enemy submarines, shone his searchlights
vertically upwards onto the clouds to guide the aircraft, until ordered
to put them out by Rear-Admiral Curteis. Stubborn to the last,
Bovell then signalled his acquiescence with his brightest 20-inch
signal projector! Nonetheless, all nine Swordfish found the carrier
and landed safely between 0200 and 0230, the returning crews all
stating that they had not seen the searchlight display, but had easily
sighted and followed the low-intensity signal lamps used by the
cruisers.

At 0306, just after the last aircraft had landed aboard *Victorious*, and following a brilliant manoeuvre by Lütjens, the two shadowing cruisers, HMS *Norfolk* and HMS *Suffolk* lost contact with KMS *Bismarck*.

For the next thirty-six hours a vast network of airborne and surface ship searches attempted to locate the elusive enemy.

While *Victorious'* strike role was now over, 825 Squadron's Swordfish were part of the search effort. In the mid-morning of the 25th, three Swordfish were put up, but they had no luck. While two managed to return to Victorious, 5H/V4337 was not so lucky, and at 1315 was forced to land at sea. Struggling into their raft, things looked bleak for the crew, Lieutenant(A) P.B. Jackson, RN (P), Sub-Lieutenant D.A. Berrill, RN (O), and Leading Airman F.G. Sparkes (TAG), especially when an aerial search came up empty. However, lady luck kept her eye on the trio; eight days later, on 3 June, they were found by the Icelandic steamer SS *Largufoss* 50 nautical miles E of Cape Farewell.

A further effort on the 26th, again by three aircraft, proved more costly. This time the missing Swordfish simply disappeared. Lost with it were three of the men that attacked *Bismarck* 30 hours earlier: Lieutenant(A) Henry Charles Michell Pollard, DSC, RN (P-age 24), Sub-Lieutenant(A) David Musk Beattie, RNVR (O-age 24), and Leading Airman Percy William Clitheroe, DSM, RN (TAG-age 25).

Thus ended the role of HMS *Victorious* in the hunt for the *Bismarck*. But 24 May did not mark the last time 825 Squadron would attack a German battleship. Some nine months later, on 12 February 1942, during the Channel dash, six Swordfish of a reformed 825 Squadron, still led by the indomitable Esmonde, would fly on a one-way mission to destiny. Among the 13 airmen killed that day were six of the 24 survivors of the *Bismarck* attack:

Lt Commander (A) Eugene Kingsmill Esmonde, DSO, VC, RN (P); age 32 (Swordfish W5984/H)

Petty Officer Airman William Johnson Clinton, RN (TAG); age 22 (Swordfish W5984/H)

Petty Officer Airman Ambrose Lawrence Johnson DSM, RN (TAG); age 22 (Swordfish W5983/G)

Sub Lt (A) John Chute Thompson, RN (P); age 27 (Swordfish V4523/F)

Sub Lt Robert Laurens Parkinson, RN (O); age 21 (Swordfish W5985/K)

Leading Airman Henry Thomas Albert Wheeler, RN (TAG) (Swordfish W5985/K)

Seven months later, on 17 September, 1942, the survivors were reduced yet again when Sub-Lieutenant (A) Valentine Kay *Norfolk*, DSC, RN (O), was killed in Swordfish DK776 while a member of 816 Squadron. As far as I have been able to determine, the remaining seventeen survived World War II, all members of a unique fraternity.

Finale – HMS *Ark Royal*

Even before the *Bismarck* crisis had begun, important events were transpiring in the Western Mediterranean. On 12 May, HMS *Furious* had departed Greenock under the protection of HMS *London*, and sailed for Gibraltar carrying 40 RAF Hurricane IIs and nine FAA Fulmar IIs of the new 800X Flight, the lot being destined for Malta. Arriving on the 18th, the 19th was spent transferring 21 of the Hurricanes and all of the Fulmar IIs (exchanged for worn out Fulmar Is) to HMS *Ark Royal*. On the 20th, Force H, commanded by Vice-Admiral Sir James F. Somerville, KCB, DSO, RN, sortied into the Western Mediterranean to begin Operation 'Splice'.

Joining the two carriers were BC HMS *Renown* (F), CA HMS *Sheffield*, and DDs HMS *Faulknor*, HMS *Foresight*, HMS *Forester*, HMS *Foxhound*, HMS *Fury* and HMS *Hesperus*.

On the 21st, amid significant confusion, seven Fulmars and 48 Hurricane I/IIs departed for Malta. While two Fulmars and one Hurricane were lost en-route, the rest reached Malta safely. Turning about, Force H returned to Gibraltar on the 22nd. For the next 48 hours, the news about the *Bismarck*'s break out captured the world's imagination. Then, just before the *Victorious* attack commenced, at 2331 on the evening of 24th, the Admiralty signalled Vice-Admiral Somerville to again take Force H to sea and "Steer so as to intercept *Bismarck* from southward. Enemy must be short of fuel and will have to make for an oiler. Her future movements may guide you to this oiler."

Leaving *Furious* behind (as she carried no aircraft), Somerville led Force H into the Atlantic. HMS *Ark Royal* was carrying five Fleet Air Arm Squadrons, believed to total 23 Fulmar II fighters and 27 Swordfish I TSRs:

807: 11 x Fulmar I/II Lt-Cdr J. Sholto Douglas, DSO, RN

808: 12 x Fulmar II Lt-Cdr R. C. Tillard, RN

810: 9 x Swordfish I Lt-Cdr M. Johnstone, DSC, RN

818: 9 x Swordfish I Lt-Cdr Trevenen Penrose Coode, RN

820: 9 x Swordfish I Lt-Cdr J. A. Stewart-Moore, RN

As British forces combed the most likely routes open to *Bismarck*, an official Admiralty communiqué told an anxiously waiting world the outcome of events thus far:

> *"After the engagement yesterday in the North Atlantic, the enemy forces made every effort to shake off the pursuit. Later in the evening an attack by naval aircraft resulted in at least one torpedo hit on the enemy. Operations are still proceeding with the object of bringing the enemy forces to close action."*

Vice-Admiral Lütjens was obviously impressed by the fact that British radar had enabled the two cruisers to keep contact with her for a night and a day, in darkness and very bad weather. At 0401 on the morning of the 25th, unaware that at last he had in fact given them the slip, he proceeded to send a long signal to Group West to outline his view of events thus far:

> *"Enemy radar gear with a range of at least 35,000 meters interferes with operations in Atlantic to considerable extent. In Denmark Strait ships were located and enemy maintained contact. Not possible to shake off enemy despite favourable weather conditions. Will be unable to oil unless succeed in shaking off enemy by superior speed . . ."*

Unable to interrupt the transmission, it was not until 0846 that Group West was able to signal Lütjens that it was their belief that contact had been lost some six hours earlier! Lütjens immediately resumed radio silence, but the damage had been done. All through the 25th and 26th *Victorious* continued to fly off her Swordfish on anti-submarine patrols and air searches, but nothing was found. At 1625 on the 25th Adolf Hitler sent a personal message to Vice-Admiral Lütjens offering, 'Best wishes on your birthday'. It was not acknowledged as *Bismarck* kept silent, steaming at a reduced speed of 20 knots for the safety of a French West Coast port. She was running short of fuel due to the hit on her oil tanks and at one point, was reduced to 12 knots to allow for repairs to the damaged forecastle. (Had *Bismarck* travelled at her full capability of 28 knots throughout, there is little doubt that she would have made that port she sought). At 1924 the Admiralty informed all ships their belief that *Bismarck* was making for western France.

That night, Force H steamed northwards into an increasingly heavy sea and a rising wind. With waves reaching more than 50 feet, Somerville was forced to reduce his speed; first to 23 knots at 2115, to 21 knots at 2340, 19 knots at 0000, and finally to 17 knots at 0112. At dawn on 26th, even HMS *Ark Royal*, with her deck 62 feet above the water, was "taking it green" and the wind over the flight deck had reached 50 knots.

Dawn saw Coastal Command renew the aerial search with vigour. At 0835 *Ark Royal* joined the effort by launching 10 Swordfish to search the western semicircle, covering the 180° arc from south-southwest through north-northeast. At half past ten that morning, Pilot Officer D.A. Briggs, RAF, flying Catalina Z of 209 Squadron from Lough Erne, Ireland, on the southernmost of the Bay patrols, sighted *Bismarck*. Although *Bismarck* immediately engaged the stranger with heavy and accurate fire, the Catalina was able to get off a fairly accurate sighting report before losing the battleship in the weather. His position report placed *Bismarck* 690 miles to the west-northwest of Brest and gave the pursuers less than 24 hours in which to intercept, after which she would reach friendly umbrella of protection afforded by the Luftwaffe, and ultimately the sanctuary of port. Admiral Tovey's only hope was to slow her down with yet another air strike, and the only carrier within striking distance was HMS *Ark Royal* coming up from the south.

Copying Briggs contact report, the two closest Swordfish altered course to intercept. At 1114, 2H (Sub-Lieutenant(A) J.V. Hartley, Sub-Lieutenant P. R. Elias, Leading Airman N. Huxley) sighted what they believed to be a German cruiser. Seven minutes later 2F (Lieutenant(A) J.R. Callander, Lieutenant P.B. Schondfeldt, and Leading Airman R. Baker) joined 2H and identified *Bismarck*. Meanwhile, *Ark Royal* fitted two ASV-equipped Swordfish with long-range tanks and sent them off at 1200 to maintain contact until relieved. At 1154 *Bismarck* broke her long silence, reporting that she was being shadowed by an enemy 'Land plane'. Thereafter, and until 2320 that night, *Ark Royal*'s Swordfish, working in pairs, maintained a vigil over *Bismarck*, keeping her under continuous observation.

Beginning sometime after noon, *Ark Royal*'s search planes began fluttering home; the last two were 2F and 2H, coming aboard at 1324. With the search planes safely aboard, the flight deck personnel began the daunting job of preparing the critical torpedo striking force to hit the enemy in conditions that bordered on the horrific. Eventually, fourteen Swordfish from all three TSR Squadrons, each armed with an 18" torpedo, were spotted. Meanwhile, in a further effort to maintain contact, Vice-Admiral Somerville ordered HMS *Sheffield* to close *Bismarck* and to shadow her with radar. In what would turn out to be a glaring omission, HMS *Ark Royal* was not informed of this action.

At 1450, after a meticulous briefing during which the strike commander, Lieutenant-Commander J.A. Stewart-Moore, was specifically informed that only *Bismarck* was in the target area, the 820 Squadron CO led the strike off. At 1520, the strike group detected a target on ASV radar; some twenty miles closer than expected. Knowing that only *Bismarck* herself was in the target area, Stewart-Moore began his attack approach and, at 1550, the Swordfish burst out of the bottom of the cloud cover and commenced their attack.

It was readily apparent that they had totally surprised their foe, as there was quite literally no AA fire. With devastating swiftness the Swordfish descended from all points of the compass dropping their deadly cargoes. Only after 11 had released did the true reason for the lack of defence fire become apparent; they were attacking HMS *Shef-field*!

Realizing that it was a case of mistaken identity and to his eternal credit, *Sheffield's* commanding officer, Captain C.A.A. Larcom, RN, ordered his guns to "on no account fire". Then, ringing down to the engine room for full speed, he calmly conned the ship through the dangerous waters, successfully dodging the six torpedoes that came his way. Of the other five torpedoes, two exploded when they entered the water and three exploded in *Sheffield's* wake.

One Swordfish, recognizing *Sheffield* after dropping, made a signal to her, 'Sorry for the Kipper', as they turned for home, still facing the challenge of returning safely whence they had come. Landing conditions had become even worse than before, and the Deck Control Officer had to attach a rope to his waist before he could stand back to the wind, holding up the 'bats'. Three aircraft crashed on the flight deck as they came on, the rising stern smashing their undercarriages, and the wreckage had to be cleared away before the others could be taken on. Fortunately, there were no crew casualties, and all were aboard by 1720. Nonetheless, they were a crestfallen band.

Although it was immediately questioned whether further air operations were even possible in the steadily worsening weather, the aircrews were adamant in their desire to have another go. Over the next 90 minutes the flight deck personnel again struggled to get the available aircraft armed, fuelled, and onto the pitching flight deck. By 1900, *Ark Royal* began turning into the 50-knot wind, the last fifteen airworthy Swordfish, four from 810, four from 818, and seven from 820 were ranged on deck and the aircrews began manning their planes.

Flt	Sqn	Aircraft	Pilot	Observer	TAG	Result
1st	820	4A	Lt-Cdr T.P. Coode, RN	Lt. Edmond S. Carver, RN	PO W.H. Dillnutt	port beam
1st	820	4B+	S-Lt.(A) S. Dixon-Child, RNVR	S-Lt.(A) G.R.C. Penrose, RN	LA R.H.W. Blake	port beam
1st	820	4C/ L9726	S-Lt. J. W. C. Moffatt, RNVR	S-Lt.(A) J.D. Miller, RNVR	LA A.J. Hayman	port beam, hit stern
2nd	810	2B+	Lt. D.F. God-frey-Faussett, RN	S-Lt.(A) L.A. Royall, RN	PO V. R. Graham	starboard beam
2nd	810	2A+	S-Lt.(A) K. S.	S-Lt.(A) P. B.	NA D.L.	starboard

Flt	Sqn	Aircraft	Pilot	Observer	TAG	Result
			Pattisson, RN	Meadway, RN	Mulley	beam
2nd	810	2P	S-Lt.(A) A. W. D. Beale, RN	S-Lt.(A) C. Friend, RN	LA K. Pimlott	port bow, hit amidships
3rd	820	5K	Lt.(A) S. Keane, RN	S-Lt.(A) R. I. W. Goddard, RN	PO L.C. Mulliner	with 1st sub-flight
3rd	810	2M	S-Lt.(A) C. M. Jewell, RN	LA G.H. Parkin-son		with 4th sub-flight
4th	818	5A	Lt. H. de G. Hunter, RN	L-Cdr. J.A. Stewart-Moore, RN	PO R.H. McColl	port side
4th	818	5B	S-Lt.(A) M.J. Lithgow, RN	S-Lt.(A) N.C. Manley-Cooper, RNVR	LA J.R. Russell	port side
4th	818	5C/V4298+	S-Lt.(A) F.A. Swanton, RN	S-Lt.(A) G.A. Woods, RNVR	LA J.R. Seafert	port side a/c jettisoned
5th	818	5K	Lt.(A) A.S.L. Owensmith, RN	S-Lt.(A) G.G. Topham, RNVR	PO J. Watson	starboard side
5th	818	5L	S-Lt.(A) J. Gard-ner, RN	S-Lt.(A) J.B. Longmuir, RNVR		jettisoned
6th	818	5F	S-Lt.(A) M. F. S. P. Willcocks, RN	S-Lt.(A) H.G. Mays, RN	LA R. Finney	Jettisoned
6th	818	5G	S-Lt.(A) A.N. Dixon, RN	S-Lt.(A) J.F. Turner, RNVR	LA A.T.A. Shields	Starboard

This time the air staff had put together an improved plan of attack. First, because of the premature explosions of virtually half the torpedoes on the previous attack, the new magnetic exploders that had been used were discarded and replaced by older, but reliable, contact exploders. Second, the new strike commander Lieutenant-Commander T. P. Coode, CO of 818 Squadron, was briefed to led the group directly to Sheffield, maintaining her vigil some 12 miles astern of *Bismarck*, get a fresh bearing to the target, and then attack. The crews realized the importance of their task. They, and they alone, could stop the *Bismarck* from reaching the safety of Brest, for it was certain that the Fleet could not possibly catch up if the Fleet Air Arm Swordfish did not slow the battleship down.

One can imagine that scene: the fifteen Swordfish ranged on the pitching flight deck, wing-tip to wing-tip; the tumultuous roar of the exhausts; the flurries of spray beating on the linen covered fuselages; the aircrews bundled in their wool-lined flight suits damp with spray; the ratings at the chocks bracing their bodies against the drive of the wind; the lead plane taxies into the centre of the deck; the Pegasus engine roaring at full power as the brakes strain too hold airframe stationary. Then, at 1910, the Flight Deck Officer waves his green flag, the pilot lets off the brakes and shifts he feet to the rudder pedals and the first Swordfish begins moving forward, racing down the deck and rising into the gale.

The group formed up over Somerville's flagship and took their departure at 1925. A little more than a half hour later *Sheffield* was sighted, and she blinkered them to proceed on a bearing of 110 degrees, distance 12 miles. Conditions were less than ideal, with seven-tenths cloud cover extending from 2,000-5,000 feet and as Coode climbed for altitude he lost Sheffield. The group was forced to orbit the area, slowly decreasing altitude, looking for a break in the clouds to relocate the cruiser until finally, at 2035, Coode relocated his guide. Armed with a new fix, the group completed its climb to 6,000 feet and, at 2040, disappeared into the grey mist at 110 knots, in sub-flights in line astern formation.

Lieutenant-Commander Coode (5A) had planned a coordinated attack with the sub-flights coming in simultaneously from different angles, forcing the *Bismarck* to divide her fire and making it harder for her to evade torpedoes. With no sign of a break in the cloud cover – down to 2,000 feet – the chances of reforming were slender, so each sub-flight was ordered to return independently.

Thirteen minutes after leaving *Sheffield*, Coode estimated that they should be in a good position and started the dive. Coode later reported 'Visibility was limited - a matter of yards. I watched the altimeter go back. When we reached 2,000 feet I started to worry. At 1,500 feet I wondered whether to continue the dive. At 1,000 feet I felt sure something was wrong, but still we were completely enclosed by cloud. I held the formation in the dive, and at 700 feet only we broke cloud, just when I was running out of height.' The time was 2055.

Most of the striking force became split up in the thick blanket of cloud, and they went in to the attack as best they could; in pairs, threes, fours, or even alone. The Commander-in-Chief stated afterwards that the attacks were pressed home 'with a gallantry and determination which cannot be praised too highly.'

Coode found he was four miles ahead and to leeward of the target. Realizing that a slow approach against the wind would be suicidal, he re-entered the cloud to close in and try another angle. This left the second sub-flight, to 'open the ball'. Lieutenant(A) D.F. Godfrey-Faussett, RN (2B) having lost Coode in the clouds, led the second sub-flight up to 9,000 feet where they ran into some icing problems before descending on the ASV's attack bearing. He and Sub-Lieutenant(A) K. S. Pattison, RN (2A) were both caught in an intense AA barrage that hit both aircraft as they made their run in from the *Bismarck*'s starboard beam, but both survived the storm of 'shot and shell'. Meanwhile, Sub-Lieutenant(A) A.W.D. Beale, RN (2P) having lost touch with the other two, returned to *Sheffield* to get a new range and bearing to the enemy. Of him and 2P we'll hear more later.

The third and fourth sub flights managed to stay together in the descent until they hit 2,000 feet, then they separated. As they cleared the clouds, four, Lieutenant H. de G. Hunter, RN (4A), and Sub-Lieutenants(A) M.J. Lithgow, RN (4B), F.A. Swanton, RN (4C), and C.M. Jewell, RN (2M) reformed in a clear patch of sky as they popped out of the underside of the cloud layer, and forged in from the port side at the same time as the second sub-flight came in from starboard. The German AA was extremely accurate, and followed them until they were seven miles from the target. *Bismarck*'s gunners seemed to be particularly attentive to 4C, which tallied no less than 175 holes in it. Both the pilot, Sub-Lieutenant(A) Swanton and his TAG, Leading Airman J.R. Seager were wounded, while the observer, Sub-Lieutenant(A) G.A. Woods, RNVR weathered the storm unscathed.

Separated from the others, Lieutenant(A) S. Keane, RN (5K), leader of the third sub-flight tagged on to Coode's sub-flight as they closed in. They popped out on the target's port side beam and immediately came under intense and accurate AA fire which hit, but did not bring down 5B, piloted Sub-Lieutenant(A) S. Dixon-Child, RN. As they withdrew, Keane's crew reported that they saw a hit on *Bismarck*'s starboard side near the funnel. While the actual location was considerably further aft, they were apparently eyewitnesses to one of the most decisive blows in modern history as, at 2105, the torpedo released by Sub-Lieutenant(A) J.W.C. Moffatt, RN (5C) struck the extreme stern of the target.

The fifth sub-flight lost each other in the clouds. As the leader, Lieutenant(A) A.S.L. Owensmith (4K), descended through the clouds at 3,000 feet he found himself the subject of intense AA fire, apparently controlled by radar. Breaking out at 1,000 feet, he found himself badly placed astern of the target, and so began to work around into a more favourable angle on her starboard side. While doing so, he saw a large plume of water rise up right aft from *Bismarck*'s starboard side. Left with the impression that he was 'flying through a wall of smoke and water' Owensmith noted that *Bismarck* was swinging around to port which seemed to be an extremely odd form of avoiding action to be taking given his angle of approach. Sub-Lieutenant(A) J. Gardner, RN (4L) made two separate attempts to close, but was met with such a concentration of fire that he was forced to withdraw.

Meanwhile the sixth sub-flight climbed to 7,450 feet where they broke the clouds. Disorientated, they too returned to HMS *Sheffield*, received a new range and bearing, and forged ahead again. Diving to attack from the *Bismarck*'s starboard side, they found themselves subjected to the combined fire of her entire AA battery. Sub-Lieutenant (A) A.N. Dixon, RN (4G), was forced to release some 2,000 yards out. His leader Sub-Lieutenant (A) M.F.S.P. Willcocks, RN (4F), having thoughts of making another approach, retained his.

While all this was transpiring, 2P, flown by the indomitable Sub-Lieutenant (A) A.W.D. Beale, RN reappeared ahead of *Bismarck* on her port bow, and attacked alone. In spite of the very intense and accurate fire they were rewarded by an enormous column of smoke and water that rose up on the port side of *Bismarck*'s deck as, at 2115, their torpedo hit home. By this point, all the Swordfish had had at least one go at the target and 13 were on their way home. This left two, Gardner in 4L and Willcocks in 4G, still striving to get in close enough to make a reasonable drop. However, as the remainder withdrew, they found themselves under extremely accurate AA fire at every turn, even when they lost sight of their quarry. Finally, both were forced to face the realization that further attempts were simply suicidal and they too turned about, jettisoned their torpedoes, and headed home. By 2125, the attack was over.

Such were the difficulties of observation that Coode reported immediately after the attack that he did not think the *Bismarck* had suffered any significant damage. As the Swordfish streamed home, HMS *Sheffield's* radar plot noted that *Bismarck* was manoeuvring erratically, and began to close in an effort to ascertain if *Bismarck* had, if fact, been damaged. At 2140 she poked out of the broken mist and found herself subjected to six well aimed salvos of 15" shells. Humbled in the extreme, Captain Larcom hastily withdrew having determined that her fighting efficiency had not diminished! At 2205, the first Swordfish began returning to *Ark Royal*. As the observers made their individual reports, it became clear that the results were more successful than first supposed, and it was first established that the *Bismarck* had been hit on the port side, then on the starboard quarter. Later still a possible hit on the port quarter was reported.

At 2300, the last of the strike planes was recovered. It had been an interesting recovery. The weather was still abominable, and five of the attacking Swordfish had been hit by the AA fire. Swanton managed to get 4C back on to *Ark Royal* in one piece, but on closer inspection was found to be damaged beyond repair and it was jettisoned. Three others crashed on landing, but miraculously, no one was hurt. Only six of the Swordfish remained serviceable and, expecting the possibility that another attack would be necessary, they were re-armed and ranged for yet another strike. Even as the last of the aircrew headed for the ready room for debriefing, the damage was confirmed by a signal from the shadowing Swordfish that *Bismarck* had made two circles at slow speed and was staggering off to the north-north west. The impossible had really occurred. Unbelievably, at the proverbial eleventh hour, those gallant young airmen, the Fleet Air Arm's own dashing 'few', had actually crippled Germany's great battleship!

At 2320, after nearly five hours in the air, the two Swordfish shadowing *Bismarck* were recalled. With *Bismarck* steering back on her pursuers, apparently unmanageable, and with the destroyers of Captain Phillip Vian, DSO, RN's 4th Destroyer Flotilla on hand, the Fleet Air Arm's role in the hunt was coming to a close. They came aboard at 2345, just before nightfall.

Bismarck's War Diary records: "Turrets 'Anton' and 'Bruno' open fire at *Rodney*" and she also records that she has been hit in return claiming the "foretop command post disabled". The British shells began to rain in and one by one the turrets are reported as being out of action. At 0931 hrs all main battery guns are silenced, forever. At 0958 hrs *Bismarck* shudders are a torpedo hit is reported midships. Multiple hits from close range are blasting *Bismarck* but still she refuses to go down and at approximately 1000 hrs explosive charges go off in the turbine room. 22 minutes later torpedoes from the Dorsetshire slam into her port side and at 1039. *Bismarck* finally sinks in position 48° 10' north, 16° 12' west.

By dawn on the 27th, the weather was, if anything, worse. Admiral Tovey closed in with HMS *King George V* and HMS *Rodney* and, at 0847, the final battle began. Realizing that further torpedoes would probably be needed to actually sink *Bismarck*, *Ark Royal*'s Flight Deck personnel strove to range a strike group made up off all of her serviceable Swordfish.

At 0900, sounds of heavy gunfire could be heard, even over the cry of the wind. Twenty minutes later *Ark Royal* turned into the wind and with a 56-knot wind over the deck, launched the twelve-plane strike. They sighted the foe, now but a battered hulk, at 1020hrs but were unable to attack as shells from the British battleships were falling all around her. As they circled overhead HMS *Dorsetshire* closed in and circled *Bismarck*, firing torpedoes from both sides. Finally, at 1036hrs the great ship capsized and sank. Having had a "ringside seat" for one of history's great events they turned and headed home, the hunt over.

The *Bismarck*'s crew had consisted of 103 officers, including the ships surgeon and midshipmen, and 1,962 petty officers and men. Only 100 were to be picked up by rescuers out of 2,065 men.

"The Bismarck had put up a most gallant fight against impossible odds, worthy of the old days of the Imperial German Navy, and she went down with her colours still flying."
Commander of the Home Fleet, Admiral Sir John Tovey

It was clear from Enigma decrypts after the death of the *Bismarck*, that the large network of supply ships that was to have supported her patrol would now be made available to U-Boats. The first to go was the *Belchen*, a 10,000t tanker, sunk off Greenland by the cruisers *Aurora* and *Kenya*. Within two weeks the Royal Navy had eliminated almost the entire network at sea, some nine tankers and supply ships sunk in the North & South Atlantic. Understandable euphoria swept the OIC; this was real operational intelligence. But risk factors were involved. The Kriegsmarine would want to know how it was possible the Royal Navy could find and destroy all these ships, spread over a large area, in a matter of 14 days. The officers of the Royal Navy ships involved asked the same question.

Royal Navy Ships Involved in the Chase

Battleships – *King George V, Prince of Wales, Ramillies, Revenge, Rodney, Repulse, Hood, Renown.*

Aircraft Carriers – *Victorious, Ark Royal.*

Cruisers – *Suffolk, Norfolk.*

Destroyers & Others – *Dorsetshire, London, Kenya, Galatea, Aurora, Neptune, Hermione, Edinburgh, Manchester, Arethusa, Birmingham, Sheffield, Achates, Antelope, Anthony, Echo, Somal, Eskimo, Nestor, Jupiter, Electra, Icarus, Active, Inglefield, Intrepid, Assiniboine, Saguenay, Lance, Legion, Columbia, Punjabi, Windsor, Mashona, Cossack, Sikh, Zulu, Maori, Piorun (Polish), Tartar, Faulkner, Foresight, Forester, Foxhound, Fury, Hesperus, H-44 Minerve, P-31 Sealion, Seawolf, Tigris, Sturgeon, Pandora.*

Hugo-Sebag Montefiorre again states:

After 1 June 1941 the code breaking picture changed overnight. All of a sudden Bletchley Park's code breakers could read Naval Enigma messages almost as quickly as the Germans. This enabled the British Admiralty to set up ambushes for the German supply ships which had made their way out to the Atlantic. They were supposed to replenish Bismarck and Prinz Eugen, as well as the U-boats, when they ran out of food, torpedoes, or fuel on their long patrols. Eight of these ships were sunk between 3 June and 2 June 1941, six of them as a direct result of using Enigma information. Another seven supply ships and weather ships were sunk during the next three weeks. But after 1 June, the Admiralty decided that it should stop acting on Enigma intelligence, even when it was available, in case the British successes alerted the Germans to the fact that their naval cipher was compromised.

Bismarck Discovered

The American film director James Cameron took an expedition on board a Russian Survey ship to the site of the sinking of the *Bismarck*. This survey ship is the largest of its kind and is equipped with two manned submersibles, Mir 1 & 2. These in turn were equipped with Remote Operated Vehicles (ROVs) and were equipped with specially designed cameras and 8kw searchlights. Along with two survivors of the *Bismarck* they arrived on site 61 years (to the day) after *Bismarck* sank. Just before dawn on the anniversary the survivors were woken to conduct the remembrance service for their dead comrades and then the dive began in earnest. On February 16th 2003 the resulting documentary was shown on Discovery TV. The first dive took three hours to reach the site (a journey which took *Bismarck* 10 minutes). The first piece of wreckage sighted was that of the Admiral's Bridge, which was as big as a 4-storey building. This was lying upside down on the ocean floor, having been sheared off by the pressure of water as *Bismarck* fell to her grave. Also sheared off was the entire stern section from the armoured bulkhead aft; about 50 metres of stern.

Captain Lindermann and Admiral Lutjens were actually on the bridge proper during the ships last moments. When the *Bismarck* turned turtle, the four main gun turrets, held in place only by gravity, dropped out of their mountings and fell straight to the bottom, landing with such an impact that the turrets disappeared into the silt, leaving their massive multi-level below-deck sections pointing towards the surface. *Bismarck* landed hard on the side of a volcanic slope, bow-first, buckled and then landed keel-first. The resulting impact sent shock waves out, causing an avalanche down the slope and taking *Bismarck* with it a distance of about two thirds of a mile. As she slid down the slope she hit the already landed Admiral's Bridge, sliding it to one side and turning it completely upside down. Finally, the *Bismarck* slewed around and came to rest.

Whilst the two Radio Room survivors watched topside on monitors, one of the ROVs entered through a shell impact hole directly into the Radio Room, where the desks where these men had once sat could clearly be seen. As the submersibles conducted their minute survey of the hull they found only about half a dozen penetrations through the actual armour-plated sides of the ship. Most of the damage done to *Bismarck* was to her superstructure. The Captain never lived to see his ship lose her fight for life. A direct hit from the *Rodney* (16-inch guns) on the main bridge, covered by 14 inches of armour, caused the door to be blasted from its hinges and the tremendous impact and concussion killed all inside instantly. At the same time the Admiral was killed.

Why did the Royal Navy fail to actually sink the *Bismarck*? First we must go back to the encounter with HMS *Prince of Wales* and HMS *Hood*. When the *Hood* was struck by a direct hit on her magazines the *Prince of Wales* was severely damaged and was preparing to withdraw. As she turned to withdraw, she fired one last salvo from her main guns. Two of these shells hit *Bismarck* in the bow, but passed straight through the un-armoured section and into the sea beyond. However, the resulting entry hole and ripped out exit hole caused tons of seawater to eventually find their way onboard, making the *Bismarck* sluggish and losing her some speed. As the *Hood* broke in two and began to sink, the aft turrets fired one departing salvo before sinking into the abyss. Bill Garzke, an expert on the *Bismarck* and author of *Battleships, Axis & Neutral Battleships of World War 2* published by the Naval Institute Press, told me that bow damage caused on the *Bismarck* by the *Prince of Wales* is untrue.

> "I have been researching the Bismarck operation for 43 years and can tell you that hit came in her 9th salvo (I believe). The 6th salvo produced the hit on the boats and the 13th produced the hit near the bridge. This was a diving shell that had an underwater trajectory"

The next attack upon the *Bismarck* involved some extremely heroic pilots who flew old, slow, Fairey Swordfish torpedo launching, biplanes off *Ark Royal*. Under an intense anti-aircraft barrage they pressed home their attacks in bad weather and a hail of bullets. They had already been in the air a few hours en route to the *Bismarck*. The

Bismarck successfully evaded all the torpedoes but one, which caught her rudder and blew a hole in the steerage section. Film footage from James Cameron's dives clearly shows the rudder not only jammed on the turn, but also actually embedded into the central of the three propellers. The result of this irreparable damage was that the *Bismarck* was stuck on a wide circular course, unable to speed away from the closing pack of Royal Naval hunters. And close they did.

Captain Lindemann announced to the crew that they were stuck and that "they could help themselves" to the stores. An attempt was made to launch one of *Bismarck*'s Arado seaplanes, packed with her war diaries and papers, but they could not get the catapult to work; the pilot was not amongst the survivors.

A request was made to Berlin for a U-Boat to race to the scene to take off *Bismarck*'s papers. Ironically it was this U-Boat, arriving hours later, that spooked the British ships into making a withdrawal, having only had time to rescue about 100 survivors, thus condemning over a thousand men to their deaths. We must bear in mind that capital ships such as *Rodney*, *King George V* and the heavy cruisers were not equipped to go chasing U-Boats. As the Royal Navy is an honourable service, to leave sailors to die must have been a very difficult call to make, but it was a case of withdraw or be killed.[12]

The well-publicised triple torpedo hit from the *Dorsetshire* did not cause the *Bismarck* to go down; the torpedoes detonated against the outer shell, rupturing it, but water tanks behind the impact area cushioned the blow and the inner shell remained intact. Again, these were clearly seen on film in the documentary. Admiral Tovey, the British Commander, had ordered his capital ships in close to finish off *Bismarck*, but as a consequence, the direct hits caused by these ships, did not have the impact required and did little damage to the main hull. The shells, being fired almost horizontally, lacked the necessary punch. Compare this to the shot that sunk HMS *Hood*,

---

[12] Baron Burkard von Mullenheim-Rechberg confirms in his book that no less than eight U-Boats in the Bay of Biscay region had been ordered to support the *Bismarck* – the U73; U556; U98; U97; U48; U552; U108; U74 the U74 and the U556 had no torpedoes left. The U74 had also been damaged previously and suffered bad manoeuvrability. Although the British ships did not have code access, they could track the U-Boats on HF/DF.

fired from 14 miles away. Proximity does not necessarily mean deadliness in naval battles.

The survivors of *Bismarck* always maintained that they had heard the orders to scuttle the ship, but the Royal Navy, hell bent of revenge for the *Hood*, did not wish to accept this. HMS *Hood* had been the flagship of the Royal Navy and her loss was felt right down to the man in the street. If the Royal Navy had announced to the world: "We caught *Bismarck* but she scuttled herself" the public would have felt cheated, as with the earlier incident with the *Graf Spee* at the River Plate.

I have always been 'in love' with the *Bismarck*. Although she was an enemy ship that killed hundreds of my fellow countrymen, she was a marvel of engineering and a beautiful ship to behold. The almost indisputable fact that she "committed suicide" rather than be killed lends more to her legend and majesty.

May she and her crew rest in peace.

The Bismarck, her bows heavy with water, heads for St Nazaire.

Fairey Swordfish torpedo-carrying aircraft on the deck of Ark Royal.

The Bismarck going down.

5. Sinking the *Scharnhorst*

Scharnhorst, a 31,100-ton *Gneisenau* class battle-cruiser, was built at Wilhelmshaven, Germany. She was launched in October 1936 and commissioned in January 1939. Her first wartime operation was a sweep into the Iceland-Faeroes passage in late November 1939, in which the British armed merchant cruiser Rawalpindi was sunk. In the spring of 1940 the *Scharnhorst* and her sister, *Gneisenau*, covered the conquest of Norway. They engaged the British battleship *Renown* on 9 April 1940 and sank the carrier HMS *Glorious* and two destroyers on 8 June, leaving only 3 survivors. In the latter action, *Scharnhorst* was torpedoed. She was further damaged by a bomb a few days later and was under repair for most of the rest of 1940. This had been as a direct result of intelligence gathered by breaking the British naval code. The Germans knew where *Glorious* was. Hugh Sebag-Montefiore, in his book *Enigma - The Battle For The Code* writes:

> ...the German cryptographers, who, unknown to the British, could read the Royal Navy's codes, were telling the German Navy the whereabouts of Britain's warships. One crucial signal, intercepted by the Germans, and read by them on June 2nd, revealed the exact position of HMS Glorious, the aircraft carrier, off the coast of Norway. It was one of the ships sent to protect the troop ships as they brought home the British Army.

Hinlsey, in Bletchley Park, issued a warning "circulated in the OIC's logbook, but it failed to receive a wider circulation" The aircraft carriers commander was never given the intelligence which might have prompted him to fly off his aircraft to see what lay over the horizon. At 1715 hrs on 8 June 1940, Glorious spotted the *Scharnhorst* and *Gneisenau* closing fast. Minutes later they opened fire on HMS Glorious reducing her to a mangled, blazing mess full of mutilated corpses.

From 22 January until 22 March 1941 *Scharnhorst* and *Gneisenau* operated in the Atlantic, sinking several ships and severely threatening British supply lines. Whilst at Brest, France, following this operation, the German ships were the targets of repeated air attacks. The resulting damage kept them non-operational into late 1941, when it was decided to concentrate German surface naval power in the Norwegian theatre. Since it was too risky to attempt the redeployment via the North Atlantic, on 11-13 February 1942 the two battle-cruisers and heavy cruiser *Prinz Eugen* made a daring "dash" through the English Channel to reach Germany. In the book *The Battle of The Narrow Seas* by Peter Scott he describes the scenario from the point of the men of the Motor Gun Boats.

When the Germans decided to risk an all out "channel dash" for their three cruisers at Brest, some authors give the impression that the British were caught napping and not ready for such an event. This maybe so to a certain extent but we must take into consideration the conditions at the time. The alternative of running the *Scharnhorst*, *Gneisenau* and *Prinz Eugen* around the northern route risked many days at sea, running into British ships constantly on patrol in these waters and giving the Home Fleet time to ready, weigh anchor and steam out from Scapa Flow for an ambush whilst constantly shadowing these three from air and sea. And U-Boats would have been warned off as a matter of course in case they were mistaken for Allied vessels. Bletchley Park would almost certainly have intercepted such signals and the Royal Navy would have been ready. Later in the war, Admiral Doenitz suspected such an occurrence had taken place but his suspicions fell on deaf ears. However, this would not have been a deciding factor with the German High Command, who did not know, and never did, that their enigma codes were broken and that Britain read all their radio traffic, albeit at a delay, sometimes only a few hours, sometimes a day or two. Whether Bletchley Park had received any radio traffic concerning the "dash" is not known, and even if they had, there could have been a delay in deciphering which occurred quite often when key codes on the enigma machine had been changed. On the days of 11th and 12 February 1943 if this was the case, I do not know.

Also to be taken into consideration was the fact that this was February, the height of the winter stormy season, the ships were at anchor in Brest and had been for some time. Air Reconnaissance was possibly grounded and, as you will read shortly, the seas were "heavy" which means of course, windy and rough! Taking all the above factors into consideration, except of course for Enigma, the Germans would have been waiting for such a time to make their run. They would have made all preparations under the strictest secrecy, especially in Brest, where the French Resistance would have eyes and ears. They would also have been waiting for such weather as this before suddenly weighing anchor and racing out at 27 knots to head for Germany, not all that far a distance away.

When spotted, the ships and their escorts had almost reached Bologne and there would certainly have been no time for any large vessels in, for example, Portsmouth to set sail. Even if they had managed to do so, they would have been following the Germans without a hope in hell of catching up given the short distances involved in the capital ships reaching Germany. Britain sent out a small force of MTB's (Motor Torpedo Boats) in an effort to hit these targets. Each MTB only carried 2 torpedoes, already loaded into their respective tubes and once fired, there would be no time to race back to Dover for a refill! It would be a one off, split second timing, hit or miss effort against fast moving targets. Targets that were, in fact, moving faster than the MTB's of that time could travel, 27 knots against 24 knots. The *Scharnhorst*, *Gneisenau* and *Prinz Eugen* would have been able, in an emergency, to probably have made a few knots more. *Scharnhorst* certainly could as we shall find out later on.

Another factor in the German's favour for a Channel dash was that they could enjoy full supporting land based fighter cover, which they did, coupled with the usual destroyer escort for these ships and plenty of E Boats to provide an outer defensive screen. An eye witness will shortly describe the fighter cover as "swarming". Quite probably, every available fighter based in Northern France was, at one time or other, involved in providing this massive umbrella over the ships.

825 Squadron attacked *Scharnhorst* during the channel dash, only nine months after attacking Bismarck, on 12 February 1942, six

Swordfish of a reformed 825 Squadron, would fly on a one-way mission to destiny. Among the 13 airmen killed that day were six of the 24 survivors of the Bismarck attack:

Lieutenant-Commander(A) Eugene Kingsmill Esmonde, DSO, VC, RN (P); age 32 - Swordfish W5984/H

Petty Officer Airman William Johnson Clinton, RN (TAG); age 22 - Swordfish W5984/H

Petty Officer Airman Ambrose Lawrence Johnson DSM, RN (TAG); age 22 - Swordfish W5983/G

Sub-Lieutenant(A) John Chute Thompson, RN (P); age 27 - Swordfish V4523/F

Sub-Lieutenant Robert Laurens Parkinson, RN (O); age 21 - Swordfish W5985/K

Leading Airman Henry Thomas Albert Wheeler, RN (TAG) - Swordfish W5985/K

Motor Torpedo Boat Attack

As these capital ships approached Bologne, a telephone rang in a small office in Dover were a Lt Comdr Pumphrey was catching up on some paperwork. It was an unsecure line and the Royal Navy Officer assumed it was the Stores. It was now 1135 hrs on 12th February 1942. In fact, on the phone, was Captain Day, the Chief of Staff. He informed Pumphrey that these battle-cruisers were now off Bologne and asked him how soon could he be ready? Pumphrey replied that his boats were at 4 hours notice to sail but would do what he could. He then dashed off to the Wardroom and told all to get ready for sea immediately then ran off to the Ops Room where they thought it was a joke. "There was a mad rush for the boats. Luckily all available MTB's were in running order". Usually mechanics would be busy doing repairs when in dock, but this time they were all in order. "There wasn't a moment to lose if we were to make an interception of ships travelling at 27 knots in out 24 knot boats. We formed up and screamed out of the harbour at full speed and passed the breakwater at 1155 hrs, 20 minutes from the telephone call! There were five of us, Boats 221, 219, 44, 45 and 48. *Scharnhorst* and

Gneisenau were something of a legend to us, and here we were, racing to attack them, in broad daylight!" Pumphrey had taken command of 221 as his own MTB was in dock and the commander of 221 had been ashore at the Stores, there had been no time to find him. They set course for No 2 buoy and the going was "pretty rough" with a strong westerly wind "but the weather was behind us so it didn't affect speed too much"

At 1210 hrs they could all see the "swarm" of fighters, Me 109s. A Squadron of these peeled away and roared low enough over the racing MTBs that "we could see the metal frames of the pilots flying goggles". The MTBs opened fire on this Squadron, MTB 45 clipped sections of wing off one Me109 but the 109s for some reason did not attack, presumably on orders to await the expected RAF bombers. At the same time, through thick patches of smoke, 10 E Boats made their appearance on a course barring the MTBs from an attack run on the cruisers. Problems struck MTB 44 when one of her engines "conked out" and she fell "miles astern". The four remaining MTBs altered course towards the E boats. The "temptation to those E Boats to turn towards us, close the range, and clean us up, must have been almost irresistible, but they resisted it. The initiative stayed with me". At 1000 yards both sides opened fire. Then the main force appeared out of the smoke screen, the *Prinz Eugen* in the lead, followed by the two battle-cruisers, 4000 yards away. The "swarm" of Me 109s still above them like angry wasps. Pumphrey noted that their armament was fore and aft and estimated speed at 27 knots. "The situation was impossible. The E boats barred the path for an MTB attack. I put on emergency speed thinking it would be a waste of time and I was right. The E boats added a knot or two, maintaining their excellent defensive position".

Pumphrey had two alternatives, try to battle a way through the E Boats or to try and fire the torpedoes at long range. The MTB's were on an ideal vector, 50 degrees on the bow of the leading battle-cruiser, but the range was "hopelessly long". Pumphrey admits to making the wrong decision and altered course to try and fight his way through the E Boats. "It was a mad thing to do, the inevitable result would have been the loss of all the boats before the range could be reduced to a reasonable one, say 2000 yards." Fate took its own strange hand and Pumphrey's starboard engine "conked out" and his speed fell back to 16 knots. Under these circumstances he had only one alternative left, to hold and to fire at 4000 yards. When the E Boats were about 200 yards away they fired their torpedoes. Even at such a short range, the fire from the E Boats scarcely touched the MTBs as the seas were "too rough". After torpedoes were away "we turned away without much hope of a hit. The whole operation was most unsatisfactory and 3 minutes after we had fired, the *Scharnhorst* and *Gneisenau* turned away at 90 degrees from us and our last hope of a hit disappeared".

One of the MTBs, 44, recovered from his dead engine, saw a brief opportunity when *Prinz Eugen* turned towards them by 50 degrees and he fired, although the target was quite distant. Pumphrey said that "after the allotted torpedo run time I saw a plume of water rise under *Prinz Eugen*'s bridge, not a characteristic torpedo hit, but what else could it have been?" The E boats then made smoke and through this emerged a Narvik Class destroyer, at least Pumphrey identified it as such, but it was in fact "Friedrich Ihn" a Maas class destroyer. The destroyer was faster than the MTB's and the situation looked desperate. Fate again took a welcome hand with the appearance of two MGBs (Motor Gun Boats), the 41 and the 43. Lt Stewart Gould, commanding, was angry at having missed "the fun" and he was in no mood "to be embarrassed by a mere Narvik". The two 63 foot boats went at the destroyer, blazing away with their Oerlikon's. Stewart Gould intended to drop depth charges as close to the destroyer as possible. The destroyer mistook them for fresh MTBs, loaded with torpedoes, and turned away to rejoin the others. MGBs do not carry torpedo tubes!

Minelayers had succeeded in laying a partial minefield ahead of the ships and caused damage which led to *Scharnhorst* being docked in Gdynia for repairs which lasted until her subsequent move to join up with Tirpitz, in Norway, the following year. This account of the Channel Dash was published in "The Battle of The Narrow Seas" by Lt Cdr Peter Scott, MBE, DSC + Bar, RNVR in 1945. He served with these "spitfires of the sea" with distinction, as did their very brave crews. Fatality rates were relatively high in these high speed "flimsy" craft.

To Norway

Repair work, a grounding and her always troublesome steam power plant kept *Scharnhorst* out of action until March 1943, when she went to northern Norway to join the battleship Tirpitz and the Lutzow plus 2 flotilla's of destroyers threatening the convoy route to the USSR. In March 1943 the *Scharnhorst* had left Gdynia heading for Norway. She had been in Gdynia for repairs following her famous channel "dash" in which she had incurred mine damage which had been laid deliberately in her path by British coastal forces. During bad weather the *Scharnhorst* slipped out of Gotenhafen and sailed to Trondheim via Bergen with a heavy escort and large air cover, under the codename of Operation Zauberflotte. She then sailed from Trondheim, accompanied by the Tirpitz, to join up with the Lutzow at Bogen Bay, not far from Narvik on 12 March 1943. On March 22 they then sailed to Altenfjord, arriving on 24th March. As this was a direct threat to the Arctic convoys the disposition of the Home Fleet had to be amended to meet any possible threat. The carriers Furious and Indomitable stood by on the Clyde and the Battleship HMS Anson sailed for Seidisfjord, Iceland. To cover for the eventuality of an Atlantic Bismarck style breakout, patrols in the Denmark Straits and the Faeroes - Iceland gap were stepped up. Additional cruisers also left Iceland to cover convoy RA53. Admiral Doenitz had only recently taken over the Kriegsmarine from Admiral Roeder. Before that he had been in charge of the U-Boat Arm. Up to this time Hitler, mindful of what had happened to the Bismarck in May 1941, refused to allow his capital ships into action unless all conditions were favourable for a victory, and that the exact positions of all the British capital ships were known, as well as the carriers, of which he was particularly wary. Indeed, men were already being drafted away from the capital ships to replace crews lost in the U-Boats and to crew new U-Boats. In February 1943, Doenitz succeeded in changing Hitler's mind and had been told that he could send his ships out at "the next favourable opportunity". Hitler had said that the "time for great ships was over, I would rather have the steel and nickel from these ships than send them into battle again". Hitler correctly pointed out that, in the Pacific, the value of capital ships had been lessened by carrier borne aircraft and that the Kriegsmarine and the

Luftwaffe could not develop satisfactory cooperation. This was to prove exactly right in the coming months. In the winter months of 1942/1943 the despatch of convoys to and from Russia had been very successful but the very presence of these ships in Norwegian waters was taking the shine of any elation that may have been felt in the Home Fleet or the Admiralty. Although a couple of merchantmen had been sunk, by U-Boats, large amounts of essential supplies including tanks and planes had successfully been delivered to Russia. Admiral Tovey, Commander in Chief Home Fleet, therefore viewed the coming months with their long arctic summer daylight hours, with some trepidation. The presence of these ships dictated everything tactically and tied down a great number of large ships which could have been used elsewhere. He recommended a halt to convoys to Russia. Events in the Atlantic were to come to the Admiralty's aid in reaching a decision. The battle against the U-Boat was reaching a climax and the decision was taken to move all available escorts to the command of Admiral Sir Max Horton, Commander in Chief Western Approaches, based in Liverpool. To say that the Soviets were not best pleased would be an understatement. Stalingrad had been relieved on 2 February 1943, so the imminent danger of a Soviet collapse had receded and Soviet industry, moved to the Urals, had recovered and was beginning to churn out massive quantities of armaments for its forces.

On the 8 May 1943, Admiral Sir Bruce Fraser assumed command of the Home Fleet. He was an outstanding gunnery officer who had played a leading role in the production of the main armament on the newest of Britain's battleships, the King George V Class. He had also been Tovey's deputy, therefore transition was minimal and he needed very little time to get to grips with the command. Parts of the Home Fleet had been sent to the Mediterranean for the invasion of Sicily and some American ships had sailed from Argentina, Newfoundland to be based at Scapa Flow with the Home Fleet, battleships *South Dakota* and *Alabama* and five US destroyers. Fraser now also had two King George V class battleships with a combined armament of 20 14-inch guns and 18 16-inch guns to deal with any possible German surface offensive.

The US Forces, though not lacking in enthusiasm, completely lacked any form of anti-submarine training. When the combined fleet sailed for ranging exercises the Americans spent more time trying to kill porpoises than U-Boats! Although no convoys were running to Russia during these months the very threat of the *Tirpitz*, etc was to remain at the forefront of Fraser's planning.

In September 1943 Fraser had a very good "picture" of the exact whereabouts of the German Battle Group, thanks to intelligence from Norwegian Resistance, Ultra signals and Air Reconnaissance. *Scharnhorst*, *Tirpitz* and *Lutzow* were anchored in inlets off Altenfjord. Due to the *Tirpitz* being damaged by the heroic exploits of the Royal Navy's X Craft, and the return to Germany of the *Lutzow*, the *Scharnhorst* was now the Royal Navy's chief concern and the only operational German capital ship in Northern waters. Ongoing repairs were still being conducted on *Tirpitz*, so for the time being, she was considered "out of it".

On 21 October Admiral Sir Dudley Pound died and was succeeded by Admiral Cunningham, fresh from victories in the Mediterranean. Within three months of his appointment, the Royal Navy would have its excellent victory in the Arctic seas. The surrender of the entire German 6th Army at Stalingrad was followed by the smashing of the German summer offensive by the biggest tank battle ever, at Kursk in July 1943. By Sept 1943 the Germans were in headlong retreat from Moscow in the north to Baku in the south. Smolensk was taken by the Red Army on Sept 25th. It was at this time that the Soviets "requested" the resumption of the Arctic convoys.

Diplomacy between the UK and USA on one side and the USSR on the other was acrimonious. One of Stalin's replies to Churchill was so bad that he refused to receive it, returning it as 'unread' to the Soviet Ambassador. Nevertheless, convoys were to resume and ships stranded in Kola since the spring had to be returned to the UK. Ten destroyers, two minesweepers and a corvette left Iceland on 23 October, along with five minesweepers and six sub-chasers being given to the Soviet Navy. The returning convoy reached Loch Ewe without incident on 14th November.

By October 1943 the German Battle Group North consisted of the *Scharnhorst*, under the command of Kapitan Julius Hintze and the 4th and 6th Destroyer Flotillas. On 17th November the 6th Flotilla was ordered back to the Baltic. The 4th Flotilla consisted of the new large Z-Type destroyers. Each was over 400 feet long with five 15cm guns and eight torpedo tubes. They were larger and faster than their British counterparts.

Rear Admiral Erich Bey took command of the Battle Group on 8th November. His previous appointment had been Flag Officer (Destroyers). He had been in command of the destroyers during the channel dash. He had little in the way of supporting staff and his orders were "unworkable", containing many restraints. Furthermore, he could not make his mind up about the use of the destroyer flotilla; whether they should support *Scharnhorst* or vice-versa.

Apparently in the German High Command only Doenitz was optimistic about using *Scharnhorst* against convoys. On December 19th Doenitz told Hitler "*Scharnhorst* will attack the next convoy". At the end of 1943, Arctic convoys to Russia were once again settling down to a routine. Due to the ever-present threat from the *Scharnhorst* escorts were, by necessity, on the heavy side, with screening destroyers being covered by cruisers and capital ships. For example, convoy JW/RA 55 was accompanied by cruisers *Belfast*, *Sheffield* and *Jamaica* and the battleship *Duke of York*.

On Dec 22nd a Dornier 217 on a weather flight sighted the convoy and reported back to Norway that it was a "troop convoy" and this was immediately interpreted as the invasion of Norway. Apart from increased air patrols and U-Boat activity, *Scharnhorst* was put on a 3-hour notice to sail. But the same day the report was rectified to simply "a convoy".

Admiral Fraser on board *Duke of York* was concerned that the convoy appeared exposed. Accordingly, he thought it worthwhile to break radio silence to make amendments to the positions of his ships. He ordered *Duke of York* and her accompanying cruiser *Jamaica* to increase speed and ordered the convoy to reverse course for a while (not an easy thing for a convoy to do); thus, should the *Scharnhorst* set sail she would not arrive in the vicinity of the convoy until after dark. He increased the destroyer screen by four, by removing them from the untouched homeward-bound convoy RA55a, as it was clear that this had totally evaded detection.

By nightfall on 24th December there was still no news of *Scharnhorst* but the two convoys were now converging and she could still mount an attack. In spite of her lack of fighting since 1941, Fraser must have had a sailor's sixth sense about the coming few days. The weather was Gale Force 8 and U-Boat transmissions were being detected by HF/DF (High Frequency Direction Finding) on more than one heading. At 0900 hrs Christmas Day, the U-716 fired an acoustic torpedo (gnat) at a destroyer, but missed.

Fraser had one ace-in-the-hole which gave him almost complete access to German naval signals. For quite some time Britain had had access to these via the enigma machine mentioned earlier, at Bletchley Park. Such signals were given the codename "ULTRA" and were treated with the utmost secrecy, to be accessed by a very select few; Fraser was one of these few.

At 0216hrs 26th December such a message arrived on board *Duke of York* stating that *Scharnhorst* had probably sailed at 1800hrs on 25 December, eight hours previously. To cover the source of the intelligence and the fact that the convoy's commodore did not have access to ULTRA, the Admiralty sent out the following signal: "Admiralty appreciates *Scharnhorst* is at sea." If this were to be intercepted by the German BDienst intelligence service it would be assumed that Norwegian Resistance had seen her slip her moorings and make her way down the fjords towards the open sea, or a patrolling submarine had reported in.

On board the British ships confidence was very high and crews felt that if they met up with *Scharnhorst* they would soon despatch her to a watery grave. It was not until 1955hrs on Christmas Day that *Scharnhorst* and the destroyers of the 4th Flotilla (Z-Type) passed through the net barrier of Lange Inlet into Altenfjord and headed up the length of Stjernfjord at 17 knots. German High Command and Group North Command were already having grave doubts, especially when the Luftwaffe reported that there could be no reconnaissance flights due to bad weather.

The German battle-cruiser *Scharnhorst* was now on her way to her destiny, heading north at 25 knots into worsening weather. Seas were washing completely over the destroyer escorts battling along with her. At 0300hrs on 26th December Bey received a signal confirming the operation was to proceed. By 0700 *Scharnhorst*'s navigator reckoned that they were now within 30 miles of the convoy and ahead of it; another 40 minutes and the convoy should be in view. At 0820 hrs, for some unknown reason, Admiral Bey turned *Scharnhorst* northwards but neglected to inform the 4th Flotilla, which sailed blindly on at 90 degrees to *Scharnhorst*, contact soon being lost, never to be regained…

The Battle of the North Cape

Time had run out. At 0926 hrs, without any warning from the radar or her lookouts, a star shell burst above *Scharnhorst*, illuminating her like a great silver ghost on a darkened sea. She had been caught by surprise. Fraser had been drawing his net tighter, marshalling his ships. He had already turned the convoy away from the raider. Force 1 was in contact and Force 2 with the *Duke of York* was steaming hard. All the British participants were aware of each other's exact positions; Fraser did not want to repeat the mistakes of an earlier *Tirpitz* encounter with the Home Fleet. Admiral Bey was unaware that British capital ships were closing in until 0926hrs.

HMS *Belfast* got a radar fix at 0840hrs which placed *Scharnhorst* between her and the convoy, thus if Bey had been a bit more determined he might have caused considerable damage to the convoy before engaging the Royal Navy; Doenitz himself was later to say the same thing.

HMS *Sheffield* got the first visual sighting at 0921hrs, signalling "enemy in sight, bearing 222 degrees, 13000 yds". *Belfast* fired the star shell but did not see the enemy. At 0929hrs the order to engage the enemy was given. All the ships except *Norfolk* had 'flash-less' cordite and therefore when the ships opened fire *Norfolk*'s gun flashes made her the prime target for the return of fire from *Scharnhorst*.

Norfolk loosed off no less than six 8-gun salvos in only two minutes – with mostly manual loading and as the cruiser ploughed through heavy seas! – a testimony to the high standard of her gun crews *Norfolk*'s second salvo smashed the mattress aerial of *Scharnhorst*'s Seetakt radar, destroying the port HA director and wounding four of her crew. *Scharnhorst* increased speed to disengage, getting up to nearly 30 knots and opened the range to 24,000 yards within 20 minutes of the first star shell. At 1020hrs contact was lost.

On board the *Duke of York* Fraser was worried. After contact was reported lost, he considered his options but his course of action was decided when he received a signal from *Belfast* at 1205 hrs: "Unknown contact, 075 degrees, 13 miles." Belfast (and Force 1) was back in contact. Fraser ordered his ships, Force 2, to turn to course and close. *Sheffield* confirmed contact at 1211hrs, followed by *Norfolk* at 1214hrs.

Force 1 and *Scharnhorst* were closing at a combined speed of 40 knots. Admiral Burnett, on board *Belfast*, had made a correct "guess" after they had lost *Scharnhorst* the first time and had moved his ships accordingly. Now they were approaching each other head on! Once again it was the *Sheffield* who announced "enemy in sight" and at 1220hrs Force 1 was ordered to "Open Fire!"

For the second time *Scharnhorst* was taken completely by surprise but when she replied her shooting was quite accurate. *Norfolk* again bore the brunt of her replies. One 11-inch shell hit X Turret, putting it out of action. Another hit *Norfolk* on the starboard side, amidships, killing eight men near the secondary damage control headquarters.

Chief Engine Room Artificer Cardey later wrote:

> *"I was standing in the middle of the compartment by the dials when there was a vivid flash and bits of metal rained down. One hit an engine room rating, who was just beside me, in the leg. Another piece of metal tore off the tops of two fingers of a man who had his hand on a lever, he did not know it had happened until a quarter of an hour later. Water began to pour down through the engine room hatches. Some fuel oil came with it, and I saw one fellow looking like a polished ebony statue because he had been covered from head to foot with the black oil. He was carrying on as if nothing had happened.*
>
> *I went across to the dials and found that the pressure was not affected. Some of the lights had gone out and there was a good deal of smoke, and we knew by the smell that the fire was raging somewhere. They were too*

busy to come and tell us what happened. Every man in the engine room had his work to do so we just carried on and only heard odd bits of information when they brought the sandwiches down and so on. We kept the engines going at full speed for six hours after the ship was hit. There was about three feet of water swishing about in the bilges below the engine room and the lower plates were covered."

And CERA Davies wrote of the 'Hostilities-Only' men:[13]

"As an old RN man I can tell you they were something to be proud of. Not one faltered, and I suppose we all were, at the back of our minds, expecting something to happen any minute."

The destroyers were buzzing round *Scharnhorst* like angry wasps. *Musketeer* got close enough to observe the hits from her guns landing. *Scharnhorst* increased speed again and began to pull away from Force 1. Burnett, on *Belfast*, resolved to shadow her until Force 2 was in a position to intercept her. The whole engagement had lasted 20 minutes. Force 1 had taken up position port side of the battle-cruiser, about 7½ miles, just outside visible range.

At 1300hrs Admiral Bey turned *Scharnhorst* onto a course of 155 degrees, which would take her home. He was following orders, but Doenitz was again critical, later stating that *Scharnhorst* could have got through to the convoy easily enough. Mystery surrounds the fact that Force 2 had previously been sighted by the Luftwaffe. Bey had received a sighting report at 1530 hrs the previous day. German intelligence had a wealth of information on their hands but little was conveyed to Bey warning him of the closing British net or of the capital ships about him.

Throughout the afternoon Burnett's ships hung onto *Scharnhorst*. Every 20 minutes or so Burnett would report direction, speed and position. It was a superb bit of shadowing, described by Fraser as "exemplary". Tovey wrote to the Captain of HMS *Belfast*:

"I was following your intercepts on the chart and I know that you and your fine ship would never let go of the brute unless the weather made it absolutely impossible for you to keep up. The combination of the gallant

---

[13] Sailors who had signed up "for the duration" and would leave the Royal Navy at the outbreak of peace

*attack you and other cruisers made on the Scharnhorst, coupled with your
magnificent shadowing, is as fine an example of cruiser work as has ever
been seen."*

Fraser could not tell if D4 (4th Flotilla destroyers) were with
Scharnhorst, so he signalled Burnett and received the reply "one heavy
ship" thus removing any doubt in Fraser's mind. Fraser now knew
that action would be joined at about 1630hrs. Burnett signalled that
he was "by himself" shadowing *Scharnhorst* at about 1600hrs. However, this was not quite true, as *Musketeer* and three other destroyers
were risking all by pounding through the heavy seas at 30 knots,
against a head sea, regardless of damage that could ensue from such a
pounding. *Norfolk* had dropped back to fight a fire on board, but brilliant work by her fire crews saw her catching up again by 1700 hrs.
Sheffield also fell back but never really caught up, being 10 miles behind *Belfast* for the remainder of the engagement. *Belfast's* captain
recorded that he could never understand why *Scharnhorst* which
must have seen *Belfast* on her radar, never turned and engaged her,
driving her off or even sinking her.

Duke of York picked up *Scharnhorst* on her radar at 1617hrs, followed shortly by *Belfast* locating *Duke of York* on her own radar. The
first thing noticed when *Scharnhorst* came into visual range was that
her guns were trained fore and aft. For the third time in the same
day *Scharnhorst* had been caught completely by surprise! For the gun
crews of *Duke of York* the waiting was over; she fired her first salvo at
1651hrs...

The first salvo from *Duke of York* hit *Scharnhorst* low down and
forward, with "A" turret becoming immediately inoperable. Destroyers were ordered in for a torpedo attack. *Scharnhorst* again recovered
from her shock and returned fire accurately. HMS *Savage* got in so
close that when *Scharnhorst* was illuminated by star shell *Savage* was
lit up as well. Cmdr Meyrick on *Savage* actually had to turn away and
increase range in order to attempt a torpedo attack. As the afternoon
wore on *Scharnhorst's* gunnery became so accurate that it was inevitable that *Duke of York* would receive some hits. The radar jammer was
put out of action and then a remarkable sequence of events took
place, which was to find its way into naval legend...

One of *Scharnhorst*'s 11-inch shells screamed right through one of the legs of *Duke of York*'s tripod foremast, travelling only feet beneath the radar office and its three occupants! The radar ceased working, even though, after checks, all appeared to be in perfect working order. Lt Bates RNVR recorded:

"I switched off all the office lights and climbed up into the aerial compartment. By feeling about in the dark and with the help of a small pocket torch, I found the aerials were pointing up to the sky. I got the aerials horizontal and re-stabilised them by their gyroscope and the echoes were restored."

The terrific shock of the 11-inch shell passing through the mast had made the aerials topple over! This episode of the battle very soon became legend, not only on board *Duke of York* but throughout the entire fleet – that the "miraculous" repair of the radar had been due to Bates having climbed the mast and held the wires together single-handedly. He received the nickname "Barehand Bates" and nothing he could say could dispel the legend, which also gained official recognition throughout Great Britain. It was after all, just the thing that the newspapers of the time thrived upon as a means of stiffening morale and resolve in a wartorn country. "Barehand Bates" received the DSC for his efforts. Able Seamen Badkin and Whitton were also rewarded for their efforts with a DSM each.

In another straddle the mainmast was hit, causing the temporary loss of the Type 281 air warning radar set and Admiral Fraser's barge was also wrecked.

Scharnhorst was yet again showing signs of getting away as she began to open up the range. By 1717hrs she was out of visual range of *Duke of York* which continued firing by radar. At 1824hrs the battleship stopped firing. Fraser signalled to Burnett that he was going to remain with the convoy as they had no chance of closing the *Scharnhorst*. Suddenly the range counters, which had been rapidly clicking up the range between the ships, started to slow down, then showed that they were again closing with the target. *Scharnhorst* was slowing down! It was thought possible that *Scharnhorst* had either switched off her radar so that the Royal Navy could not detect the emissions or that it was out of order, but survivors picked up later recalled that announcements were heard about contacts to starboard. But nobody ordered the main guns to be trained in that direction and indeed, when the alarm sounded, most of her gun crews were stood down!

The *Duke of York*'s first salvo scored a hit above the waterline, a second wrecked the already inoperable "A" Turret. The consequent explosion detonated charges in "A" magazine which spread to "B" magazine. Both magazines had to be partially flooded by the damage-control teams. At this time the gunnery from *Scharnhorst* was, at best, piecemeal. The crews manning the 11-inch guns fought well and hard but closer quarter secondary weapons were badly handled with countermanding orders being given regarding types of shells to be loaded. In the case of the 105mm guns, the crews were below decks, having been stood down due to the badly protected positions of their guns. *Scharnhorst*'s speed fell down after a 14 inch shell hit the starboard side and put a boiler out of action. It was recorded on the bridge of *Scharnhorst* that her speed dropped from 29 knots down to 22 knots rapidly.

At this time the destroyers of Cmdr Meyrick were now rapidly gaining on the battle-cruiser. HMS *Savage* and HMS *Saumarez* were 10,000 yards off the stern and HMS *Scorpion* and the Norwegian destroyer *Stord* were off the starboard beam. *Scharnhorst* fired upon them when they were within 8,000 yards, but as her 105mm guns were stood down she lacked proper anti-destroyer armament. *Savage* and *Saumarez* drew most of the enemy's fire but *Stord* and *Scorpion* appeared not to have been spotted, coming in from the south east. Both fired torpedoes at *Scharnhorst*. For the Norwegians aboard *Stord* there was vengeance in the air, a unique chance to strike back at the enemy occupying their country. Lt Cmdr Storeheill of the Royal Norwegian Navy was determined not to miss this opportunity of pressing home his attack to the limit. *Scorpion's* commander remarked that they thought *Stord* was going to ram *Scharnhorst*, so determined was Storeheill's attack. Only one torpedo was seen to hit and it is impossible to determine from which destroyer this came. Meanwhile *Scharnhorst* presented herself to *Savage* and *Saumarez* who duly launched torpedoes at 1853 hrs and *Savage* recorded three hits on the battle-cruiser. *Saumarez* was badly beaten up on her approach, slowing to only 8 knots due to damage, but she still managed to fire off four torpedoes. Again three hits were recorded, one in a boiler room.

The cruisers *Belfast* and *Jamaica* and the Battleship *Duke of York* were witnessing a pyrotechnic display of tracer and gun flashes. By this time the radar on *Duke of York* had been repaired and she was tracking *Scharnhorst* at 22,000 yards. The Battleships Fire control was able to switch between visual and radar firing effortlessly. *Scharnhorst* turned directly towards Force 2 and the range came down quickly. Then she turned 90 degrees to them and *Duke of York* and *Jamaica* opened fire at 10,400 yards. This appeared to again have caught *Scharnhorst* out; the *Duke of York* salvo hit aft, causing immense damage, and the next few salvos were fired in rapid succession, literally tearing *Scharnhorst* apart. Bey signalled to Berlin at 1730 hrs that he was "surrounded by heavy units" and at 1825 hrs, "We shall fight to the last shell."

Norfolk now began firing from the north but had to check fire due to difficulties in identifying one unit from another. *Belfast* was also now firing and registering hits. The death of *Scharnhorst* was now as inevitable as imminent. Her speed had fallen off to 5 knots but she held steady, steaming north.

Lt Vernon Merry, RNVR, who was Admiral Fraser's Flag Lieutenant, wrote:

> *"Every time we hit her, it was like stoking up a huge fire, with flames and sparks flying up the chimney. Every time a salvo landed, there was this great gust of flame roaring into the air, just as though we were prodding a huge fire with a poker".*

At 1920hrs Fraser ordered *Belfast* and *Jamaica* in closer to the stricken *Scharnhorst* and told them to finish her off with torpedoes. Meanwhile *Duke of York* continued salvo after salvo in quick succession until, at 1928 hrs, she checked fire to allow *Belfast* and *Jamaica* to fire their torpedoes. Only light, uncoordinated fire was coming from *Scharnhorst* as *Jamaica* fired three torpedoes, but one misfired and she claimed no hits. Shortly afterwards *Belfast* also fired, one of which may have hit. Burnett claimed to his dying day that *Belfast* administered the "coup de grace". Both cruisers came about to fire their remaining torpedoes. *Jamaica* fired three but could not see any hits due to the thick smoke enveloping *Scharnhorst* but at the correct time for the torpedo run underwater explosions were heard and it was assumed that two torpedoes had hit home. *Belfast* broke away as the sea became "infested" with *Musketeer*, *Matchless*, *Virago* and *Opportune* of 36 Division. These four had had a long, hard slog through heavy seas to make this battle.

Fisher's four destroyers would not be put off their prey at the last minute so *Belfast* steamed away to assume an outlying position and the four destroyers raced in on the attack. They got in so close that they could "smell the fires burning" as she was pounded again by the battleship. At 1930 hrs *Matchless* and *Musketeer* attacked on her port side whilst *Opportune* and *Virago* her starboard. *Opportune* fired two salvos, claiming two hits. *Virago*, less than two months out of her builders and with a crew who had never been to sea before, fired seven torpedoes at 2,800 yards and observed two hits. *Matchless* then fired four torpedoes and observed at least three hits. *Matchless* was having problems bring her tubes to bear, as the heavy seas had strained the gears, turned for another go but as she came in *Scharnhorst* was not there – she had gone down.

No ship actually saw her go down but a distinctive heavy underwater explosion was both felt and heard in the ships above. Helmut Boekhoff, survivor, recalled that he turned and saw, in the light of a star shell, the *Scharnhorst* turned right around and he could see a propeller still turning. Then all of a sudden he saw he go down, come back up again, then suddenly, she was gone. After she had disappeared he felt a "tremendous trummel" in his stomach and legs as there was a big explosion underwater.

At 1948 hrs *Belfast* fired a star shell but all they saw was a raft covered with oil-soaked German sailors, "it was a dreadful sight". They thought at the time that the sailors were screaming, but as Helmut Boekhoff recalls: "The men were screaming and shouting "*Scharnhorst* - hip hip hooray, hip hip hooray and he was certain that a song was coming up "On A Sailors Grave, No Roses Grow". After the explosion underwater he turned to the other sailors, some swimming between bits of rubbish and clinging onto other pieces, still shouting "Heil our Fuhrer" and "*Scharnhorst* - hip hip hooray" and he thought to himself "pscht, what a waste".

Fraser ordered all ships out of the immediate area whilst ships with torpedoes still on board "just in case" and a destroyer, equipped with a searchlight, was sent in to check the area. *Matchless'* searchlight piercing the Arctic night. In a superb piece of seamanship, Lt Comdr Clouston, *Scorpion's* Captain, stopped up wind of the survivors, keeping them in the lee, calm water, and drifted in gently. Those he was able to rescue spoke in sincere admiration of his skills. *Scorpion* succeeded in rescuing 30 men although all around drifted bodies, obviously dead. Fraser asked *Scorpion* for confirmation that *Scharnhorst* had gone down, which Clouston confirmed. At 2035 hrs the *Duke of York* broadcast at full power to Scapa WT "*Scharnhorst* Sunk". At 2136 hrs came the reply "Grand. Well done". I would imagine that the German High Command in Berlin heard that signal!

Fraser wished to save as many German sailors as possible but at 2040 hrs he received an ULTRA traffic signal stating that U-Boats in the area had been freed of all restraints of attacks on warships. One wolf pack was known to be in the region and this indicated that German High Command was only too well aware that *Scharnhorst* had gone down. Reluctantly Fraser ordered all ships from the area and resume passage to Kola. *Saumarez*, badly mauled in the attack, made her own way slowly and, after pausing to bury her dead, arrived safely at Kola on 27th December in the evening, a few hours after the rest.

Survivors were able to give some details of the end of the battle-cruiser. From when the *Duke of York* had opened fire at 1901 hrs, the *Scharnhorst* had been pounded to pieces. "C" Turret had been able to fire right to the end, when ammunition ran out shells were passed from "A" Turret. Not one of the *Duke of York*'s salvo's had penetrated the heavily armoured deck, but had wrought havoc above, leaving only mangled wreckage. As none of her medical staff had survived the sinking it was assumed that they had stayed with the wounded to the end – a similar scenario to the sinking of the *Bismarck* 2½ years earlier. Above the deck the P1 15cm mounting had been destroyed. The hangar was hit and the aircraft destroyed thereby causing a large fire. The starboard 105mm mounting had been hit, a shell landed near the funnel, also on the starboard side and another 'tween decks on the port side. Most of the superstructure was a mangled mess with medical teams trying to climb through to reach wounded sailors. The starboard anchor had been shot away. "B" Turret was hit and ventilation was out of action. When fired, the guns released thick acrid smoke into the turret causing the men breathing problems. The upper deck was littered with bodies which were washed overboard as the ship heeled.

Gunfire did not sink the *Scharnhorst*, it was the torpedoes which sank her in the end. I think here comparisons can be drawn with HMS *Hood*, which, although planned, did not have an armoured deck. A shell from the *Bismarck* hit her through the deck into a magazine which, in an instant, blew up the entire ship. The *Duke of York* hit *Scharnhorst* with 14 x 14 inch shells, not one of which penetrated the deck. Helmut Boekhoff again: "the ship was on fire from stem to stern". He had climbed up the main superstructure to the top of the bridge before being thrown into the water as the ship capsized. The Executive Officer, Fregattenkapitan Dominick, was seen be calmly helping seamen on with their life jackets. The Captain, Hintze, gave his life jacket to a sailor who had lost his own. Wilhelm Godde, another survivor, made a point in mentioning that at no time did discipline lapse or panic set in. Both Rear Admiral Bey and the Captain survived the sinking and were seen swimming in the water, but both drowned although Hintze was very close to being rescued by Scorpion.

No Celebration

Out of a ship's company of 1,900 men, only 36 were rescued. These were taken to Kola and transferred to the *Duke of York* for shipment to the UK. After a brief moment of panic and visions of Siberia when they were put aboard a soviet tug, they relaxed when it was clear they were not being handed over to the Soviets. They were very well looked after on board the battleship. *Duke of York* arrived at Scapa Flow on New Years Day 1944. She received the cheers of all assembled ships companies. An emotional homecoming. Admiral Fraser told his men to celebrate Christmas. Messages of congratulations flooded including the First Lord of the Admiralty, President Roosevelt and even from Marshal Stalin. But it was also a time for reflection. The sailors of the Royal Navy (and the Royal Norwegian Navy) were only too aware that nearly 2000 sailors had gone to their deaths in the bleak waters of the Arctic. An officer on board the *Sheffield* wrote: "All that is left of a 26,000 ton ship was some 36 survivors. One couldn't help feeling a little sorry for those who had perished. It was a cold dark night, with little chance of survival in those icy waters. However, it might just as easily have been one, or indeed, all of us"

Little exultation was evident aboard the ships that took part in the Battle of The North Cape. It had been too grim for that and, by necessity, remoteness of actions at sea precludes any hate between sailors. This was, of course, countered by an intense pride in what had been achieved, doing what they had been trained for in a ship built for that very purpose. Also consider the possible hundred's of civilian merchantmen whose lives had been spared by the failure of the *Scharnhorst* to break through to the nearby convoys and by the diligence of men like Burnett, who would not let go.

And what of these two convoys that these ships protected so well? RA53a got through to the UK unscathed. Only a single sighting by a solitary Luftwaffe plane indicative that the Germans were even aware of its passing. Convoy JW55b, on its way to Kola had several U-Boats in contact, but by the 27th this had dwindled to just a single submarine. The others had been called off to go to the battle area to both search for survivors and, as the ULTRA signal inferred, to attack any Royal Naval vessels found nearby. On Dec 29th, the convoy arrived safely at Kola with just one straggler, *Ocean Gypsy* coming in late, some hours behind. Convoy RA55b left Kola on New Years Eve 1943, consisting of 8 ships and arrived safe and sound at Loch Ewe on 8th Jan 1944.

The sinking of the *Scharnhorst* had finally eliminated all the surface threats to Arctic convoys, although *Tirpitz* was still under repairs following damage inflicted during the Royal Navy's X Craft attack. *Tirpitz* would continue to affect Home Fleet planning throughout the summer of 1944 but would take no further action against the Allies, being sunk at her moorings at Tromso on 12th November 1944 by bombers of the Royal Air Force using several 12,000lb "tallboy" bombs. She had been moved there after previous carrier-borne air attacks had damaged her. But, her new berth was 200 miles nearer the UK and within range of the RAF bombers. Strangely, in all the attacks leading up to the sinking of the *Tirpitz*, not a single Luftwaffe plane challenged the RAF which enjoyed complete autonomy over the sky's of the Norwegian fjords.

Captain Parham of HMS *Belfast* recalled years later that, "…the best way of remembering that day would be to read the despatches whilst being rocked in a fridge, lit by a single candle, with someone banging on the outside with a hammer."

In spite of the awesome firepower from the *Duke of York*, she did not inflict fatal damage on the *Scharnhorst*. The general credit for this now lies on the brave destroyer of the Royal Norwegian Navy, the *Stord*. She made her very courageous attack, closing to within 400 yards of the big guns (one shell would have sunk her) and delivered a torpedo attack which completely changed the course of the battle.

Since the "official" story has been written there emerged another player in the World War, the secret role of Enigma. When these stories were revealed and more, they went a long way to explain how certain events took place. One such is the *Scharnhorst*. Here is the role played by enigma.

The Role of Enigma in the sinking of the *Scharnhorst*

Due to the withdrawals of U-Boats from the Atlantic in 1943, the role of Enigma diminished but was counterbalanced by the assistance it gave to a grateful Royal Navy in the Arctic Ocean. Not only did the U-Boat threat remain in the region but also the convoys to Murmansk and Archangel were within range of Norwegian based German bombers and also surface ships were in Norway's Fiords. *Tirpitz* was out of action, crippled in Trondheim Fiord and the *Lutznow* had fled back to German National waters. But, still alive, and very much kicking, was the *Scharnhorst*. Her presence tied up much of the Home Fleet in Arctic waters. Admiral Fraser was receiving enigma reports on the state of readiness of *Scharnhorst*. Fraser, on board *Duke of York*, personally took convoy JW55A to Kola in December 1943 much to the surprise of the Russians. He then returned to bring convoy JW55B which was due to leave Loch Ewe, Scotland on 20 December 1943.

As JW55B sailed Fraser received notice that *Scharnhorst* was on 3 hours readiness, and on Dec 21st was back on 6 hours notice. Then he was informed on 22nd December that, on 21st December, *Scharnhorst* was back up to 3 hours notice. Enigma decoding had become relatively fast but there were delays, counted in hours, when codes were changed. News received on Dec 23rd was such a case.

Part of the German coding system on enigma was the Offizier Procedure for anything of utmost importance, normally one off messages. The method involved an officer setting up an enigma with the same settings as normal, but using different plug board settings. The list of settings changed only once a month. After encoding his message, the transcript was then handed to an operator who encoded it yet again.

But Bletchley Park managed to work around even this extra hurdle using cribs which often contained the word "fort" or "continuation" (fortsetzung) and the time of origin of each message. Leslie Yoxall, a 26 years of age mathematician, exploited yet another German oversight. As soon as the board settings were discovered, they were valid for the remainder of the month. Yoxall managed to decode a message containing only 80 characters, whereby the normal message length required was in the region of 200.

Nevertheless, it took 48 hours to inform Fraser that, on Dec 22nd, *Scharnhorst* had been told to make ready for sea. This coupled with enigma news of increased Luftwaffe reconnaissance warned him that something was about to happen. If the Offizier Code has been more readily decoded he would have heard that

"Battle Group is to be at 1 hours notice from 1300 hrs 25th December. *Scharnhorst* to acknowledge".

It took 31 hours for this message to reach Admiral Fraser on the battleship *Duke of York*. But by this time it was too late to influence events.

Even when a message could not be decoded it was not the end of matters. Harry Hinsley, Bletchley Park, used a method that, if messages were more frequent than normal, then something really major was occurring, or about to occur. He phoned Denning in the OIC at the Admiralty and related this fact. When he had first arrived at this conclusion, nobody took any notice of him, and the Royal Navy lost HMS *Glorious* and several destroyers to *Scharnhorst* and *Gneisenau*. Now, when Harry spoke, people listened.

Fraser was informed that *Scharnhorst* has sailed when a message warned a patrol vessel to expect *Scharnhorst* to pass her at approximately 1800 hrs 25th December. Fraser recorded that, at 0339 hrs 26th December, he received a signal stating that *Scharnhorst* was at sea. Fraser was too far from convoy JW55B to be of any use. He broke radio silence to order JW55B to steer to the north, away from *Scharnhorst*. The Germans picked up Fraser's messages but did nothing to inform *Scharnhorst* or to recall her. Even when a Luftwaffe reconnaissance aircraft called in to report "5 warships, one apparently big" to its base still the Germans did nothing. The aircraft has found Fraser but not the Vice Admiral's Cruiser Group which was already engaging the *Scharnhorst*. Back at Bletchley Park another mathematician, Pondered, read the penultimate signal from *Scharnhorst* to base timed at 1819 hrs which he sent onto the Admiralty at 2347 hrs, he wondered if the message intercepts had had any bearing on the outcome. *Scharnhorst* succumbed to the guns of the Royal Navy at about 1945 hrs that same evening.

The Scharnhorst.

Rear Admiral Erich Bey.

A Motor Torpedo Boat (MTB).

6. The 'U-Boat Peril'

"The only thing that ever really frightened me during the war was the U-Boat peril"
Winston Churchill

Of approximately 40,000 German sailors who went to sea in the U-Boat, 30,000 failed to return. When war began, Britain saw Germany's big ships as the main threat to her sea trade, and so did the Germans. It was intended that Germany's surface raiders would savage the merchant fleet on which Britain depended for much of her food, most of her raw material and all of her oil. Germany's U-Boats were to operate in coastal waters, sweeping up anything left by the battleships. Both Britain and Germany were wrong, the real naval menace to Britain's survival was to be the U-Boat. At least one man knew this, Admiral Doenitz, Chief of the U-Boat Arm and later on Grand Admiral of the entire German Navy. He could have been wrong too if Hitler had delayed his war with Britain until all the battleships planned for the German Navy had been built. As it was, Doenitz was certain that, with enough submarines, he could win the war at sea. He had proved it to himself 29 years before.

"In October 1918, I was Captain of a submarine in the Mediterranean, near Malta. On a dark night I met a British convoy, with cruisers and destroyers. I attacked and I sank a ship. But the chance would have been very much greater if there had been a lot of submarines. That's why the idea of a wolf pack, to put the submarines together, to attack together. In all the years from 1918 until 1935, when we had submarines again, I never forgot this idea"

Under water, the 1939 U-Boat was very slow, but on the surface it was faster than any convoy of merchant ships. With its low silhouette, it could not be seen easily, especially at night, but its targets were outlined clearly against the sky and with radio, the U-Boats could assemble quickly into a hunting pack. Doenitz knew that Britain would try to protect her essential Atlantic trade by a system of convoys escorted by warships. To attack these convoys Doenitz wanted 300 U-Boats, when the war started he had only 27 and these boats had long dangerous voyages from their base before they could reach their targets. When France fell, Doenitz gained new bases much nearer the shipping routes. In fact, when en route to Lorient, just after the capitulation of France, Karl Doenitz and his Adjutant were asked to provide a lift to two refugees travelling west. They turned out to be two German Jews escaping Germany. Doenitz said to them when he dropped them off in Le Mans, "Give my regards to England"!

His sea wolves would return to their French ports as heroes. One special hero was Otto Kreschmer, who sank over 250,000 tons of British shipping. In October 1940 he joined the first real wolf pack:

"I remember that there was a signal that there was a convoy coming in from America to England, and that its position was not known. Doenitz ordered all submarines to the west of Ireland to form a sort of recce line to let the convoy pass through. When the first submarine was sighted, the convoy made a signal of contact, this regular line was dissolved automatically, every boat was free to move into the attack"

Grand Admiral Raeder demonstrated a touching faith in his Fuhrer when he addressed a U-Boat crew on Gunnery exercises in spring 1939. The Fuhrer, Raeder said, had promised him that under no circumstances would there be a war against Britain, for that would mean "Finis Germaniae". Doenitz, always open with his crews, admitted that given the circumstances, he could not believe it and as a commander he had to be prepared. All he could do was demand a U-Boat Arm of 300 boats; only this number would be able to enforce a blockade of England. Within 6 weeks the unthinkable had happened, Poland was invaded and Britain and France had declared war on Germany. Doenitz had made no secret of his foreboding, but it still came as a shock to him and his men. Propaganda fed it to the people that Germany had been forced into this war. The Kriegsmarine were unprepared. Britain and France had more than 10 times the amount of warships. The Kriegsmarine could not see how they could win a war at sea, the situation, to their eyes, was desperate. The 3000 men of the U-Boat Arm were well trained but only had 57 boats and most were small 250 ton "ducks". These were coastal vessels. Only 27 boats were capable of going into the Atlantic.

They sailed mainly from Baltic and North Sea ports, their crews enthusiastic but had little experience. For the first 18 months U-Boat activity against British supply lines was small. During the invasion of Norway by the Germans there were no U-Boats in the Atlantic at all. In the summer of 1940, France fell and the U-Boat gained the use of the ports in the Bay of Biscay. British destroyers relied on ASDIC, which could give the range and bearing of submerged U-Boats by using sound. Lack of escorts for the convoys meant the U-Boats could attack convoys at will. However Britain placed too much importance to ASDIC which only worked properly in ideal conditions, not what the Atlantic Ocean is exactly famous for. Too few escorts were running right over U-Boats and not detecting them. Tactics were none existent in the Royal Navy for dealing with convoys and convoy attacks. Ships, when attacked, would steam off in all directions, scattering across the ocean, the escorts spent much of the time in attempts to round them up. Belligerent Captains of merchantmen would disobey instructions and one ship was noted as displaying a "bright white light" on its stern by an escort returning to catch up with the convoy following an attack. This was a Greek freighter in convoy SC7.

The main attack boat favoured by Doenitz was the Type 7, differing little from its WW1 counterpart. Powered by two large diesel engines capable of 17 knots. Air for the engines was channelled through a pipe within the conning tower to ensure maximum distance from the sea. A U-Boat spent 90% of its time on the surface. Once the order was given to dive, the engines were shut down, power being drawn from the boat's batteries. Undersea, the U-Boat was capable of little more than seven knots, and this only for an hour. At two knots it could stay submerged for a maximum of 36 hours. It was then obliged to surface to replenish air and batteries. On the surface a U-Boat had the necessary speed to overtake a slow moving convoy, but if submerged it was almost impossible. Here too, it was almost blind.

By the spring of 1940 Jurgen Oesten was commander of U-61:

"All the boats we had during the war were basically surface craft that had the ability to dive. Out of the 20 ships I sank, 19 were sunk whilst I was on the surface. At night, if you were closer to your target than 3000 to 4000 meters, then from the bridge of a normal merchantman, the conning tower does not appear above the horizon. You offer only a small silhouette to your target, almost invisible."

By 1935 the Admiralty knew a great deal about the nuts and bolts of the U-Boat but very little about tactics. This was quite surprising, as Doenitz had published a book, *Die U-Bootswaffe*, in 1939, in which he made no secret of his methods and tactics. In this he noted the importance of night attack and the thoroughness with which his crews had been trained. The Admiralty also might have consulted its own submarine service, which had practised night attacks of its own.

A U-Boat was a 220-foot home to 43 men. Young and fit, the crew were aged from 20–23; the commander was about 28. Almost half the crew lived in the bow compartment, the main arsenal. There were four tubes and about ten torpedoes. A further two torpedoes could be fired from the stern and two more carried in pressure-proof containers in the upper deck. Life became more comfortable with each torpedo fired! Sharing a bunk with a crewman on the opposite watch, each man turned into a still warm bunk. Beside each bunk was a small locker for a handful of personal possessions. There was no need for clean clothes or razors and precious little for soap.

Within days of leaving port, the appearance of the crew changed, marked by a life without sunlight. Faces were pasty white and bearded, eyes black-rimmed. Clothing soon became thick with diesel and brine. Water was for drinking only, and whilst it was possible to wash with seawater soap, no such effort was made. Two toilets were on board but one was filled with food with more than 40 men sharing the other. The smell of diesel was prominent, as was the smell of food and of men; put all this into a pot and stir and you had the unique U-Boat smell. Some men used cologne to mask the smell, but most just took it for granted.

Beyond the bow compartment was the officers and chief petty officers quarters. Life was a little less bleak for the nine men who ate and slept here. The Captain had his own bunk and a little writing desk next to the radio room. The officers ate on a little table in the middle of the passageway, meals being constantly interrupted by traffic to and from the bow compartment.

At the heart of the submarine was the Control Room, packed with an array of equipment, valves, dials and gauges – the battle HQ of the submarine. Here were the ballast tank and diving plane controls. One of the U-Boat's two periscopes was operated from here, the other, a longer attack periscope, was housed in the coming tower above. Next came the petty officers' compartment and the tiny galley. The cook had a three-ring range, two small ovens and a 40 litre boiling pot. Meals were surprisingly good, their quality helping to relieve the hardship of being on board although fresh food did not last well. Everywhere was damp due to a constant dripping of leaky valves and condensation and in this close atmosphere, food began to gather a thin film of green mould within days. After the fresh food either spoiled or ran out they resorted to tinned food.

Beyond the galley was the engine room, with its clattering thumping diesels and then last of all, the electrical compartment with two 375 horsepower electric motors. For most of the war patrol a four-man watch was maintained up on the conning tower. Horst Elfe, second officer on board U-99, records:

"We had to endure some pretty massive Atlantic storms. It could not have been worse. No U-Boat could be controlled at periscope depth in that, it had to be well under or on top. Surface attacks were unthinkable because nobody could see, move, aim or anything. People only thought of their own survival in these seas."

Admiral Sir Andrew Cunningham observed that although it took three years to build a ship, it took 300 years to build a tradition and the first losses at sea, especially that of the *Royal Oak*, delivered a jolt to the public; nevertheless their belief in final victory remained unshaken. At first the Royal Navy attacked everything that appeared to be moving. Reports of U-Boats sightings were everywhere. One lookout on an Isle of Man Lighthouse reported a periscope six miles away (even on a clear day it would be a lucky observer who spotted a periscope at 1000 yards!) Nevertheless HMS *Walker* was sent out from Liverpool to chase a contact that was a waste of time before it began. At 25 knots *Walker* could be there in two hours, but given a U-Boat's speed, it could have been anywhere within a 10-mile circle, which is a lot of sea to cover with one ship and ASDIC with a range of just 2000 yards.

Convoys could only be escorted from Britain to a line 300 miles west of Ireland. The rest of the Atlantic could be reached by the U-Boat. From July to October 1940, 144 unescorted ships were sunk and 73 badly escorted convoy ships were sunk. U-Boat commanders had discovered a flaw in ASDIC – it could NOT detect a submarine on the surface!

Doenitz developed the wolf pack attack system, whereby several U-Boats, operating together, attacked convoys. On the night of September 21st 1940, Convoy HX72, a fast convoy consisting of 41 merchantmen, was attacked and 11 were sunk. The commodore of the convoy was sure at least two U-Boats had taken part in the attack. The senior officer of the escorts agreed. There was a suggestion that U-Boats were beginning to co-ordinate their attacks. It was altogether unexpected and some influential voices in Naval Intelligence were sceptical (the same "stick-in-the-mud" who thought aircraft unnecessary, perhaps).

Slow convoy SC7 was to put the matter beyond doubt. The Canadian port of Sydney saw the motley collection of ships get underway in the first week of October 1940. SC7 was not expected to make more than 8 knots and many of its 35 ships would struggle to make half of that! The oldest, Norwegian tanker *Thoroy*, was 47 years at sea. Most of the ships had spent the past two weeks at various ports loading cargo. The SS *Fiscus* was loaded with 5-ton steel ingots, a floating brick! Frank Holding, a Liverpudlian, recalled how apprehensive the crewmen were about the forthcoming two weeks at sea with this cargo. "If you had that sort of cargo you had no chance. Once a ship like that got hit, it went down like a stone." Holding counted himself lucky to be aboard the SS *Beatus:* a "dirty old tramp steamer – she had the smell of sugar and oil on her. The cooks were Chinese and the engine room crew were Indian, so there was only me and another Liverpool lad [who were English]." As Assistant Steward, Holding's lot was slightly easier:

"We had privileges over the deck crew and the engine room. They lived in the Forecastle, maybe 8 to 10 bunks to a room. But I was in a room with just the galley boy. We were always told that if we were sunk by a U-Boat they would leave the rest of us, only taking the Captain or the Engineer. We feared machine gunning."

Two friends, Eddie and Billy Howard looked him up at Three Rivers; they were on the *Creekirk*, loaded with iron ore. By 5th October SC7 was assembled and ready for sea. At the pre-sailing briefing some Royal Naval Officers complained about the "bloody-minded skippers" (those who considered they were better off on their own). For the first eleven days, only one sloop was to be their escort. Only as it approached home waters could the convoy expect any more protection. Some of the ships had been fitted with a 4-inch gun on the stern, but the sailors considered it of little use.

A little after midday the first ships weighed anchor and set off; it would take most of the rest of the day to get the remaining ships "on station" – nine columns with three or four ships in each column. For merchantmen used to an empty horizon it was taxing to try to keep station. Four days out SC7 ran into bad weather and immediately some ships began to fall back. One of the largest ships, the 6,000-ton *Empire Miniver*, was one of these, with turbine trouble. Captain Robert Smith remarked to the Admiralty that: "we were peering into the darkness when, to our amazement, we saw a bright light on our port bow. When we drew up we found it was a Greek steamer. It had been visible to us for 6 miles!" So much for the warnings given at the conference. Some belligerent captains thought they would be better off on their own.

In the early hours of 16th October one of the stragglers emitted a distress call – submarine attack! The convoy's lone escort, HMS *Scarborough*, could do nothing. Cargo and crew were lost. Spirits were raised when, on the horizon, two escorts were spotted. HMS *Fowey* and HMS *Bluebell* had arrived from Liverpool, but there was no plan for coordinated action in the event of attack. Late that night, the watch on the bridge of U-48 spotted the moonlit silhouette of a ship. As the U-Boat closed it became clear that it was a convoy, a large one, and weak. Lorient received a transmission giving reference and speed. A group of five U-Boats was ordered to find, close and attack...

U-48 went in first, instead of waiting for the others and soon spotted the largest ship, the 9,500-ton tanker *Languedoc*. The first torpedo went through her side, sending up a column of fire and water into the sky. Two minutes later a second hit the freighter *Scoresby*. Inexperienced, the escorts remained to pick up survivors while the convoy steamed on, unescorted. The following evening another U-Boat damaged a ship.

By nightfall on 18 October, three escort vessels were shepherding the remaining 31 ships, but just over the horizon waited six U-Boats in a line across the path of the convoy. Among them were U-100 commanded by Joachim Schepke and U-99 commanded by Otto Kreschmer, both renowned "aces".

Just before midnight they struck. All around ships were burning, blowing up, sinking. It was absolute chaos. The escorts could do nothing but collect survivors. ASDIC was useless, radar not fitted. Only 12 ships reached port and the only reason these 12 survived was that Otto Kreschmer had received word that convoy HX79 was coming into range behind them. The U-Boats turned their attention to this new convoy, sinking twelve and damaging two out of 49.

Many of the convoy escorts during this stage of the war were old vintage WW1 destroyers, sloops and corvettes, unsuited for anti-submarine warfare. Kretchmer's U-99, using high-speed night-attack tactics (which Admiral Doenitz had written about in 1939) sank nine of 17 ships from convoy SC7. ASDIC, of course, could not find U-Boats on the surface.

The crippling losses of allied shipping during the early years of the war were out of all proportion to the number of enemy submarines at sea. Rarely were there more than 12 at sea at any one time. It was not until after the war that the Allies discovered that the Germans knew the codes being used by the convoy radios. U-Boats were also accompanied to sea by Condor aircraft of the Luftwaffe. The Condor, a long-range reconnaissance bomber, would report shipping movements to the U-Boats, but sank quite a few ships themselves.

In the North Sea in late 1939, faulty torpedoes caused U-23, under the command of Kretschmer, to take three torpedoes to finish off

a small freighter. Having only one torpedo left, Kretschmer entered
the Orkney waters near Kirkwall. Inside the bay sat a neutral tanker,
the *Danmark*, 10,500 tons. The U-Boat crew could see men on deck
smoking cigarettes and the neutral tanker made no effort to hide
herself. When the torpedo exploded, all eyes went skyward, thinking
it was the Luftwaffe. Nobody thought a submarine would penetrate
the bay. Sailing right past the lookouts, U-23 slipped away as gunfire
was directed into the air.

The sinking of the *Danmark* marked a new phase in the war. She
had flown the flag of a neutral country. By January 1940, the Prize
Regulations governing Conduct of Nations at War at sea were being
deliberately ignored. To disguise this U-Boats were told to choose
their targets with care, hoping the Allies might think that the
unlucky ship had hit a mine. The Admiralty did assume mines and
swept the area. Both of the U-23's sinkings were attributed to mines.
It was not until U-Boats were sighted on the surface by aircraft that
the Admiralty faced the grim truth.

In December 1940 convoy losses promised to reach such an extent
that defeat through starvation threatened Britain. What were needed
were more escorts guarding more closely controlled convoys, with
better detection gear. In return for bases, the US handed over 50
WW1 vintage destroyers. Old, it was true, but they filled the gap.
Also fast escort destroyers were released from invasion duty when it
became apparent that the danger had passed. Shipbuilding increased
too. More significantly, British scientists invented a small "resonant
cavity magnetron" which would soon provide the essential radar system to catch U-Boats on the surface. What was known to the U-
Boat commanders as the "happy time" was about to come to an end.
But the U-Boat menace continued and bitter battles were to be
fought on the Atlantic during 1941.

After America's entry into the war the U-Boats had a second
"happy time" *'Die Glückliche Zeit'*. The USA did not enforce blackout
on its eastern coastline and as a consequence the coast of Florida was
lit up with miles of lighting. Ships passing by were silhouetted
against these lights, making them easy prey for the 21 U-Boats Doenitz had sent there. By June 1942 they had sunk no less than 505
ships, many within sight of the Florida beaches.

Apart from shortages of technology, training and escort vessels, the lack of long-endurance aircraft to cover convoys didn't help. The Americans wanted their Liberators for the Pacific; the British wanted the Lancaster for Bomber Command. It was the Germans who first demonstrated the value of air supremacy. In late 1940 they had established Focke Wolf Condor Squadrons along the Biscay coast which could operate up to 800 miles into the Atlantic Ocean. In the first two months of 1941 they alone sank 46 ships, totalling 167,822 tons. The U-Boats sank only 60 in the same period. In spite of warnings from England, via Enigma, an Anglophobic Admiral King, C-in-C Eastern Seaboard, refused to act.

In 1941 ships sunk by U-Boat equalled 432 (2,171,754 tons), ships sunk by aircraft equalled 371 (1,017,422 tons), adding up, with those sunk by other means, to a total of 1,299 ships. Britain and her allies could not build ships fast enough to replace them. But 1942 was far worse... 1,644 ships were sunk and U-Boat strength rose from 91 in January to 212 by December.

Even so, the tide was turning, imperceptibly. By the end of 1942 Britain had small escort carriers in the convoys and Liberators could, on occasion, be spared. Sunderland flying boats operating from Iceland could help on the northern route. A British invention, 'the hedgehog', a multi-barrelled mortar which threw a pattern of 24 depth-charges ahead of the attacking ship, and 'the squid', which did the same with three depth-charges, removed the problem of attacking a U-Boat with depth charges over the stern. The new radar could detect a submarine on the surface; it was also small enough to be fitted, in time, to Coastal Command aircraft. New tactics were also learnt. With the formation of hunter/killer groups of destroyers and groups such as Captain Walker's 2nd Support Group, consisting of 'Black Swan' class sloops, escort commanders were now freed from the task of deciding whether to chase submarines or remain with the convoy.

In September 1942 the first hunter/killer group, under the command of Johnny Walker, was at sea, ready to race to assist any convoy judged to be sailing into danger – firstly, to strengthen the convoy's defences, then to drive off the U-Boats and chase them to their destruction, leaving the escorts to continue with their job.

By January 1943, losses reached 203,000 tons. In February losses reached 359,000 tons. In March 1943, Convoy HX229 left Halifax. On March 13th it was found, accidentally, by U-653. Dropping back it sent off a report and Doenitz sent 12 U-Boats which wreaked havoc amid the convoy's 11 columns. eight ships were sunk in the first attack, two more the next night. In the meantime, another group came across convoy SC122, even larger than HX229 [SC122 was a slow convoy, HX229 was fast].

By the night of 18/19 March, the two convoys had practically amalgamated, but so had their attackers; between them they had 25 U-Boats. By the morning of 19 March, 21 ships of the two convoys had been sunk. If the convoy had not arrived within range of aircraft on the morning of 20 March more would have been lost. In fact, an arriving Liberator sank one U-Boat. In that one encounter 140,842 tons of allied shipping was sunk, bring the March 1943 total to 627,000 tons, one of the worst months of the war.

During April hunter/killer groups were released from the Mediterranean and Roosevelt ordered more Liberators over the Atlantic. By May 41 Liberators were operational. In the middle of that month a large convoy was scattered by a storm south of Greenland. twelve U-Boats took advantage, sinking nine ships, but two support groups arrived from Nova Scotia, the gales dropped; the returning U-Boats were driven off, and then chased, some being sunk. Four were destroyed by depth charges the first night, two sunk by bombers the next day and two collided in the darkness and sank.

The next convoy lost three ships, but the Germans lost also three U-Boats. The next convoy lost two ships for the loss of two U-Boats and two damaged. The next two convoys arrived unscathed, leaving six U-Boats sunk in their wake. In April the total of shipping sunk was 245,000 tons lost for a tally of 15 U-Boats. May saw 165,000 tons lost for 40 U-Boats sunk. In June 18,000 tons were lost and 17 U-Boats sank. The tide was indeed turning.

Doenitz kept his remaining boats in port while he tried to find new tactics. During June 1944 he tried to use them to undermine the D-Day invasion, but they were beaten off with the help of Captain Johnnie Walker's ships, which were deployed to screen the invasion regions.

The Battle of the Atlantic was effectively over. It had been a very close-run thing but the U-Boat was never to be a deterrent again. As Hitler always thought of the U-Boats as a defensive organisation, to keep the Allies busy whilst he waged his war in the east, Doenitz continued to send his men out on suicidal missions, knowing that their probability of returning to base was virtually zero. U-Boat Commanders complained to Doenitz that the Allies were listening to their signals, to which he replied: "Impossible, the code machines cannot be broken". But they *were* broken and we *were* listening!

However great the U-Boat threat was, they actually only sank about 1% of the totall tonnage of shipping crossing the Atlantic Ocean. Unfortunately, the Admiralty's own code had been broken by B-Dienst, the German Intelligence Service and they fed convoy details, when known, to Doenitz. It's amazing that the Germans never recognised Enigma information contained within Admiralty signals!

The U-Boat 'Ace' Commanders

Germany's ace U-Boat Commander Otto Kreschmer – also known as 'The Wolf of the Atlantic' – was captured alive and imprisoned in Canada. Men spoke with awe of the destructive ability of his U-Boat, which carried a "golden horseshoe" upon her conning tower; they also spoke with respect for her commander, who fought with honour and humanity. Kretschmer would bring his U-Boat along-side ships he had destroyed, toss cigarettes, brandy and medical supplies to the occupants of the lifeboats and set them on the right course for home. Kretschmer's war did not, however, end with his capture. From his prison camp in Canada he organised an astonish-ingly efficient espionage group and kept HQ back in Berlin supplied with an incredible amount of accurate military information. This and more can be found in the book *The Golden Horseshoe* by Terence Robertson but, like his other book, *Walker RN*, it quite possibly is now out of print. Otto Kreschmer survived the war to become a dip-lomat. An interview with him, and other U-Boat survivors, can be seen on an excellent video tape narrated by Julia Somerville entitled *Battle of the Atlantic* (Luther Pendragon Productions, 1995, RGI 3037

@ £13.99). Also included is some extremely rare footage of "ace" U-Boat killer Captain Johnnie Walker in action.

Another of the U-Boat aces was Erich Topp, commander of the 'Red Devil' U-552. In 1936 he was serving aboard the cruiser *Karlsruhe* but a personal encounter with Admiral Doenitz led him to volunteer for the U-Boat Arm. In 1937 he reported to the Neustadt Training School but his first sight of a U-Boat was a huge disappointment. Here too he experienced the unique smell and the high humidity, but these soon wore off and he began to feel 'at home'.

At 0116hrs on 14 October 1939 the British Battleship *Royal Oak* was torpedoed whilst in the 'protected' anchorage at Scapa Flow. She took 15 minutes to sink the 13 fathoms to the bottom, drowning 833 crew. The U-Boat responsible was U-47, commanded by Günter Prien. Prior to this, on 3 Sep 1939, at the outbreak of war, Günter Prien had sunk the *Bosnia*, a British Merchant ship. Two days later he added two more. Returning from Scapa Flow, he was received by Adolph Hitler and awarded the Knights Cross of the Iron Cross. In June 1940, Prien was given a 'group' – U-47 plus six others. This group accounted for 32 merchant ships equalling 175,000 tons. Prien sank four of five ships lost in convoy SC2 in Aug 1940. It was also Prien who spotted HX79, calling in five others that sank 14 ships, three of which went to Prien. On 6 March 1941 Prien spotted the convoy OB293, calling in four other boats. Initially losing four ships, the convoy was stoutly defended. The Germans initially lost one U-Boat and one severely damaged. Keeping the convoy in sight, using surface speed, Prien neglected to watch his flanks. HMS *Wolverine* surprised him and sank him with all hands. In some quarters it is alleged that Prien was sunk by one of his own torpedoes, but this is unproven; credit for his "kill" remains with *Wolverine*. Prien's personal "tally" included 30 ships equalling 165,000 tons. He was posthumously awarded the Oak Leaves to his Knight's Cross.

U-100.

Admiral Doenitz.

7. The *Wilhelm Gustloff*

This is the story of the sinking of the *Wilhelm Gustloff* and the deaths of a staggering 10,614 passengers[14] – a maritime disaster which to this day many people know nothing of at all. The Germans kept it quiet at the time, for obvious reasons, and to the Allies at that stage of the war it was of no consequence.

The ship docked in January 1945 at Gotenhafen (Gdynia), Poland to remove German refugees from the path of the oncoming Soviet Red Army; its mission to take them to Kiel in Germany. She was built to accommodate 1,850 passengers and a crew of 400, but when she set sail on her final voyage she was carrying an estimated 600 tons of humans, which reputedly settled the ship an estimated extra 15cm in the water. Some original estimates included amongst the passengers: 918 naval officers and men, 373 German Women Naval Auxiliaries, 162 wounded soldiers of whom 73 were stretcher cases, and 173 crew, all fleeing from the advancing Red Army.

The ship was built in 1937 as a luxury liner by Blohm & Voss of Hamburg. Carrying the name of a murdered Swiss Party official[15] and the Swastika on her funnel, she weighed approx 25,500 tons, had a length of 650 feet and was the crown jewel of the *Kraft durch Freude* (Strength through Joy) Nazi Organization (KdF). Deutsche Arbeitsfront of Hamburg were her owners. She was also used as a troopship during the Spanish Civil War and as a hospital ship and a floating barracks for U-Boat crews. She had a sister ship, the *Robert Ley*.

Shortly after noon on January 30th 1945, the *Wilhelm Gustloff* slipped her moorings and put to sea but 30 kilometres off the Polish

---

[14] This is the largest estimate as many of the passengers were undocumented by the normally fastidious Germans.

[15] The Wilhelm Gustloff was named after a man considered by some during that time to be a German martyr. He had been the leader of the Party in Switzerland and he was murdered in 1936. His name was chosen for the largest liner of the KdF fleet and in 1937 when it was launched, his widow christened the bow on its maiden voyage.

coast she was spotted by a Soviet submarine (the S-13, commanded by Alexander Marinesko) and was hit by three torpedoes at 9:08pm (Gotenhafen time) on January 30th 1945. The first torpedo struck near the bow (and as she went down bow-first was probably the shot that sank her), a second just aft of the first by the 'E' Deck swimming pool and the third amidships in the Machine Room.

The *Wilhelm Gustloff* was neither marked as a refugee ship, nor as a hospital ship and carried no anti-aircraft armaments. At that time she was being operated by the Kreigsmarine as a Troopship. Anti-torpedo measures had not been considered by the Captain. Some sources believe that a small minesweeper accompanied the *Wilhelm Gustloff*, others state she sailed alone. When the ship sank it was at first estimated that about 6,000 people were on board but the post-war German military later raised this to 8,000 and one survivor estimated 9,000. What is known is that only 964 people were rescued. 400 members of the Women's Auxiliary of the Kreigsmarine were sitting in the empty swimming pool when the second torpedo hit, killing them almost instantly.

As the passengers fought to gain the lifeboat decks, killing many in the ensuing stairwell crushes, they found that the lifeboats had not been swung out, the task of the crew in such an event. The crew had vanished after the first hit. Many hundreds of people died in the freezing Baltic waters but the vast majority went down with the ship.

George Duncan writes the following:

> "Indescribable panic reigned as the ship listed and sank in about ninety minutes near the Danish island of Bornholm. Rescue boats picked from the stormy seas 964 survivors, many of whom were landed at Sassnitz on the island of Ruegen and taken on board the Danish hospital ship Prince Olaf which was anchored in the harbour."

Karl Hoffmann, survivor:

> "The surging mass of people attempted to storm the lifeboats, hardly anyone hearing the command "women and children first.""

A female survivor stated:

> "I saw the ship settle at the bows and go down, bow-first, like an arrow..."

The refugees were desperate to get away from the vengeful Soviet Red Army, which was now driving relentlessly westwards, spurred on by the words of Ilya Ehrenburg:

"Kill! Kill! In the German race there is nothing but evil; not one among the living, not one among the yet unborn but is evil! Follow the precepts of Comrade Stalin. Stamp out the fascist beast once and for all in its lair! Use force and break the racial pride of these German women. Take them as your lawful booty. Kill! As you storm onward, kill, you gallant soldiers of the Red Army."

Not every Russian soldier was a butcher or a rapist, of course, some still had a sense of morality and decency. Alexander Solzhenitsyn was one of these. He was a young captain in the Red Army when it entered East Prussia in January 1945. He wrote later in his *Gulag Archipelago*:

All of us knew very well that if the girls were German they could be raped and then shot. This was almost a combat distinction.

In his poem 'Prussian Nights' he describes a scene he witnessed in a house in the East Prussian town of Neidenburg:

Twenty-two Hoeringstrasse.
It's not been burned, just looted, rifled.
A moaning by the walls, half muffled:
the mother's wounded, half alive.
The little daughter's on the mattress, dead.
How many have been on it?
A platoon, a company perhaps?
A girl's been turned into a woman,
a woman turned into a corpse...
The mother begs, "Soldier, kill me!"

For his failure to take Ilya Ehrenburg's directive to heart, Solzhenitsyn was reported by the political commissar in his unit as not being 'politically correct' and was packed off to the *gulag* – a Soviet concentration camp.

Divers went down to survey the wreck of the *Wilhelm Gustloff* not so long ago and found that the complete central portion of the ship was a collapsed mangled mass of twisted metal. The torpedoes could not have done such damage nor could the depth of the water; she was not that far down.

So, what caused the collapse of the superstructure? Apparently, in the Cold War, Soviet divers had found the wreck, identified it, and set demolition charges in order to destroy it. Why? Some think it may have been because she could have been carrying looted Russian treasures, which she wasn't.

Maybe it was just a Soviet Naval exercise in demolition and nothing sinister at all?

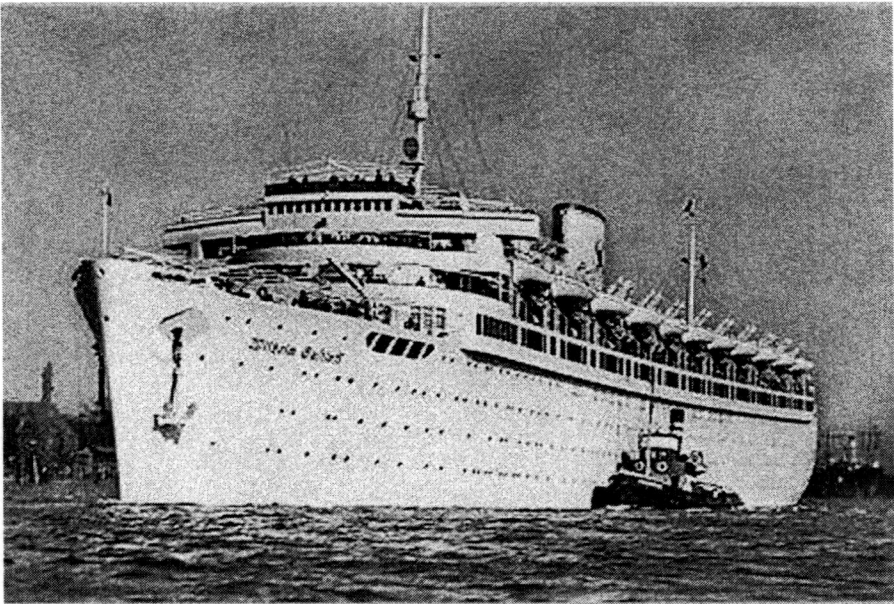

The Wilhelm Gustloff.

8. Exercise 'Tiger'

Exercise 'Tiger' was to have been one of the final, large-scale exercises prior to the biggest invasion in history, D-Day. Although technically an incident involving US soldiers, this tragedy took place almost wholly at sea, involving German E-Boats (*Schnellboots*), Landing Craft and Naval vessels.

At Torcross in Devon, on the edge of Slapton Sands, I met Ken Small, author of the book *The Forgotten Dead*, who signed a copy for me. He was sitting by a Sherman Tank, which, thanks to his efforts, had been retrieved from the seabed to become a memorial. In his book Ken tells of a walk along the beach following January storms and his subsequent discovery of various artefacts turned up by the hammering of the waves. What came of those finds led him, and through him, us, to an extraordinary sequence of events. When I told Ken of my attempts to build a section on my website about this incident he gave me permission there and then to use whatever I wished from his detailed book.[16]

In World War 2 German listening posts were quite adept at cross bearings, triangulation and finding locations based on the interception of radio signals. During the occupations of Holland and France, agents who stayed on air too long were quickly captured using this expertise. In 1944 German listening posts along the Atlantic Wall in France were picking up prolific signals emanating from American Forces on exercises in the South West of England. Much of the communication was in plain English. The Americans were about to practice for the D-Day Landings at 'Utah' Beach using Slapton Sands, which resembled 'Utah' in many ways, including the cliffs which lay behind the 1,800-year-old shingle barrier and beach.

---

[16] In March 2004 I received an email from a lady at BBC Radio Devon informing me of Ken's death earlier that month, which was something of a shock. I knew he had been unwell but was unaware how serious it was.

In 1943, 3,000 local people, their animals and all their belongings had been evacuated from the Slapton and Torcross area for almost a year whilst the beach was used for practice landings. One old man committed suicide rather than leave his home. Live ammunition was being used and a local hotel was destroyed in the landings. I heard one tale of a local boy who worked for pocket money at a local US base. One day he arrived as normal only to be told by a Military Policeman "go home kid, there's nobody here anymore". He was handed a $10 note left for him by the Stores Sergeant.

Operation Tiger involved 30,000 soldiers, including troops from the Infantry Division, 279th Combat Engineers and 70th Tank Battalion, US Army. Landing craft were used to deploy the soldiers and their equipment onto the beaches, where they were supposed to beat the enemy. A convoy of ships set sail from local ports, including Dartmouth and Plymouth. Escorts were provided by the Royal Navy. HMS *Scimitar*, a destroyer, was to take the lead with a corvette, HMS *Azalea*, bringing up the rear. The first sign of things going wrong on the exercise came when HMS *Scimitar* was rammed and holed by another vessel and ordered to remain in port. Nobody thought to inform the Exercise Commander of this fact. The convoy started without an escort and the corvette HMS *Azalea* had no radio contact with the Landing Craft.[17]

The pages of Ken's book contain several 'versions' of what happened, but I trust the dedicated research he carried out so painstakingly and think that his book probably contains the nearest to the truth that we are ever likely to hear. Emails received by me later bear testimony to the near truth of Ken's research. There are many eyewitness reports in his book which I trust a great deal more than the so-called "official" history (I am of the firm belief that history is the opinion of the writer in most cases).

In brief, what happened is this: as the convoy sailed into Start Bay, the westernmost corner of Lyme Bay, German E-Boats found them and opened fire on the defenceless convoy, killing 749 soldiers. This was on the evening of 27th April 1944. German Intelligence had lis-

---

[17] A typing error in the frequencies has been cited as a likely cause; the ships did not have the same information.

tened to the American radio traffic and dispatched nine E-Boats from their home port of Cherbourg to create this large-scale disaster.

Landing Craft 507 and 531 were sunk and 289 was badly damaged. To put the losses in perspective – they were four times greater than on D-Day itself at Utah Beach. General Eisenhower immediately ordered all bodies to be recovered, especially those of a certain ten officers who had in their possession maps of the actual landing at Utah Beach. All bodies were duly recovered and the whole sorry episode 'hushed up'.

So, what actually happened? It was 0200hrs on 28th April 1944. Since the moon had just gone down, visibility was fair. The sea was calm. A few hours earlier, in daylight, assault forces of the US 4th Infantry Division had gone ashore at Slapton Sands, a stretch of beach along the south coast of England that closely resembled one on the coast of Normandy codenamed 'Utah', where a few weeks later US troops were to storm ashore as part of history's largest ever amphibious assault – D-Day. The assault at Slapton Sands was known as Exercise 'Tiger', one of several rehearsals conducted in secrecy in preparation for the momentous invasion to come. So vital was the exercise of accustoming the troops to the combat conditions they were soon to face that commanders had ordered the use of live naval and artillery fire, which could be employed because British civilians had long since been relocated from the region around Slapton Sands. Individual soldiers also had live ammunition for their rifles and machine guns.

In the early hours of 28th April, off the south coast in Start Bay (part of Lyme Bay) a flotilla of eight LSTs (Landing Ship Tank) were sailing toward Slapton Sands, transporting a follow-up force of engineers, chemical and quartermaster troops not scheduled for assault but to be unloaded in orderly fashion along with trucks, amphibious trucks, jeeps and heavy engineering equipment. Out of the darkness, nine swift German torpedo boats suddenly appeared. On routine patrol out of the French port of Cherbourg, the commanders had learned of heavy radio traffic in Lyme Bay. Ordered to investigate, they were amazed to see what they took to be a flotilla of eight destroyers. They hastened to attack.

German torpedoes hit three of the LSTs. One lost its stern but eventually limped into port. Another burst into flames, the fire fed by gasoline in the vehicles aboard. A third keeled over and sank within six minutes. There was little time for launching lifeboats. Trapped below decks, hundreds of soldiers and sailors went down with the ships. Others leapt into the sea, but many soon drowned, weighed down by waterlogged overcoats and in some cases pitched forward into the water and drowned because they were wearing their lifebelts around their waists rather than under their armpits. Others succumbed to hypothermia in the cold water. Finally, when the waters of the English Channel ceased to wash bodies ashore, the toll of the dead and missing stood at 198 sailors and 551 soldiers, a total of 749, the most costly training incident involving US forces during World War II.

Whilst all this was unfolding, Norman Hine, who was a sailor aboard one of our own Motor Gun Boats (MGBs) of Coastal Services, which was on patrol in the vicinity, recalls seeing flashes from the battle but says they received no orders to intercept the E-Boats or to investigate and knew nothing of the tragedy taking place nearby.

Allied commanders were not only concerned about the loss of life and two LSTs (which left not a single LST as a reserve for D-Day) but also about the possibility that the Germans may have taken prisoners who might reveal secrets about the forthcoming invasion. Ten officers aboard the LSTs had been closely involved in the invasion planning and knew the assigned beaches in France; each had a map showing these beaches. There was no rest until those ten could be accounted for: all of them had drowned.

A subsequent official investigation revealed two factors that may have contributed to the tragedy, a lack of escort vessels and an error in radio frequencies. Although there were a number of British picket ships stationed off the south coast, including some facing Cherbourg, only two vessels were assigned to accompany the convoy, a corvette and a World War I era destroyer.

Damaged in a collision, the destroyer (HMS *Scimitar*) had put into port and her replacement vessel came to the scene too late. Because of a typing error in orders, the US LSTs were on a radio frequency different from the corvette and British Naval headquarters ashore.

When one of the picket ships out in the Channel spotted German torpedo boats soon after midnight a report quickly reached the British corvette – but not the LSTs. Assuming the US vessels had received the same report, the commander of the corvette made no effort to raise them. Whether an absence of either or both of those factors would have had any effect on the tragic events that followed would be impossible to say, but probably not. The tragedy off Slapton Sands was simply one of those cruel happenstances of war.

Meanwhile, orders went out imposing the strictest secrecy on all who knew or might learn of the tragedy, including doctors and nurses who treated the survivors. There was no point in letting the enemy know what he had accomplished, least of all in affording any clue that might link Slapton Sands to Utah Beach. Nobody ever lifted that order of secrecy, for by the time D-Day had passed, the units subject to the order had scattered. Quite obviously, in any case, the order no longer had any legitimacy, particularly after General Eisenhower's Supreme Headquarters, Allied Expeditionary Force (SHAEF) in July 1944 issued a press release telling of the tragedy. Notice of it was printed, among other places, in the soldier newspaper *Stars & Stripes*.

With the end of the war, the tragedy off Slapton Sands, like many another wartime events involving high loss of life, such as the sinking of a Belgian ship off Cherbourg on Christmas Eve, 1944, in which more than 800 American soldiers died, received little attention. There were nevertheless references to the tragedy in at least three books published soon after the war, including a fairly detailed account by Capt. Harry C. Butcher (Gen. Eisenhower's former naval aide) in *My Three Years With Eisenhower* (1946).

The story was also covered in two of the US Army's unclassified official histories: *Cross-Channel Attack* (1951) by Gordon A. Harrison and *Logistical Support of the Armies*, Volume I (1953) by Roland G. Ruppenthal. It was also related in one of the official US Navy histories, *The Invasion of France and Germany* (1957) by Samuel Eliot Morrison. In 1954, 10 years after D-Day, US Army authorities unveiled a monument at Slapton Sands honouring the people of the farms, villages and towns of the region "who generously left their homes and their lands to provide a battle practice area for the successful assault in Normandy in June 1944." During the course of the ceremony, the US commander of the North Atlantic Treaty Organization, Gen. Alfred M. Guenther, told of the tragedy that befell Exercise Tiger.

All the while, a detailed and unclassified account of the tragedy rested in the National Archives. It had been prepared soon after the end of the war by the European Theatre Historical Section. For anybody who took even a short time to investigate, there clearly had been no cover-up other than the brief veil of secrecy raised to avoid compromise of D-Day. Yet, in at least one case, WJLA-TV in Washington – the news staff pursued its accusations of cover-up even after being informed by the Army's Public Affairs Office well before the first program aired about the various publications including the official histories that had told of the tragedy.

I have had emails from relatives stating quite categorically that they were never informed as to the circumstances of their loved ones deaths. Some, in fact, found out for the first time through my own web pages about the event! So why, 43 years after the event, had there been a sudden spate of news stories and accusations?

This had its beginnings in 1968 when a former British policeman, Kenneth Small, moved to a village just off Slapton Sands and bought and operated a small guest house. Recovering from a nervous breakdown, Mr. Small took long walks along the beach and began to find relics of war: unexpended cartridges, buttons and fragments from uniforms. Talking with people who had long lived in the region, he learned of the heavy loss of life in Exercise Tiger. Why, Mr. Small asked himself, was there no memorial to those who had died? There was that monument the US Army had erected to the British civilians thanking them for vacating the region during the run up to D-Day, but there was no mention of the dead Americans. To Mr. Small, that looked like an official cover-up.

From local fishermen he learned of a US Sherman tank that lay beneath the waters a mile offshore, a tank lost not in Exercise Tiger but in another rehearsal a year earlier. At considerable personal expense and with the assistance of a Cornish businessman Mr Small managed to salvage the tank and place it on a plinth just behind the beach as a memorial to the Americans who had died. The memorial was dedicated in a ceremony on the 40th anniversary of D-Day.

How had the tank got onto the seabed? This tank had a missing plate underneath the hull which had gone unnoticed until they tried to "launch" it. The tank filled up with water, turning to steam on the hot engine, mistaken for smoke, and went straight to the bottom.

On 25th May 2002 I met Mr Small alongside this tank (incidentally, we were both born in Hull in Yorkshire). I had travelled down with my wife and daughter to Tiverton, the next morning continuing down to Slapton Sands to take some images on my digital camera. I was delighted to meet Ken and after we talked for a while I took his photograph alongside his Sherman and bought from him a copy of his book "The Forgotten Dead", which he autographed for me. He also gave me permission to reproduce some images and notes from his book. My 470-mile round trip was well worth it, if only to meet Mr Small in person.

I read his book and my first impression was of a cock-up on a monumental scale – American soldiers as young as 19 in some cases slipping from life rafts and succumbing to the cold, deep water; LSTs floundering about in circles, not knowing what they were supposed to do; officers killed outright and leaderless men jumping into the flaming sea; lifeboats unable to be launched due to rusted-up release pins. So many soldiers died due to complete incompetence and severely disabled equipment. Soldiers were even ordered not to return fire on the E-boats as "it may give positions away"(!).

Another point from Ken's book is the complete and utter intransigence of the British Authorities – from Local Council level to Westminster – as compared to the friendly warmth and help he received from the American authorities, in particular Beverly Byron in Congress. I am dismayed and amazed by the lack of support from the British Army, probably the RAC Centre Regiment at Bovington Camp Dorset. At the time it was the 3rd Royal Tank Regiment. From "we will be delighted to help" to their 11th hour pull-out with no explanations, leaving Ken in the lurch, with no backup to remove the tank from the channel, until a kind civilian helped out with the right gear. As an ex "tankie" myself (1st Royal Tank Regiment) it leaves me a bit shame-faced. The Royal Navy did assist by providing a ship to raise the tank from the seabed and get it to within hauling distance of the shore. I would also like to add here my own greetings to those wonderful people of Kansas who made Ken so happy and welcome on his trip to a function in that State.

That ceremony prompted the first spurt of accusations by the British and American press of a cover-up, but they were soon silenced by publication of two detailed articles about the tragedy: one in *American Heritage* magazine co-authored by a former medical officer, Dr. Ralph C. Greene, who had been stationed at one of the hospitals that treated the injured; the other in the respected British periodical *After the Battle*.

Those were carefully researched, authoritative and comprehensive articles; if anybody had consulted them three years later, they would put to rest any charges of a cover-up and various other unfounded allegations. Ken Small, meanwhile, wanted more. Although persuaded at last that there had been no cover-up, he nevertheless wished for an official commemoration by the US government to those who had died. Receiving an invitation from an ex-Army major who had commanded the tank battalion whose lost tank Mr Small had salvaged, he went to the United States where the ex-Major introduced him to his congresswoman, Beverly Byron, who as it turned out is the daughter of General Eisenhower's former naval aide, Captain Butcher.

With assistance from the Pentagon, Congresswoman Byron arranged for a private organization, the Pikes Peak Chapter of the Association of the US Army in Colorado, where the 4th Infantry Division is stationed, to provide a plaque honouring the American dead. She also attached a rider to a congressional bill calling for official US participation in a ceremony unveiling the plaque alongside Ken Small's tank at Slapton Sands. Information about that pending ceremony, scheduled for 15 November 1987, set the news media off. There were accusations not only of a cover-up but also of heavy casualties inflicted by US soldiers, who presumably did not know they had live ammunition in their weapons, firing on other soldiers. Nobody questioned why soldiers would bother to open fire if they thought they had only blank ammunition, or why a soldier would not know the difference between live ammunition and blanks when one has bullets and the other has not (as an ex-serviceman myself, I certainly knew whether I had 'live' ammo or not!). Nor was there actually any evidence of anybody being killed by small arms fire.

There surfaced a new an allegation (almost certainly a hoax) made earlier by a local resident, Dorothy Seekings, who maintained that as a young woman she had witnessed the burial of 'hundreds' of Americans in a mass grave (she subsequently changed her story to individual graves). Dorothy Seekings also claimed that the bodies were still there. At long last somebody in the news media (a correspondent for BBC television) thought to query the farmer on whose land the dead were purportedly buried. He had "owned, lived and worked on that land all his life," said the farmer, "and nobody was ever buried there."

This tallies with US Army records that show that in the first few days of May 1944, soon after the tragedy, hundreds of the dead were interred temporarily in a World War I US military cemetery at nearby Blackwood. Following the war those bodies were either moved to a new World War II US military cemetery at Cambridge or, at the request of next of kin, shipped back to the United States.

In March 2005 I received an email claiming that there were indeed soldiers buried near Slapton and also that bodies had been shipped across the Channel and buried in France. The controversy refuses to lie down!

Yet many like Ken Small continued to wonder why it took the US Government 43 years to honour those who died off Slapton Sands. Those who wondered failed to understand US policy for wartime memorials. Soon after World War I, Congress created an independent agency – the American Battle Monuments Commission – to construct overseas US military cemeteries, to erect within them appropriate memorials and to maintain them. Anybody who has seen any of those cemeteries, either those of World War I or of World War II, recognizes that no nation honours its war dead more appropriately than does the United States. Only the American Battle Monuments Commission, not the US Army, Air Force or Navy, has authority to erect official memorials to American dead, and the American Battle Monuments Commission limits its memorials to the cemeteries, which avoids a proliferation of monuments around the world. Private organizations, such as division veterans' associations, are nevertheless free to erect unofficial memorials but are responsible for all costs, including maintenance. Soon after the end of the war, veterans of the 1st Engineer Special Brigade, which incurred the heaviest losses in Exercise Tiger, did just that, erecting a monument on Omaha Beach to their dead, presumably to include those who died at Utah Beach and those who died in preparation for D-Day. At Cambridge, there stands an impressive official memorial erected by the American Battle Monuments Commission to all those Americans who died during World War II while stationed in the British Isles. That includes the 749 who died in the tragedy off Slapton Sands, and there one finds the engraved names of the missing. Long before 15th November 1987, the US Government had already honoured those soldiers and sailors who died in Exercise Tiger.

The Media Response

"It was a disaster which lay hidden from the World for 40 years . . . an official American Army cover-up."

"That a massive cover-up took place is beyond doubt. And that General Dwight D. Eisenhower authorized it is equally clear."

"Generals Omar N. Bradley and Eisenhower watched "the murderous chaos" and "were horrified and determined that details of their own mistakes would be buried with their men.""

"Relatives of the dead men have been misinformed – and even lied to – by their government."

"a story the government kept quiet ... hushed up for decades ... a dirty little secret of World War II."

What was that terrible event so heinous as to prompt those accusations of perfidy 43 years later from the British news media from some American newspapers and in a particularly antagonistic three-part report from the local news of the ABC affiliate in Washington D. C. WJLA-TV?

In preparing for the Normandy Invasion the United States Army conducted various training exercises at Slapton Sands in Start Bay and in the nearby Tor Bay, beginning on December 15th 1943. Slapton was an unspoilt beach of coarse gravel, fronting a shallow lagoon that was backed by bluffs that resembled Utah Beach. After the people in the nearby village were evacuated, it was an almost perfect place to simulate the Normandy landings. The training was long and thorough. The culmination of the joint training program was a pair of full-scale rehearsals in late April and early May.

TIGER was the code name of the training exercise for the Utah Beach assault forces under Admiral Don P. Moon. It was held from April 22nd to 30th 1944. The troops and equipment embarked on the same ships and for the most part from the same ports from which they would later leave for France. Six of the days in the exercise were taken up by the marshalling of the troops and the embarkation of the landing craft. During the night of April 26/27 1944 the main force proceeded through Lyme Bay with mine craft sweeping ahead of them as if crossing the channel.

Since German E-boats, which were high-speed torpedo boats capable of operating at speeds of 34-36 knots, sometimes patrolled the channel at night, the British Commander in Chief, Plymouth, who was responsible for protecting the rehearsal, threw patrols across the mouth of Lyme Bay.[18] These patrols consisted of two destroyers, three motor torpedo boats and two motor gunboats. Another motor torpedo patrol was sent to watch Cherbourg, one of the ports where the German E-boats were based. The E boats, according to a German sailor, slipped through this screen without even seeing them. Following the "bombardment" on Slapton Sands, the exercise "landings" were begun during the morning of April 27th, and the unloading continued during the day and the next when a follow up convoy was expected.

This Convoy T-4 consisted of two sections from two different ports. The Plymouth section, LST Group 32, was composed of USS LST-515, USS LST-496, USS LST-511, USS LST-531, and USS LST-58, which was towing two pontoon causeways. The Brixham section consisted of USS LST-499, USS LST-289 (see image below), and USS LST-507. The convoy joined with HMS *Azalea* as escort and proceeded at six knots in one column with the LSTs in the same order as listed above.

---

[18] According to another version - above, these patrols were already in place and NOT as cover for an operation that maybe they did not even know about!

When the convoy was manoeuvring in Lyme Bay in the early hours of April 28th they were attacked by nine German E-boats out of Cherbourg that had evaded the Allied patrols. No warning of the presence of enemy boats had been received until LST-507 was torpedoed at 0204hrs. The ship burst into flames and survivors abandoned ship. Several minutes later LST-531 was torpedoed and sank in six minutes. LST-289, which opened fire at E-boats, was also torpedoed but was able to reach port. The other LSTs plus two British destroyers fired at the E-boats, which used smoke and high speed to escape. This brief action resulted in 198 Navy dead and missing and 441 Army dead and missing according to the naval action reports. Later Army reports gave 551 as the total number of dead and missing soldiers.

The final training exercise 'Fabius' took place between May 3rd and 8th, without any enemy attacks. LST 508 missed the action and survived due to a pre exercise collision in the channel with a freighter. Consequently her crew lived on instead of ... [see email reprinted later in this chapter]

To keep the Germans from possibly learning about the impending Normandy Invasion, casualty information on Operation TIGER was not released until after the invasion. On August 5th 1944 Supreme Headquarters, Allied Expeditionary Force (SHAEF) released statistics on the casualties associated with the Normandy Invasion, which included information about the German E-Boat attack on April 28th. This information was also published in the August 7th issue of *The Stars and Stripes*, the daily newspaper of the US Armed Forces in the European Theatre. The Textual Reference Branch, National Archives and Records Administration, 8601 Adelphi Road, College Park, MD 20740-6001, holds the originals of both these sources.

Over the years, details on the training exercises and the resulting losses have appeared in such published sources as Samuel Eliot Morison's *The Invasion of France and Germany, 1944-1945* (1957), volume XI of his 15-volume *History of United States Naval Operations in World War II*, and Roland Rupenthal's *Logistical Support of the Armies* (1953) and Gordon Harrison's *Cross-Channel Attack*, which are both part of the multi-volume series United States Army in World War.

The report printed in the above paragraphs also makes the mistake of claiming that it was actually Omaha beach that these exercises were in place for – conflicting reports; conflicting information. I amended it to read Utah. I think it is apparent that Eisenhower and his General's DID hush up news of this disaster, but only so that military security and secrecy could be maintained. How many more lives would have been lost if the Germans found out anything? Eisenhower himself said that if the maps were not found, the whole "show" was off. According to information contained above and on the net, the "secrecy" surrounding this exercise was in fact "made public" after the successful Normandy landings. (See email printed later in this chapter; according to this account, relatives were told nothing). I am no expert and do not claim to be, but this is one incident that may never be successfully and satisfactorily sorted out.

Events according to the official Tiger web site:

> What began as a top secret naval operation to prepare US Army and Naval forces for the June 6th D-Day Invasion, would end with one of the highest losses ever suffered in combat by the US Army and Navy in WW II.
>
> At 0135hrs on the morning of April 28th 1944, eight Tank Landing Ships (LST's) and their lone escort, the British corvette HMS AZALEA, were en route to the landing area. Slapton Sands was selected because its beach looked every bit like the beaches at Normandy that would be code named Utah and Omaha by the allies. The eight LST's of LST Group 32, formed convoy T-4. They were the support group for elements of the 4th & 29th Infantry, 82nd Airborne and 188th Field Artillery Group already ashore at Slapton Sands.
>
> The LST's were carrying the 1st Engineer Special Brigade, the 3206th Quartermaster Company from Missouri, the 3207th Company and 462nd and 478th combat truck support companies as well as other elements of the US Army's engineer, signal, medical and chemical corps along with some infantry. Miles south in the mouth of Lyme bay, lay the bulk of the Tiger naval force. Protected by the cruiser USS AGUSTA and the new British "O" class destroyers HMS ONSLOW and HMS OBEDIENT as well as the Tribal Class destroyer HMS ASHANTI and a covering force of motor torpedo boats. Anchored along with LST's 55 and 382 they would be of no help to the ambushed LST force of T-4. Attacking in the pitch black night, 9 German Navy "E" boats (torpedo) struck quickly and decisively. Without warning LST 507 was torpedoed first. Explosions and flame

lit the night. At 0217 LST 531 is torpedoed. It sinks in six minutes. Of the 496 soldiers and sailors on her, 424 of them died. It would be on this ship that the state of Missouri would lose some 201 of its boys of the 3206th. LST 289 tried to evade the fast German "E" boats but was hit in the stern. LST's 496, 515, and 511 all began firing at their attackers, LST 289 joined in returning fire while lowering landing craft to pull it out of harms way.

At 0225hrs the LST 499 radioed for help. Minutes later the lead ship, LST 515 sent out an urgent and chilling message. "E' boat attack". Radio stations along the coast pick up the dramatic calls for help, unaware of the top secret operation underway, the calls go unanswered. Only after an alert radio operator heard the words "T-4", did the Naval Command realize the calls were from "Tiger" and send help. By 0240hrs the horror was slowly realized. Two LST's sunk, a third lay crippled. Of the 4000 man force nearly a fourth were missing or killed. Official Dept. of Defence records confirm 749 dead, 551 US Army and 198 US Navy. The death toll makes "Tiger" the costliest battle to US forces at that point in the war after Pearl Harbour. On April 28th 1944 the LST's darkest yet finest hour occurred. When, for one hour, the men and ships of Convoy T-4 fought the greatest naval battle ever faced by an LST force in history. Against superior enemy warships, the Tiger amphibious force held its own. The German attack did not stop Exercise Tiger. Landing operations resumed later on the 28th. It is a credit to the tenacity and determination of the soldiers and sailors involved in Exercise Tiger, that the D-Day invasion at Normandy occurred as planned. The events surrounding Exercise Tiger were officially declassified in early August 1944, two months after the Normandy Invasion. On April 28th 1996 Secretary of The Navy John Dalton stated in his remarks "Tiger....was the LST's finest hour."

In Peter Scott's book *The Battle of The Narrow Seas* (1945) he makes a vague reference to the disaster at Slapton. As he was on the planning staff at Portsmouth "Plot" prior to D-Day, he would have been ideally placed to learn of this catastrophe. He refers to E-Boat successes prior and during D-Day. He writes:

"Only once in that time did the E Boats achieve anything of consequence. That was during an invasion exercise when they got in amongst a convoy of landing craft in Lyme Bay and wrought serious devastation

and heavy loss of life; it was their sole success although they were at sea night after night".

Even in this brief reference Scott gives the E-Boats undue credit. The vast majority of American losses were from alleged friendly fire from their own forces on the beach! At the time of writing his book (1945) he must have known of the real reasons over 900 US servicemen met their deaths.

Emails

From Ray Holden (HMS *Kite* Association):

> *I saw an ITV documentary about Slapton. That is how I came to hear about it. Veterans of Slapton appeared on it, one of them was coxswain of an LST. These veterans openly cried when describing how they were pinned down on the beach by friendly fire. They even described from what direction the machine gun was firing. Dozens of men were killed and apparently were posted as being killed in action. In my own personal opinion this is where the cover up came in.*

I hope my American friends will forgive me but this seems to be "nothing new". How many times do we hear of US forces bombing Allies and their own? Gulf War - all British losses down to "friendly fire" and Afghanistan - how many "friendly" deaths? Iraq too - "friendly" deaths. I suspect that the "dozens" of US soldiers that allegedly died by friendly fire can only be resolved by exhuming bodies and checking for bullets - I doubt if survivors of these families would like to find that out! Apparently some American soldiers were also killed by Royal Naval gunfire when they crossed lines they were supposed to remain behind - or did their officers not pass the orders on? More mystery, more supposition and more conspiracy theories?

I have since found a newspaper report dated 1997 in which witnesses clearly state that they saw US soldiers being "mown down" by their own troops![19]

---

[19] Oral Histories - Exercise Tiger, 28 April 1944
(http://www.history.navy.mil/faqs/faq87-3g.htm)

Recollections by Lt Eugene E. Eckstam, MC, USNR, (Ret.), a
medical officer on USS LST-507.[20]

*More lives were lost in one exercise practicing for D-Day than during
the invasion of Utah Beach on 6 June 1944. That rehearsal was called
"Exercise Tiger." Planning for the greatest amphibious operation in history required many such exercises, each designed to test the readiness of
plans for the invasion of Normandy and the efficiency of the troops.
Duck, Fox, Muskrat, Beaver, and Trousers preceded Tiger, and Fabius
followed. Each was larger than the last, and the later ones used live ammunition.*

*Because it resembled Utah Beach, these exercises used Slapton Sands,
a beach on the English Channel east of Plymouth in (Start Bay part of)
Lyme Bay. Other smaller exercises were held many places in southern
England, especially at Woolacombe.*

*Exercise Tiger involved some 300 ships and 30,000 men. Thirty of
the ships were LSTs (Landing Ship Tank), which loaded at Plymouth,
Brixham, and Dartmouth. The first units landed at H-hour, the morning of 27 April 1944. H-hour was delayed 1 hour, causing landings and
shelling to coincide. And not all ships got the message.*

*Convoy T-4 consisted of eight LSTs bringing up the rear and due to
land at H + 24 hours. I was on LST-507, which was last in line. The
convoy circled Lyme Bay at 4 knots. Only one British escort vessel accompanied us, another remained in Plymouth with a hole in its bow.
Much later, a replacement was sent, but too late to effect the tragic outcome of Exercise Tiger. German E-boats (torpedo boats) plied the
Channel and Lyme Bay several times a week and the night of 27-28
April was one of them.*

*I was a brand new Naval Reserve medical officer, fresh out of an ab-
breviated senior year and internship, totally unprepared for what was to
follow. I knew only about the role of such physicians on LSTs and this
training was short.*

*My first assignment in January 1944 was Great Lakes Naval Train-
ing Station in Illinois. I followed the other physicians on the North
Shore electric train to the Great Lakes Naval Hospital and checked in.*

---

[20] Adapted from: "The Tragedy of Exercise Tiger," Navy Medicine 85, no. 3 (May-
Jun 1994): 5-7.

The next morning I found the difference between Hospital and Main-side! I was assured all the paperwork would be transferred. It wasn't, as I later discovered.

At the recruiting centre, Mainside, we examined an average of 1,700 recruits a day. In a week I became an expert in haemorrhoids, hernias, and right ears. Then I, and perhaps 50 other new physicians, reported to Lido Beach, Long Island. A few thousand hospital corpsmen of all ranks were there too. Thus, individual outfits of Foxy 29, the code name for our medical unit, were formed by taking two physicians and an assortment of 40 corpsmen. We were supposed to drill and train our "men." After the brass saw hilarious marching formations colliding, the Marines took over.

Our training at Lido Beach was the introduction to the LST and its uses as a medical evacuation ship. We had some exposure to gas warfare, and endured unpleasant contacts with several chemical agents. Units shipped out at regular intervals on LSTs. We left on 10 March 1944.

As LST-507 was dropping off cargo and loading supplies in various English ports, our medical unit was sent to Fowey for a week of intensive training on chemical warfare and general first aid. This all added up to very little preparation for an invasion with major casualties.

When our medical unit reported back to LST-507, it was in Brixham and had loaded some 290 Army personnel. The tank deck held 22 DUKWs (amphibious trucks) with jeeps and trucks topside, all chained to the deck and fully fuelled. Army troops were everywhere.

Loading occurred 24 April 1944. We and two other LSTs sailed from Brixham on the afternoon of 27 April to join five LSTs coming from Plymouth. Only recently I found that our British escort had been warned about E-boats in the area, but the U.S. forces had not been given the correct radio channel to monitor. We sailed along in fatal ignorance.

General Quarters rudely aroused us about 0130. I remember hearing gunfire and saying they had better watch where they were shooting or someone would get hurt. At 0203 I was stupidly trying to go topside to see what was going on and suddenly "BOOM!" There was a horrendous noise accompanied by the sound of crunching metal and dust everywhere. The lights went out and I was thrust violently in the air to land on the steel deck on my knees, which became very sore immediately thereafter. Now I knew how getting torpedoed felt. But I was lucky.

The torpedo hit amidships starboard in the auxiliary engine room, knocking out all electric and water power. We sat and burned. A few casualties came into the wardroom for care and, since there was ample help, I checked below decks aft to be sure no one required medical attention there. All men in accessible areas had gone topside.

The tank deck was a different matter. As I opened the hatch, I found myself looking into a raging inferno which pushed me back. It was impossible to enter. The screams and cries of those many Army troops in there still haunt me. Navy regulations call for dogging the hatches to preserve the integrity of the ship, and that's what I did.

Until the fire got so hot we were forced to leave the ship at 0230, we watched the most spectacular fireworks ever. Gas cans and ammunition exploding and the enormous fire blazing only a few yards away are sights forever etched in my memory.

Ship's company wore life jackets, but the medics and Army personnel had been issued inflatable belts. We were told only to release the snaps and squeeze the handles to inflate. Climbing down a cargo net, I settled into the 42 degree F. water, gradually getting lower as the life belt rose up to my arm pits. The soldiers that jumped or dove in with full packs did not do well. Most were found with their heads in the water and their feet in the air, top heavy from not putting the belts around their chests before inflating them. Instructions in their correct use had never been given.

I recall only brief moments of hearing motors, of putting a knee on a small boat ramp, and then "awakening" half way up a Jacobs ladder. I was on the only American ship, LST 515, to rescue survivors. This was at dawn, about 0600. I had been in the water over 2 hours fully dressed and insulated. Those that had stripped to swim, only God knows where they died. Drowning and hypothermia were the two major causes of death. I often wonder if many "dead" victims were really in a state of hibernation, and what would have happened had we been able to immerse them in warm tubs. But who ever heard of a tub on an LST in wartime? We couldn't even do a reliable physical exam under the circumstances.

Both dead and alive were taken to Portland. The dead went on to Brookwood Cemetery near London where they were buried individually. The rumour of mass graves is false. We got dry clothes, courtesy of the American Red Cross and then an exam at an Army field hospital in

Sherborne. An Army physician, Dr. Ralph Greene, was there and later did the first American research on Exercise Tiger.

After a month's leave, all were reassigned and most boarded other LSTs for the invasion of Normandy. Others were given shore assignments. For me, Normandy was a piece of cake. LST-391 made one run carrying Rangers Headquarters Staff to Omaha Beach. We took 125 injured from Utah Beach to England. The Army tent dispensary at the beachhead had done an excellent job with these men. Our supplies contained only about six 20 cc syringes with 1½-inch needles. We gave 1 cc (20,000 U) of penicillin every 3 hours to each of the next 20 men with the same syringe and the same needle, but with no withdrawal of the plunger. After a brief boil, syringes and needles were reloaded. There was no other way to keep the schedule. In England, the medical group was detached to stage for the Pacific.

When I got home, I tried to re-establish my pay and insurance records. Great Lakes Naval Hospital did not transfer my life insurance to Mainside! And me with a fairly recent bride.[21]

Email from Deb in Kansas (her father was on LST 289):

"Good additional material for my children to use in educating history teachers who are not aware of this exercise. Also, my father states he was sworn to secrecy and it was NOT brought forth to the public following WWII. There are many families who lost relatives that will state the same thing. What they were told was not the truth about the situation of their loved ones death."

Email Received 18th Dec 02.

Hi Mike, Just by chance I came across your report on Ken Small's book. I now live in Sarasota, Florida, but spent a large part of my life in Paignton, Devon. My wife and I ran a small guest house there. One day, out of season, we had an American gentleman knock on our door looking for accommodation. It turned out that he was involved in the Tiger fiasco and had come over to retrace his wartime steps. His name was Harold Wilson and he was a professor at Florida University in Talahassee (small

---

[21] All the files of Eugene E. Eckstam, who has done extensive research on Exercise Tiger, are/have been/being transferred to the Centre for War & Peace, Department of History, University of Tennessee, Knoxville, Tennessee.

World Huh?) As we were fairly quiet at that time we had the chance to run him around to his old haunts. His stories, and the way he reacted to seeing Slapton again, were amazing. He said nothing had changed. Every corner we took on the coastal road ... .he knew what was around the corner. It was like he had never left. We kept in touch for a while and then got no replies to our letters. When we moved over here about 10 years ago we tried again, but got no response. We still have a son and his family living in Paignton and on one of our return trips we went to Slapton and met with Ken and purchased one of his books. We have lent it out to many American friends and they are all amazed that this had happened, totally oblivious of the sad loss of life in "practice" in 1944. I was also saddened to read in your pages that the US STILL have not learned much from their mistakes in the past, Friendly fire is still a major cause of death to America's allies. Hopefully they get it right next time, God forbid that there is a next time, but that seems unlikely. Congratulations on an excellent Web page, wishing you continued success, George Layland.

Email received 15th March 2004.

Having logged on to and read your page about Exercise Tiger, I write, representing my older Brother John who is almost 80 years old and as a 19 year old serving in the British Naval Coastal Forces on the night of the 28th April 1944, he was serving on HMS RML 532 and was within 5 miles of the attack on the LST convoy. He also spent 2 hours of the following morning in the waters of the channel recovering the bodies of young American soldiers. Jim Cullen.

Email received 16th March 2004.

I was a Lieut. (XO (Executive Officer & Navigator) on LST 508 that was ordered and scheduled for the Tiger Exercise, but on the way to pick up the Army, was in heavy fog in the English Channel where it was struck by a freighter in convoy going in the other direction. The bow anchor was torn off and the bow door damaged. It would not open, thus the LST 508 returned to Falmouth for repair. Orders were obtained to permit burning and welding all night. Repair could not be made in time and the LST 507 took our place. And as you reported, was sunk. And yes, it was all kept secret. Our pay records went down with the LST

*507 and we received no pay for a couple of months. As I recall the LST
508 was on way from Falmouth to Plymouth to pick up our load for the
Tiger Exercise, but failed do to the collision in the fog as mentioned in my
prior message. (As I recall our orders were marked SECRET and the
ship's log would have not indicated the destination prior to arrival, thus
even with the log I could verify that Plymouth was correct.) Our ship's
officers and crew felt great sadness hearing of the loss of LST 507 where
many were close friends. When back in Falmouth, England my commanding officer, Lt. John G. Holmes, of LST 508 reported to our
Flotilla Commander who was surprised at seeing him. Our ship, LST
508 was about to be reported lost based on the collision report. No doubt
some of this confusion resulted from the sinking and damage of those in
the Tiger Exercise. As you may imagine the talk on the LST 508 "What
if ?" when it was learned the LST 508 had been sunk. Cdr. E. F.
Freeman, USNR (Ret.)*

As you can see from some of the above messages, families were
certainly not told of how soldiers had died but only that they had
died. Many would have gone through their lives believing that their
loved ones had died in action on some foreign land, not been killed
in an incident which should never have occurred. The official com-
muniqués mentioned in earlier pages are 'economical in the truth'.

LST 289 before…

… and after Operation Tiger.

Slapton Sands.

Ken Small with the recovered Sherman tank.

9. HMS *Kite* – An Unnecessary Fate

How did a 56-year-old ex-soldier get involved with the story of HMS *Kite*? It all started back in my youth when I had a model of the battleship *Bismarck*. I was always besotted by the beauty of this piece of marine engineering. I also used to read a lot of WW2 books, I remember Paul Brickhill's *The Dam Busters* and *Reach For The Sky* – the story of Douglas Bader. Then, much later in my life, along came the ability to research various items on the Internet. This led to a small site in which I published some results of my research, albeit on a small scale. Then, when I bought my own domain, it expanded into a virtual full-time "hobby" and my site grew and grew. My computer-widowed wife was not altogether amused and probably is still not!

My web-page on *Bismarck* was published and then came pages on U-boats. A friend suggested, after I told him about Captain Walker RN, that I do a page on him – which I did... and which led to an e-mail from Ray Holden of Stourport, who asked me quite simply "Have you ever heard of HMS *Kite*?" I replied that apart from the fact that she was one of "Walker's Own" – very little.

From then onwards, it was a matter of putting together all the information that began to flood into my computer from Ray, Christine Chaplin and others. After many hours of research and following up all the little leads, here we arrive at the definitive saga of one of "Walker's Own" that didn't come back. I then was invited to attend a function in Braintree, the 'home town' of HMS *Kite* and then a memorial service in Liverpool. Here I was very fortunate to meet the grandson of Captain "Johnnie" Walker, Captain Patrick Walker, RN (Retd). The family resemblance is certainly there. I also met Lionel Irish, one of only two survivors from HMS *Kite* still with us (the other being Reg Holmes). I also met members of Captain Walker's Old Boys Association, now sadly an association no more. The days and years are catching up on these stalwarts and their standard has now been officially "laid up" in Bootle Town Hall. There is now a stone memorial in Braintree & Bocking Public Gardens inscribed simply:

"In Remembrance of the 217 Men of HMS Kite, Braintree & Bocking's Adopted Warship Who Lost Their Lives on 21st August 1944."

The story of HMS *Kite* has never been told before, until now. The sinking of a warship in wartime is not exactly uncommon, but the reasons that she did sink are very definitely uncommon. The loss of life on HMS *Kite* ranks alongside the losses of *Bismarck*, *Scharnhorst*, HMS *Hood*, and the tremendous losses in the U-Boats. She suffered the loss of over 95% of her crew – only nine reached shore safely – while 217 men died, as a result, in my opinion, of command errors.

The crewmembers of HMS *Kite* being members of the exclusive fraternity of Captain Johnny Walker, were all highly trained.

After the death of Capt Walker in July 1944, *Kite* was seconded from her Support Group to arctic convoy escort duties and she left on her last voyage from Loch Ewe in August 1944. But let's come back to the present... Picture the scene, you are walking past some church or other, your not taking really much notice but you see some people walking slowly out of the church, they are wearing military regalia, maybe berets, maybe just blazers with badges on the breast pockets. It may cross your mind that these are former soldiers, sailors or airmen who have been remembering dead comrades or suchlike. You hurry on, the bus will be here soon and you do not want to miss the first footy game of the season on television... At 1500 hrs on Sunday August 20th 1989 such an occasion took place. It was a Choral Evensong Memorial Service at the Liverpool Anglican Cathedral. This particular Service was dedicated to the crew of HMS *Kite*.

Now, in the year 2004/5, when I am writing this, such memorial services are fairly "commonplace". It is, after all, 60 years now since 1944 when all those memorable, and not so memorable, events took place: 60 years since the death of Captain Walker, since D-Day, since the debacle of Exercise Tiger ... and since the death of HMS *Kite*.

I attended one such occasion in Liverpool in July 2004, the Laying up of the Standard of Captain Walker's Old Boys Association. But let's stop and look at this one in a little more detail. What exactly was this ship, HMS *Kite*? Who were these people walking out of such a commanding building in the centre of Liverpool? At the bottom of the dedication book to this memorial service something more sombre greets the eye:

"torpedoed by U344 on 21 August 1944 in the Barents Sea - loss of 217 lives".

Those of you who really know your World War Two history will no doubt remember all about Captain Frederick John Walker DSO & 3 Bars and his amazing successes against the U-Boats ... but HMS *Kite*?

HMS *Kite* was built by Cammell Laird shipyards on the banks of the River Mersey in Birkenhead and was launched on 13th October 1942. She was a Black Swan Class Sloop of 1,250 tons and was armed with three 4-inch guns, two 2-pounder guns, two 4-barrelled pom-poms, two 20mm Oerlikon guns and two 3-inch twin machine guns. She carried four rail throwers for depth charges, of which she carried 110 in total. On the 9th April 1943 she was one of the founder members of Walker's 2nd Escort Group, the first of the Hunter Killers.

Captain "Johnnie" Walker, Commanding 2nd Support Group issued the following order to his ships, the first paragraph read:

Second Support Group Operating Instructions (SG2)

Object

The Object of the Second Escort Group is to destroy U-Boats, particularly those which menace our convoys.

This being a significant difference between those and the standard orders of an escort group which was "the safe and timely arrival of the convoy".

Another abstract from Walker's Operating Instructions read:

"Our object is to kill, and all officers must fully develop the spirit of vicious offensive. No matter how many convoys we may shepherd through in safety, we shall have failed unless we slaughter U-Boats. All energies must be bent to this end."

His tactics still form the principles of basic training in anti-submarine operations today. Once at sea, Walker quietly but firmly clamped down with an iron hand. He made it clear that the task of the group was to destroy U-Boats and that all they did from then onwards was directed to this end. Since the outset of the war, it had been generally accepted that escorts would stay close to their charges to ward off U-boat attacks. Walker, then holding the rank of commander, had achieved his successes by ignoring this principle and hunting his victims well away from their quarry. On one occasion he sank two U-boats 40 miles away from the convoy he was protecting. In high places at the Admiralty there were powerful forces at work seeking to brand Walker as a lucky heretic. Only his success and the unqualified backing of Admiral Sir Max Horton, C-in-C Western Approaches, prevented Walker from being posted ashore.

While Admiral Horton was in a possibly favourable mood Walker persuaded him to try a revolutionary theory: six modern, fast, specially equipped sloops, freed from the fetters of convoy duty, should be given a roving commission to hunt down U-Boats in their most vulnerable grounds, the Bay of Biscay – which they crossed when beginning or completing their patrols – and far out in the Atlantic where they surfaced with impunity because the sky was clear of aircraft.

In the spring of 1942, Walker took command of the Second Support Group, the first of the new striking forces. From the bridge of *Starling*, his own sloop, he drilled *Wild Goose*, *Cygnet*, *Wren*, *Woodpecker* and *Kite* until they became a team, swinging into action with few orders and fewer mistakes. The first few weeks were uneventful and gave the crews time to work up, before spending a few days in Iceland prior to leaving on 21st May.

In June Walker found an opponent worthy of his guile, Kapitänleutnant Gunter Poser, commanding officer of U-202. This U-boat was returning home after a special mission in which it had landed Nazi agents in the United States on Long Island's Amagansett Beach (these agents were all captured and, I believe, executed). It was U-202's ninth operational trip of the war and 27-year-old Poser was a quick-witted, capable captain. U-202 transmitted a long signal while surfaced and the Group homed in on her position in line abreast. On June 13, Poser's officer of the watch sighted mastheads through the periscope and called him to the control room. Poser took over the eyepieces and immediately he identified them as destroyers. He ordered diving stations and within a few seconds U-202 was down to 500 feet. Poser had met Walker's Second Support Group hunting in fresh pastures.

On *Starling* the asdic (sonar) was already indicating a contact. The captain told the asdic officer of his intention to attack and *Starling* surged forward, the "ping" of the asdic echo sounding from the hull of U-202 becoming faster as the range shortened. Then came the order to fire depth charges. Tons of high explosives rolled from the stern rails and shot from throwers on either side of the quarterdeck. Ten charges dropped through the water towards the enemy. For a few seconds there was silence. Then miles of ocean and the waiting sloops quivered as the blasting charges exploded. Huge columns of water boiled to the surface and sprayed up into vast fountains astern of *Starling*. The great cascades subsided; but of the U-Boat there was no sign. Walker settled down to the waiting game. The enemy was proving tough to hold and hard to find…

During exercises, Walker had evolved a form of attack known as Operation 'Plaster'. It called for three sloops steaming in line abreast to roll depth charges off their sterns. Now he ordered *Wild Goose* and *Kite* to join *Starling* and the three sloops duly steamed forward, dropping a continuous stream of charges in the naval equivalent of an artillery barrage before an infantry attack. The sea heaved and shook under the impact of the explosions as twisting and turning and leaving a trail of charges the ships 'plastered' the area.

In three minutes, 86 depth charges had rocked and shaken the attackers almost as much as they had U-202. The U-Boat settled deeper and deeper as the control room crew watched the depth gauge. Down to 700… Much more and the submarine would crack under the tremendous pressure. 750… Poser's eyes would have been fixed on the controls, and his mind listening to the creaks and groans reverberating from the straining hull. 800… the engineer officers will have warned. 850… Poser snapped out his commands: "Level off and keep her trimmed at 800 feet. Steer due north, 3 knots."

Far above, Walker was talking to his officers: "No doubt about it. She's gone deeper than I thought possible and our depth-charge primers won't explode below 600 feet. Very maddening indeed." He grinned and continued. "Well... long wait ahead. Let's have some sandwiches sent up. We will sit it out. I estimate this chap will surface at midnight. Either his air or batteries will give out by then."

It was shortly after noon on June 13. By 2000 hrs Poser had taken several evasive turns without result. He could not shake off his tormentors. At two minutes after midnight his air gave out. He ordered reluctantly, "Take her to the surface." Without any audible warning, U-202 rose fast through the water to surface with bows high in the air. Her crew leaped through the conning tower hatch to man her guns, and Poser shouted for full speed in the hope of outrunning the hunters. On *Starling's* bridge, the tiny silver conning tower was visible in the moonlight. "Star shell...commence," ordered Walker. One turret bathed the heavens with light. Then came the crash of the first broadside from all six sloops laying a barrage of shells around the target.

A dull red glow leaped from behind the conning tower of the U-boat. A dimmed lamp blinked from *Starling*, and firing ceased while Walker increased speed to ram. Then he saw the jagged remains of the conning tower ablaze and shouted in triumph. U-202 was obviously too damaged to escape. He ran alongside, raking her decks with machine-gun fire and firing a shallow pattern of depth charges that straddled the submarine, enveloping her in smoke and spray. Poser clutched the hot periscope column, drew his revolver and shouted a last order: "Abandon ship! Abandon ship!" The cry was taken up and passed through the U-Boat. Poser turned to say goodbye to his officers. Rather than be captured, he was taking his own life. At 0030 hrs the battle was over - 16 hours after it had begun.

When the Second Support Group returned to Liverpool with U-202 and two more killings to its credit, Walker learned that his elder son, Timothy, had joined the crew of a British submarine (*Parthian*) operating in the Mediterranean. The following month, Admiral Karl Döenitz, commander of the U-boat fleet, threw 150 U-boats against the increasingly busy Atlantic convoy routes. Johnnie Walker again led his striking force into the Bay of Biscay to meet the enemy at his departure points.

On July 29, alerted by aircraft, the enemy came in sight on the horizon, three conning towers in line ahead. Walker's inherent love for the dramatic came to the fore. He beckoned to the signalman and ordered, "Hoist the General Chase." For a moment the signalman was confused. Then he ran up a signal used only twice before in the Royal Navy, once by Sir Francis Drake when he chased the Spanish Armada from the English Channel and again by Admiral Horatio Nelson at the Battle of Trafalgar. Off the leash at last, the five British sloops sallied forward. On *Starling's* bridge, Walker waved his cap in the air as though urging her to greater efforts as the guns of the entire group thundered a broadside at the unsuspecting U-Boats. In 30 seconds, all three had been hit from a range of four miles, making diving impossible. Ten minutes later it was all over.

Six In One Trip

This is written by Commander D.E.G. Wemyss, Captain of HMS *Wild Goose*, who served under, then took over from, Johnnie Walker with 2nd Support Group:

U592 - 31 January (Type VIIC)

The U-Boat was abaft my beam when I started to turn towards her, and the noise of a number of ships propellers in her hydrophones must have drowned the noise of my ship's increase in speed at the start of the attack. At any rate she made no move to get out of the way, nor did she get off her torpedoes in any hurry as I came charging in, and it looked as if the attack was unexpected up to the last moment. Then I imagine there came a cry from the U-Boat's hydrophone operator of "Propellers – Fast! – Loud! – Getting Louder!" and "Himmel!" from the Captain as he swung his periscope round and caught sight of us coming. He acted fast and in time, for he dodged our pattern of depth charges alright. His mind was, however, no longer occupied by thoughts of attacking and sinking anyone, which meant we had achieved our objective. His next intention, to get safely away from all this, could be dealt with in the manner we liked best, in slow time.

My chief fear during the run in to attack was that I should get there too late to put the enemy off his stroke. The asdic contact was good and the attack more or less ran itself, but try as I could to stop them, those big ships would come on. Of course, the whole thing was over very quickly, though it seemed to take ages at the time. Six depth charges produced an immediate response. With relief I saw the carriers turn and present their sterns, which meant that even if the torpedoes had been fired, they would now miss. With fresh heart we were now free to proceed with the second part of the programme. There is not much more to tell. Conditions were very good indeed and the enemy proved strangely docile after his early show of spirit. We regained out contact after the attack and had it confirmed, first by *Magpie* and then by the "Boss" on *Starling*. The *Magpie* had a go but missed and was told to rejoin the screen. The Boss then ordered an Extra Special and charges rained down. Debris and oil in sufficient quantity appeared and that was the end of the hunt.

U762 - 8 February (Type VIIC)

The weather held beautifully fine and the night of 8 February was clear and moonlit. My ship was out in the deep field on the convoys port bow when a shout from the port lookout drew the Officer of the Watch's attention to a U-Boat on the surface. It was a nice bit of work as the enemy was fully a mile and a half away, with little but the conning tower showing and I am glad that the lookout, Able Seaman J G Wall, was well decorated for it.

We turned towards her at once but before I got to the Bridge or the guns had opened fire, she dived. The asdic team, however, did their stuff and it was not long before we had contact, had told the Boss about it, and he ordered to hang on until he could team up as usual. The U-Boat made no use of her speed or violent manoeuvre to shake us off, while, since we knew she had a long way to go before she became a danger to the convoy, we kept quiet as well. The two ships approached each other in this leisurely manner on opposite courses until it was clear that the U-Boat would pass more or less directly under the ship. I do not suppose that the U-Boat realised she had been spotted before she dived, nor apparently, did she hear anything on her hydrophones, as her next action caught us completely by surprise and made me feel extremely foolish. She put up her periscope not more than 20 yards from the ship! The lookout saw it and gave a yell, I followed his pointing arm and there it was in the moonlight, a good two feet of it! The U-Boat Captain evidently intended to have a good look around and I trust he was even more surprised at what he saw than we were.

My first reaction was to go full ahead and drop a pattern, a really good shot with the port thrower would score a bull on that periscope. I had hardly got out the orders to the engines, and the depth charge party had hardly taken action, when I looked in the water alongside and realised we could never make it. We might damage the U-Boat but we could never get enough way on the ship to avoid blowing our own stern off. She was too close for the 4-inch guns and the only action was the result of some quick thinking on the part of the men stationed at the close quarter weapons.

Ordinary Seaman R.W. Gates on one Oerliken got off a pan of ammunition and I think the stripped Lewis gun got off some rounds. At any rate, tracer hopped all around that periscope, we thought we saw sparks fly off it, we hoped the fellow at the other end got an eye bath, and then it disappeared. Having persuaded the depth charge party not to fire, we tried to withdraw to a more convenient range to collect ourselves and to carry out the Bosses orders, but found that the enemy had made up his mind to beat it in exactly the same direction! We simply could not get away from him and the situation seemed to be getting out of hand when order was restored by the arrival of *Woodpecker*. She had been told to join in the hunt as well and had beaten *Starling* to it. When she had contact there were two of us on the job and matters could proceed properly. She ran in for the attack dropping her depth charges and the contact disappeared. Up came *Starling* and was directed to the spot. "Come over here" Walker signalled to Pryce (*Woodpecker*), "and look at the mess you have made". I circled round them whilst they examined their handiwork and then we dispersed to our station again.

U 734 - 9 February (Type VIIC)

That action finished at about 1am. Not long after 4am I was once more flying up to the Bridge to learn that the radar watch had detected another U-Boat on the surface. The sequence of events was the same as before she dived before we could get the guns off, we got the asdic contact, told the world and was told by the Boss he was coming. I knew however that this time he was a good long way off and would be a couple of hours reaching me. Hang on as I would, but be stared at through a periscope twice in one night was more than anyone could stand, and so I determined to have a smack at this one straight away. We might lose contact in the commotion, but we would just have to pick it up again if we missed, and anyway, it would keep her quiet until we could attend to her properly. It worked out according to this plan. The pattern produced no evidence of damage, but we picked up the trail after our attack and followed it without trouble as the U-Boat made no real effort to shake us off. The Boss turned up at 6.30am and between us, we put in two extra specials. The first one winged her and after that she laid a trail of oil wherever she went, the second one got her. Again, we got debris, but no survivors.

U 238 - 9 February (Type VIIC)

As soon as the Boss was satisfied we went on our way again to a fresh incident. From snatches of intercepted signals we gathered that *Kite* had picked up a second U-Boat at the same time as our own, which with the *Magpie* to help, she had been hammering ever since. The enemy had proved to be a tougher, more wily, opponent than the other two, so that with all their patience and perseverance had not managed to hurt her much, although she had not succeeded in getting away. We sped along at a brisk pace to join the struggle, a matter of 30 miles away and, on arrival, I was put on patrol to keep the Ring, while the Boss mixed it with the others in the middle. After all the drama of the night, this was a welcome spell of quiet, though it was good to keep our leader going at it with undiminished vigour. There was some hard slogging still for him to do, with this agile customer side stepping attack after attack. The *Kite* had to be pulled out of the struggle to join me as ring keeper because she was practically out of depth charges, then at last, the end came. Our scientists ashore may not have been very pleased at the way it was done, but that is a technical joke not worth telling here. Suffice to say that *Magpie* was duly blooded and the Groups 3rd victim within 15 hours was safely gathered in.

U 424 - 11 February (Type VIIC)

It was just before midnight on the following night, as we reached the end of our beat, that we found one, and once again, my ship was in luck. The moment was an awkward one, as the group was engaged in the changing of direction of search which meant that we were not in formation to keep clear of one another. I told the rest what I had found, and our new senior officer tried to confirm the contact, at first without success. We went through a hair raising time and had to stop the ship to avoid a colleague, and then start the attack from only 400 yards range. The explosion of the patterns lifted the stern of the ship but she still held together, and the instruments still worked so the battle could proceed. Conditions for some reason were not as good as usual and an uncomfortable time followed when we lost and regained contact and lost contact again while trying to follow the U-Boat, which was snaking freely. The *Woodpecker* got contact firmly though she was not certain that she had a genuine submarine echo, attacked it for luck, without result. They then lost it altogether and it looked as if this whole operation would turn out a frost until Wilkinson, promoted to Leading Hand, and his asdic team announced a firm contact, well clear of consorts. It was astern and at long range which sounded unlikely but the team were so confident that I begged to be excused and went after it.

It got better as we got closer until we were not only confident we had the right thing but knew enough about it to attack. The proper thing would have been to wait for assistance but this groping around was tiring people and so in we went. We lost contact on the way but were determined to have a bang and complete the attack. After that, we waited. There was no contact, but instead we were rewarded with sounds. First of all I was told that my listeners could hear a noise as though someone was banging metal with a hammer. That went on for a few minutes and then followed a sharp crack, two more muffled explosions came next and then silence. We had heard what submariners call 'breaking up noises' which came from a ship as she sinks after disappearing from view. It seemed fair to assume that what we had heard were breaking up noises from a U-Boat. And, as other ships present had also heard them and none of us had a contact it was decided to hunt no further. We formed up and went away. At 5pm we were back and what a sight met our eyes! An oil patch covered several square miles and in the middle was a large quantity of debris. "The U-Boat is sunk," signalled the *Starling*, "You may splice the mainbrace".

U264 - 19 February (Type VIIC)

At daybreak the convoy was clear of attack but it was certain that U-Boats would be found not far astern of the convoy, and so, that is where Captain Walker took the Group to hunt for them. We started the search at 9am and by 11am *Woodpecker* had contact. She had plenty of depth charges and so she and *Starling* hunted whilst the rest of us kept the ring. This time it was a long hunt. A series of attacks had damaged the U-Boat until her leaks got beyond the capacity of her crew to keep under. So her Captain decided to abandon ship. He used the last of his high-pressure air to get to the surface, the crew got out and the U-Boat sank. We got off some shots when she broke surface but soon realised it was a waste of ammunition. The whole crew was picked up.

We were informed by Sir Max Horton that, on our return home to Liverpool, he intended that we should be cheered into harbour. And what a welcome they gave us! We steamed up the channel into the River Mersey in line ahead and turned to port in succession to enter the lock into Gladstone Dock, and there was the crowd. Rows and rows of our comrades from the escort ships were there together with the Captain and Crew of the battleship *King George V* which was in dock nearby. Masses of WRENS who were making as much noise as all the rest put together, merchant crews, crews from allied ships and dock workers. Strung up was a hoist of flags which read, "Johnnie Walker, still going strong".

To Loch Ewe - 1944

In early August 1944, shortly after the untimely death of Captain Walker in Liverpool, of exhaustion, HMS *Kite* was detached from her sister ships, after having engine trouble and was sent north to Loch Ewe to form part of the escort for convoy JW59. She was commanded by Lt Cmdr Seagrave, a temporary commander, as her normal captain had broken his legs in a docking accident. He had a habit of standing on the gun turret directing docking operations, a hit too hard and he had fallen off. Seagrave was a submariner by trade and held the DSC. Operation Victual was the largest convoy to date ever sent to Russia. Vice Admiral FHG Dalrymple-Hamilton commanded JW59 and had chosen as his "flag ship" HMS *Vindex*, the escort carrier. She had better command facilities than the cruiser. The convoy consisted of 28 freighters, 14 were loaded with explosives, 2 tankers, 2 escort oilers (to refuel the escorting ships en route) a rescue ship to deal with any seamen or sailors adrift due to sinking and a special crane ship to help with the dilapidated, overworked unloading facilities in Murmansk. Also in the convoy, going to Russia were 12 MTBs (Motor Torpedo Boats) and a Royal Sovereign class battleship being given to Russia. At 1500 hrs, 15 August 1944 the 20th Escort Group steamed through the gate followed by the first freighter. The last ship passed through at 1700 hrs. HMS *Kite* and HMS *Keppel* took up their positions as Advanced Starboard Attack Party. Destroyer HMS *Keppel* was a veteran of convoy duty. The convoy had an uneventful passage, passing east of Jan Meyer Island she was spotted by a lone Ju 88. Ahead, in a patrol line, lay the "Trutz" Group of U-Boats consisting of the U344, U668, U394, U363 and the U997.

At 2045 hrs on August 20th HMS *Keppel* gained a contact on her starboard quarter. *Kite* joined her and a Fairey Swordfish from HMS *Vindex*, the escort carrier. The Swordfish watched as *Keppel* and *Kite* blasted away with hedgehogs and depth charges. They hunted throughout the night, anti gnat foxer's streamed. At 0400hrs 21st

August, the convoy altered course which it had been holding since 17th August, where joined by the Heavy escort, to a heading of 50 degrees in the direction of Spitzbergen, from where it would alter course again, later to round Bear Island and down to Kola Inlet.

Anti-Gnat Foxers were a very simple device. Short pieces of metal pipe each on their own short lanyard were attached to a steel wire cable. These were paid out to the stern of the ship and simply towed along which of course caused them to rattle together. A noise greater than the ships engines was achieved which FOXED the acoustic torpedoes. Not having these streamed correctly, or indeed having them at all, was the cause of her doom. Capt Walker hated them and always left them behind on the dockside. Walker actually lost one ship to an acoustic torpedo, the *Woodcock*, but also, when on *Starling*, foiled one by dropping a shallow set depth charge over the stern and then sinking the U-Boat concerned.

At 0644 hrs HMS *Kite*, after a long a fruitless hunt, had slowed down to clear her tangled foxers which had become twisted about one another. The sensible thing, in hindsight, would have been to sever the cables and leave them to sink. This was standard operating procedure. Knowing full well that a U-Boat had been detected, her Captain sailed a straight course, at 4 knots, a perfect target! She was hit by two torpedoes fired by U344, on the starboard side. The ship heeled over at once. Men on the deck and on board HMS *Keppel* got a brief glimpse of the U-Boat as it surfaced briefly to assess his attack and for the Kapitan to pass on a sighting report which resulted in a fresh line of U-Boats forming up ahead of the convoy, being established by the U703, U354, U365 and U711. HMS *Kite's* stern broke clean away, floated off for a few seconds, then sank. Her bow floated for a minute then also sank at a steep angle.

At 0730 hrs, with HMS *Peacock* and HMS *Mermaid* now in attendance, HMS *Keppel* stopped to pick up survivors. There were about 30 men in the water when *Keppel* started to pick them up, but only 14 were rescued. Arctic waters, temperatures at or near freezing point, a human cannot survive for too long in these conditions. Of the 14 saved, five died not long after reaching the deck of *Keppel*. (Ray Holden's brother Tom, was one of these five). These men are recorded, to this day, as "Missing in Action" although, as you will shortly see, signals sent from *Keppel* confirmed their deaths and burial at sea. 217 officers and men lost their lives. Lionel Irish, one of the nine to survive, recalls that he had been on the mess deck and someone had gone on deck to get something to drink, he had left the bulkhead door open and Lionel, in his shorts, went up to close it, just as the torpedoes hit. He recalls sliding down the deck into the sea. He does not know what happened to his shorts but was rescued without them. He had clung onto some debris until rescued. It all happened so quickly. Lionel has already told Ray Holden that he witnessed Tom's death on board *Keppel*. Yet the Admiralty failed to convey the official news of his death to his worried family.

An account of the Sinking of HMS Kite – 21st August 1944 by AB John Mackay – Asdic Operator, HMS Keppel.

I was asleep in my hammock when I was woken by an explosion, shortly followed by a second. I was up and into my boots as action stations sounded. I already had my duffel coat on as we were ordered by the captain to sleep fully clothed in case we ourselves were hit by a U-Boat torpedo. I made my way onto the upper deck and headed for my action station, HMS *Kite* was astern of our position and sinking fast. Within no more than a minute of me reaching the upper deck HMS *Kite* was fully submerged. I made my way to the bridge, where my action station was, and carried out a sweep of the surrounding area but could not pick up a contact with the U-Boat. The *Keppel* circled the survivors as we continued to look for the U-Boat responsible for sinking HMS *Kite* until support arrived. When both HMS *Mermaid* and *Peacock* arrived the *Keppel* then drifted amongst the survivors who were scattered far apart. I had been ordered to go to the foc'sle with a hard line, where I saw a large number of the men covered in thick oil and clinging to carley rafts or bits of wreckage.

I was stood alongside AB Pritchard when a carley raft with two men on it came towards us. AB Pritchard threw his line out to the men but it fell short. One of the men on the raft shouted 'are you too old to throw a line'. As both AB Pritchard and myself were a lot older than the rest of our crew it was not uncommon for our own shipmates to comment on our age. The men in the carley raft must have been wondering who had been sent to rescue them as they drifted aft where they were eventually hauled onboard. Many of the survivors on wreckage tried to swim to the *Keppel* and I saw several seamen drown as they did not have the energy to make it to us. I still believe that a lot more would have made it if they had held onto whatever wreckage they were clinging to and waited until we could launch our own whaler. I suppose panic and fear take control of you in such an awful situation.

After we had collected all the remaining survivors we headed back towards the protection of the fleet and I went below to our mess. One of the survivors was in our mess telling us of his ordeal. I remember some of the *Keppel* crew members trying to make light of what had happened to him by asking him how it was he had only got his feet wet. He told us that he had jumped from the deck of the sinking *Kite* straight into a carley raft. We gave him the nickname of 'CAT'. It was not long before we were given our orders to leave the fleet again and search for the u-boat that had sunk HMS *Kite*.

Unfortunately not all that were rescued by us from the icy waters of the North Atlantic survived and both myself and AB Pritchard, being older members of the crew, were detailed to prepare the dead seamen for burial. This entailed wrapping their bodies in canvas, putting weights at their feet and sewing up the canvas putting the last stitch through the nose (old navy superstition).

My duty at the burial service was to place the dead seamen one at a time on a sloping board and cover them with the Royal Navy flag. We held onto the body and flag whist a short service was carried out. The officer leading the service would then give us the signal to release the body into the sea and to their grave. Each individual received the same service whether they were an officer or not. Only a few of our crew attended these services as our new orders were to search for the u-boat that had sunk HMS *Kite* and the *Keppel* had to be fully manned.

As witnessed from HMS Mermaid

Tony Green in a letter to me described the scene from the *Mermaid*. "The biggest ship in the convoy was the large and (we hoped) menacing, but (we feared) tempting presence of a "Royal Sovereign" class battleship renamed *Archangel*, which was being lent or given to the Soviet Navy. She loomed, a grey and inviting target, close to the middle of the convoy, her ship's company no doubt hoping that the surrounding freighters would stop any torpedoes, which a keen U-Boat commander might try to fire in their direction and win glory for his boat. Also sailing with us were two examples of Winston Churchill's brainwaves; freighters which had been converted to small aircraft carriers. Although able to fly off only a few fighters, they contributed in large measure to a feeling of added security against enemy reconnaissance aircraft. The short flight deck, however, made landing, especially in bad weather, very risky and most pilots had to land in the drink and hope to be picked up by an escort willing to stop and thereby chance a torpedo. At that time of year, the continuous daylight gave the convoy a slight advantage over the U-boats in that they were unable to surface to recharge their batteries, an operation which could take several hours, without running the risk of being seen by a sharp-eyed lookout. The weather remained fine, the sea was almost glassy smooth and the first three days passed uneventfully. That tended to build the apprehension, which increased one morning when a German reconnaissance plane was shot down. The rest of the day passed without further incident. The convoy, still intact, steamed another 300 miles closer to Kola. A few remarks about the clothing we wore whenever we put to sea: the "regulation" working rig was blue combination cotton overalls worn over anything we cared to put on whether in harbour or at sea. (In small ships one wore almost anything that was warm in contrast to shore establishment, battleships, carriers and cruisers, where your cap was never "flat aback" and "number three's" was the usual uniform).

Our First Lieutenant, or Second-in-Command, St. John Benn, was a regular service "two-ringer" – a ring on one sleeve was missing – no older than twenty-five. He maintained a personal sea-going dress code which would have given any big-ship officer apoplexy:

knee-boots with long white sea socks turned over the top, a stained uniform, shiny with wear and minus a button or two, a thick white submariner's polo-neck sweater and a greasy cap from which the tarnished crown and oak leaves cap-badge drooped, secured only by a couple of loose threads. A movement among many of the lower deck ratings to emulate his apparent disdain for the king's uniform quickly developed. (Benn further won our acclaim by demonstrating that he was not only a good seaman, but also someone whom we could trust) We began to come back from leave with various unusual items of civilian clothing; coloured sweaters, scarves and trousers were all represented. Jimmy (the universal nickname for any executive officer) only blinked when someone emerged from the messdeck one morning wearing a bowler hat. He was quite calm about it. "I haven't objected to what you wear so far, but I must put my foot down. Go and find your issue cap, unless you want to go on First Lieutenant's report." The skipper, too, favoured unusual though thoroughly practical dress in the shape of a blue, quilted combination in the style of Winston Churchill's "siren suit".

The convoy was now about 600 miles inside the Arctic Circle in the latitude of Bear Island. Such an indirect route gave us some protection against air attack from German bases in Norway. The day after the false alarm, Red Watch had the forenoon watch. We had just come up onto "B" gun deck (in front of the bridge) and were standing about chatting and having a quiet smoke while surveying the ships on our starboard side. It was the usual grey scene, a low overcast sky, a slightly darker sea, and grey ships as far as the horizon. Tankers carrying gasoline, freighters loaded with ammunition, others with armoured vehicles, guns and trucks in their holds and aircraft fuselages packed on their upper decks. Suddenly a muffled detonation made *Mermaid* quiver. Astern of the convoy, our sister ship *Kite* had been torpedoed. The confusion aboard her must have been indescribable. Watches were changing, with almost the entire ship's company on the move; the watch being relieved would have been looking forward to breakfast and sleep and the new watch would have been thinking about the next monotonous four hours. *Kite* sank in one minute. Only nine of her ship's company survived. It was some consolation to learn that the attacking U-boat (U344) was soon after sunk by aircraft action, likely a Sunderland coastal command flying boat from a base in Scotland. (Actually it was a Fairey Swordfish from HMS *Vindex*, the accompanying Escort Carrier) (At the official enquiry into the loss of *Kite*, it was revealed that the captain, who was actually a submariner with little or no experience of commanding a surface vessel, had ordered that the ship reduce speed to a crawl to allow the anti-acoustic torpedo gear being trailed astern to be reeled aboard, and that the course be maintained in a straight line rather than the customary anti-submarine zig-zag, both of which conditions made *Kite* an easy target. And that's how it was remembered by Tony Green, on board HMS *Mermaid*.

Another eyewitness account from the decks of *Keppel* came in an email from a man called Harry Busby who met up with Ray Holden. This is Harry's account:

"I was an A/B Torpedoman on HMS *Keppel*. I was closed up on the after torpedo tubes, leaning against them and me and my mate were looking across towards HMS *Kite* on *Keppel*'s starboard quarter. We were discussing what nice lines these sloops had. Suddenly two huge balls of fire blotted out HMS *Kite* and when it cleared she was nowhere to be seen. *Keppel* immediately turned towards *Kite* and circled around her position but could find no ASDIC contact. She wasn't allowed to pick up survivors until HMS *Peacock* and HMS *Mermaid* arrived from the port side of the convoy. I recall that it seemed like hours but later found out it had only been 40 minutes, during which all that time those poor devils had been in the freezing water.

Eventually *Keppel* cut engines and gently nosed her way alongside a group of survivors, some of them drifting along the side down stern, we could not make out faces only blobs of thick stinking fuel oil. Men were hanging through the guardrails trying to clutch hold of them but could not get a grip because of the slime. About 15 men drifted around the stern end and the No 1 ordered the launching of the whaler. At first the disengaging gear would not slip which lost a few minutes but eventually the whaler was dropped into the water. The whaler collected all the 14 men who were brought back to *Keppel*. No 1 came down to the stern where men were throwing grappling hooks and using boat hooks but all the men in the water appeared to be naked or semi naked and there was nothing to "hook onto". The Skipper sent a message to No 1 to say that he would have to turn the screws because the Foxer gear (the cause of Kites demise in the first place!) was sinking down towards the screws. No 1 asked him to belay that order but the screws started to turn and all the survivors at the stern were sucked under. The bodies of the five men who died were laid out against the torpedo tubes. A three badgeman, A/B Pritchard, was given additional rum and he sewed the bodies up in canvas, the last stitch going through the nose in traditional Royal Naval fashion, and the bodies weighted. A small funeral service was held and the bodies confined to the deep, again, in Royal Naval fashion - all received a true Royal Navy burial at sea." And yet the Admiralty still state "missing presumed dead".

Joe Bennett was a Stoker on HMS *Keppel* when *Kite* was sunk. He has been in touch with Ray Holden who passed on his eyewitness account from the decks of the *Keppel*. At the time of the *Kite* sinking Joe had been sent on deck to get a container of drinking water. He took the opportunity to grab a bit of fresh air. *Kite* was on his starboard quarter. Just after he returned to the boiler room he heard two large explosions. He explained that the sound of explosions, within the confines of the engine room, were magnified. There is no way to tell if it is your ship that is the target or that it is your ship doing the attacking; you just wait and see. Orders came down to increase speed and a change of course was evident. The P/O Stoker told Joe to nip up and have a look. He could not believe his eyes - the only way Joe could explain what he saw was "A complete mess". Other men stood around the guard rails in disbelief, only wreckage and oil remained where *Kite* once was. There follows some historical information on the *Keppel* which, for the sake of history, I shall reprint here. When *Keppel* was launched she had 4 boilers rooms, these exhausted through two boilers to each of her two funnels which were flat sided funnels. Capable of a top speed of 36 knots, normal for destroyers. *Keppel* retained her two funnels until the day she was broken up. The old V and W destroyers had two funnels flat sided and one round - these were the destroyers which had the forward flat sided funnels removed. The after round funnel became known as "woodbine" funnels. Woodbine was a brand name and a byword for cigarettes; a "woody". Joe (and Harry Busby) were most indignant when a brand new ship with only one funnel wanted to pinch one of theirs; Joe - "what the hell do they want another funnel for; they only have two boilers!"

Also on board the *Keppel* was Leading Stoker Jack Boxall, number D/KX 157985. He joined in the fruitless search for survivors, which included a search for his own brother who was serving aboard HMS *Kite*. George Boxall, Stoker First Class, was never found.

Thanks to some hearsay and the investigative efforts of Alan McMillan, of Dublin, (another "friend of HMS *Kite*") we believe that quite a few of the crew of HMS *Kite* came from Eire. A retired British Admiral lived close to a fishing village in County Cork and local lads who wanted to join "Crown Forces" went to him for a reference. In 1936 the IRA murdered the Admiral for recruiting for Crown Forces.

The surviving sailors finally got to shore, where a photographer was waiting to take their pictures, one Petty Officer Payne flatly refused to be part of such propaganda when his shipmates were dead and hid around the superstructure until the whole circus had disappeared. The nine who made it ashore were: Charlie Bonsall, Brannigan, Lionel Irish, Frank Webb, Reg Holmes, Johnson, Sharples and Bradley.

Frank Webb had two sons, Steve and Rob, who I had the pleasure of meeting not so long ago. They remarked how they came so very close to not being there at all! Rob lives in Vancouver, Canada. They remember their late father with extreme love and fondness.

The next day, August 22nd 1944, a Fairey Swordfish from HMS *Vindex* was on routine patrol when, upon coming out of a cloud, she found herself abaft a U-Boat running on the surface towards the convoy. The pilot, Gordon Bennett, immediately went into the attack and dropped three depth charges. Two fell to starboard and exploded harmlessly (?) but the third landed on the deck of the U-Boat, rolled forward and became wedged under the jump wire for'ard. The U-Boat dived and 10 seconds later the depth charge exploded at its setting – 20 feet. The stern rose out of the water and sank back out of sight. This was U344, which had sunk *Kite*; it went to the bottom with all hands.

I got hold of a copy of a letter that Gordon Bennett wrote to Clem Bray on 24th November 1989 in which he describes the attack on U344. The letter is obviously replying to some points Clem Bray had raised. They may not make sense but the main gist is the attack on the U344. There are some lines not readable, but here is the letter:

Dear Clem; Thank you for letter, clippings and booklet. This latter I intend to attach to the back of my log book. What I had not realised was, for size, your massive complement. We had always thought you carried about 130, and even though in the same service it was not in wartime the general habit to enquire when meeting, about details. Very sad, especially young A/B Alfred J Spry, name identical with that of my maternal grandfather.

Ken Poolman had in 1972 written the more general Escort Carrier 1941 to 1946 (See below), which is how we came to have some contact (Ian Allen). On Page 143 of that he writes – 'Lieutenant Gordon Bennett and Sub Lieutenant PS Crouch sank U345 on August 22nd.' (Actually Couch, not Crouch). I had a letter from him in 1982 and last para reads "It seems from MOD records that the U-Boat you sank in the morning of August 22nd 1944 was Pietch's U344, which had sunk the Kite the day before. Hans Jurgen Sthamer's U354 damaged the Nabob and sank the Bickerton in the evening of the same day (22nd) and was sunk by escorts on the 24th."

354 had done its work against the Tirpitz attacking force way over to the west and had to do some hard steaming to join up with the Trutz Group to the east with which Kite was involved. It is likely that he was still catching up when I met him on the surface on the 23rd and although I got after about 40 minutes skirmishing D/C's (depth charges) down on him I believe I did him no harm. It may have been another, but he seems to have been on the starboard zone where Peacock etc could have met him the next day. The U344 sinking was fully confirmed. Glancing at my letter to you 26th Oct, I see I mention Rajah instead of Nabob it should be.

As German records become publishable and the thirty year rule expired there has been so much published and I should think that everyone intimately involved in all the minor parts like mine must wonder how the accounts can be so inaccurate. *My own observer could not surely be so far off track in debriefing yet the various witnesses must have used the ships logs. U344 looked ugly wet-black and was doing about 3 knots when sighted and curving twelve or more when D/C's were released. I sighted her from a level 1300 as I had found some useful little cloud up there. Main point is that she was less than a third of a mile away, so my attack was a twisting steep dive, engine cut back to the safe revs and Couch and I didn't discuss his colour, in fact, I very much doubt that he even looked out until after D/C's away. Also there would be (here a sentence is unreadable) three D/C's right on her would have killed just about all. I should guess that the body and the swimmer would be the Captain and the gunner the body most likely the latter, as I think he could have been near the head of the shaft and got blasted out. A quicker end for them all than your "Kite" lads.*

Good luck with your hunt for survivors. Surprising that they themselves have never got round to finding each other. You must have been very fond of Kite to go to the trouble. I was equally fond of Vindex and her splendid management.

Kind Regards,

Gordon Bennett.

PS: Also if - which I very much doubt - Couch R/t'd "Tantivy" it would not only have been un-Couch like by nature, but technically wrong. He would have sent "Contact - Attacking", possibly three times, though all I did was ask him to send it once, get his camera out port side and hang on![22]

Signals confirming that the events were passed by *Keppel* to "shore" are reproduced here:

To *KEPPEL* and KITE from SO ESCORTS

Take starboard quarter action in diagram number 2 (20.2230B)

To SO ESCORTS from *KEPPEL*

Am investigating contact on starboard side [TOR: 2340]

---

[22] On the letter was a telephone number near Derby. I found out the code and rang the number, but its current user had never heard of Gordon Bennett and I suspect he may no longer be with us, the number having being reallocated by BT. *Author*

Am attacking with depth charges [TOR: 2341]

My estimated position 135 ZZ 7

To SO ESCORTS from KITE

Am about to attack with depth charges [TOR: 2353]

To SO ESCORTS from: *KEPPEL*

I am resuming my station. KITE in company 188 ZZ 15[TOR: 0121B]

To: SO ESCORTS from *KEPPEL*

KITE torpedoed [TOR: 0642]

To: SO ESCORTS From: *KEPPEL*

My estimated position is 194 ZZ 12 miles [TOR: 0644]

And finally:

To: SO ESCORTS From: *KEPPEL*

KITE has been sunk [TOR: 0655]

And so, the nine survivors made it ashore and the enquiry about what happened was to begin.

The Board of Inquiry

Here is a copy of a letter circulated by Admiral Sir Max Horton dated 24th August 1944:

SECRET

OFFICE OF COMMANDER IN CHIEF WESTERN APPROACHES

DERBY HOUSE LIVERPOOL

25th AUGUST 1944

BOARDS OF ENQUIRY

In amplification of the instructions given in paragraph 1 of Form S 1360, I wish to bring to the attention of officers concerned my views on the conduct of Boards of Enquiry.

2. The task of a Board of Enquiry is usually to investigate some occurrence which has been brought about by a failure of personnel, material or organization. The main object of the investigation is to obtain such information as will enable us to guard against a repetition of the same, or similar occurrence. This means that we must find out who, if anyone, was responsible for the failure and whether the fault lies inside or outside the ship itself; it may be with some authority or department, or civilian firm, or some individual in the ship.

3. Unless specifically so ordered it is not the duty of a Board of Enquiry to propose disciplinary action but, for the reasons given above, it is essential that their Finding should specify in detail what persons in the ship (under the general responsibility of the Commanding Officer) were responsible for what happened and the precise degree in which each acted incorrectly or failed to act. This is a matter which is frequently glossed over or not clearly pressed to a definite conclusion; it is, however, important that he who has failed should be left in no doubt how and where he went wrong, so that he may profit by the experience and act correctly on a future occasion. If on the other hand the Board reach the conclusion that no person in the ship was in any way responsible for the occurrence they must clearly state this opinion in their Findings.

4. The Admiralty have directed that members of Boards of Enquiry investigating accidents, losses of stores etc, before coming to any conclusion which imputes blame to any person, should consider carefully:

(i) whether his apparent fault was due to negligence or inexperience or both

(ii) whether, having regard to his previous experience in similar operations, it was reasonable to entrust him with that particular duty.

The Board's opinion on these points should be included in their Findings.

5. It is also an important part of the duty of every Board of Enquiry to make recommendations for the future prevention of similar occurrences.

6. Every officer who convenes a Board of Enquiry in the Western Approaches Command is to furnish the President with a copy of this memorandum, which is to be attached to Form S.136Q and included in the minutes.

7. The special attention of Administrative Authorities, who have the subsequent handling of the reports of Boards of Enquiry, is called to my memorandum No W.A.190P of 15th June 1943, which was addressed to Flag Officers in Charge and Captains (D).

MAX HORTON Admiral Commander in Chief

Distribution:

Flag and Naval Officers in Charge R.A.C.O.B. (W.A) Commodore (D) Western Approaches Captains (D) Belfast, Liverpool, Greenock Commanding Officer, HMS IRWELL

And a copy of the Convening Order:

SECRET

Office of Flag Officer in Charge GREENOCK

8th September 1944

S.1360 MEMORANDUM

You are to assemble on board at Navy House, Clarence St, Greenock, at 1000 on Sunday 9th September, as a board of whereof Commander A H Thorold, OBE,DSO,RN of HMS Cygnet is to be the president and hold a full and careful investigation into the circumstances attending:

THE LOSS OF HMS KITE

2. The enquiry is to be conducted in accordance with the directions contained in Kings Regulations and Admiralty Instructions Chapter XI. and Commander in Chief, Western Approaches Memorandum No WA4190P of 25th August 1944 (copy for the President only).

3. The report of the Board is to be accompanied by the minutes of evidence taken, and is to contain an expression of opinion on the merits of the case as disclosed by the evidence, including a statement of the causes of the occurrence.

4. The questions in the minutes are to be numbered consecutively, and the name and rank or rating of each witness are to appear at the head of each page on his evidence.

5. The reports and minutes are each to be signed by the members of the Board and are to be in triplicate.

6. The original report is to be sent herewith for the purpose of the enquiry, and is to be returned with the report of the Board, together with this memorandum.

7. The Commanding Officer, HMS ORLANDO has been informed and directed to afford the Board all the necessary facilities.

8. Unless the president has something to communicate he is to send the reports when completed, not to bring them.

9. A shorthand writer has been detailed from the Office of the Flag Officer in Charge, Greenock.

To: COMMANDER A H THOROLD, OBE, DSO, RN HMS CYGNET

Signature

LIEUTENANT COMMANDER F L COX, RNVR HMS ORLANDO Rank: REAR ADMIRAL

LIEUTENANT T W LANCASTER, DSC, RN HMS CYGNET

(Copies to: Commanding Officer, HMS Orlando, Captain (D), Greenock

The Board of Inquiry

The list of witness and questions asked were as follows:

Questions	Asked to
1 to 35	Petty Officer JRL Payne D/JX 154993
36 to 53	Leading Seaman EC Bradley D/JX 136903
54 to 71	Leading Seaman D Brannigan D/SSX 23262
72 to 83	Able Seaman C Bonsall D/JX 419597
84 to 91	Able Seaman AP Sharples D/JX 563041
92 to 101	Able Seaman GH Johnson D/JX 368812
102 to 117	Able Seaman L Irish D/JX 351286
118 to 158	Able Seaman R Holmes D/JX 369266
159 to 182	Able Seaman F Webb D/JX 418056
183 to 201	Lt John Arthur Douglas RN[23]
202 to 210	Sub Lt Raymond William Hall RNVR[24]
211 to 213	Petty Officer JRL Payne D/JX 154993 (recalled)

---

[23] HMS *Keppel*
[24] HMS *Keppel*

PETTY OFFICER JOHN RICHARD LEWIS PAYNE Off No: D/JX 154993

Witness called and cautioned

Q1   Are you Petty Officer John Richard Lewis Payne Off No: D/JX 154993?

A1   Yes Sir

Q2   Were you serving in HMS KITE on the 21st August 1944?

A2   Yes Sir

Q3   Would you tell the Board what you know of what occurred in HMS *Kite* at the time of the explosion, or the first you know about it?

A3   I had the morning watch Sir, when it happened. We were getting the PNM's in. The speed was too fast to get the PNM's in and the Petty Officer who was on deck with me went on to the bridge and asked the Officer of the Watch if he could reduce speed. He said he would reduce speed to 6 knots. I went up on the port side of the boat deck and he stopped heaving in on the floats and we were trying to get the turns out of the wire. Then the explosion happened.

Q4   What was the actual state of the foxers at the time?

A4   The port PNM wire was wrapped round the displacer towing wire and the starboard PNM was in the rattling position.

Q5   What type of floats were you using?

A5   The old displacers Sir

Q6   What was your actual duty as regards getting in the foxers, were you for'd or aft?

A6   Well I had no actual duties at all Sir, because I was in action on the pom pom deck and the other Petty Officer asked me to give him a hand. I went down on the other side of the boat deck. The other Petty Officer was on the quarter deck and was Petty Officer of the Watch.

Q7   Where were you at the actual time of the explosion?

A7   I was on the pom pom deck at the actual time of the explosion Sir.

Q8   What was the original speed before the bridge was asked to reduce?

A8   I am sorry Sir, I don't know what actual speed we were doing. The other Petty Officer came down and told me that they were going to reduce to 6 knots.

Q9   As far as you know, had speed already been reduced when the explosion occurred?

A9   Yes we had already dropped speed.

Q10   Now I think you had better go on with what happened from the explosion onwards.

A10   There was an explosion on the starboard side aft and I was knocked over, and while I was getting up there was a second explosion. The ship started to heel over very fast; I climbed off the pom pom deck and ran along the port side and the ship was right over then Sir. I took off my sea boots and coat and ran down the ships side and jumped into the water.

Q11   How far off do you think the explosion was?

A11   One was aft of the companion ladder Sir, on the quarter deck. That is were all the dirt and so forth came from Sir   anyway, when I looked.

Q12   At that time had there been only one explosion?

A12   Yes Sir and about three or four seconds later another one. They seemed to blend into one, but there were definitely two explosions.

Q13   Where do you estimate the second explosion occurred?

A13   On the starboard quarter Sir.

Q14   Was there any difference between the violence of either explosion?

A14   No Sir, they were both the same and very quick together. That is only my estimation though Sir, I am not sure.

Q15   As far as you can see, did one appear to be further for'd or further aft than the other?

A15   The first was further for'd and the second further aft Sir.

Q16   What happened after you got into the water?

A16   When I jumped into the water I was gasping for breath. The water was very cold and I got hold of a life buoy in the water. I could see the stern disappearing. I was on the life buoy Sir, I don't know for how long. There were 4 of us on it, and then I saw a Carley float and swam to that Sir.

Q17   Had you got a life belt on?

A17   Yes but it was not blown up.

Q18   Were you wearing a piece of rope tied round you?

A18   No Sir

Q19   Were there, to your knowledge, any particular orders in the ship about the wearing of lifebelts and lengths of rope whilst at sea?

A19   We always had to wear a lifebelt Sir, but there were no particular orders about wearing a rope.

Q20   Do you know if many of the ships company did wear pieces of rope?

A21   I was Captain of the Quarter Deck Sir in one or two in my division did, but not very many.

Q22   Did you at any time sight anything resembling a U-Boat?

A22   No Sir

Q23   Did many people float clear of the ship?

A23   I jumped over the port side Sir and there were only about a dozen in my estimation who followed me over the port side. A lot of people seemed to go over the starboard side though Sir.

Q24   Were any orders given as regards abandoning ship?

A24   No I didn't hear any orders given Sir.

Q25   Can you say at all how long you think the ship floated for?

A25   She seemed to go very quickly to me Sir, in less than a minute after we got hit I should think. She heeled right over and went down in less than a minute it seemed to me

Q26   Do you know anything of the state of the watertight doors at the time?

A26   Well they were very strict about them Sir. They should have all been closed below decks Sir.

Q27   After you got onto the raft, how many were there with you on the raft?

A27   There was only one on when I got on, and then after a while 3 more came on Sir.

Q28   Did they all remain on the raft until you were picked up?

A28   Yes Sir.

Q29   How were you actually picked up by HMS *Keppel*?

A29   She steamed right up to us Sir. They were going to lower the whaler but the sea fetched us right up to the ships side Sir.

Q30   Did they hoist you out?

A30   Yes but I don't remember much about that Sir.

Q31   Did you hear any explosion at all after you were in the water?

A31   Yes Sir, I heard I think it was two, and I asked the chap who was on the Carley Float with me what he thought it was and he said he thought it would be the depth charges going off.

Q32   Were any of the depth charges set to any depth to your knowledge?

A32   To my knowledge, No Sir, they were all set to "safe".

Q33   Was primer placing gear fitted?

A33   Yes Sir.

A34   No Sir, the bows were just disappearing. When I heard these explosions I could see the stern sticking up, about 200 yards Sir and she was going down at the bows.

Q35   From that you mean the ship had split into two bits?

A35   Yes Sir

Examination of witness terminated

Witness withdrew

LEADING SEAMAN ERNEST CHAPMAN BRADLEY Off No: D/JX 136903

Witness Called and Cautioned

Q36   Are you Leading Seaman Ernest Chapman Bradley Off No: 136903?

A36   Yes Sir

Q37   Were you serving in HMS *Kite* on the 21st August 1944?

A37   Yes Sir

Q38   Will you tell the Board about the explosions and subsequent action in HMS *Kite*?

A38   We were asleep down the for'd mess deck Sir. On the first bang nearly all the mess deck woke up, and the second bang followed immediately after. Then we got up the hatch and got over the port side. We got out of the way of the ship going down and I swam with 3 others to the float. When we got on the flotanet we were about 50 or 60 yards away from the ship on the port side. Then we were floating about for a few minutes and I saw the conning tower of a submarine about 150 to 200 yards on the starboard bow.

Q39   Do you mean the conning tower or the periscope?

A39   The conning tower Sir.

Q40   How long did the conning tower stay up?

A40   The water was a bit sloppy Sir and swinging us around, and I only had one glimpse of it. I told the Petty Officer on the float to duck because I thought they were firing at us, but we found afterwards it was depth charges from our own ship exploding under the water.

Q41   How many explosions did you notice?

A41   Under water explosions Sir?

Q42   Yes?

A42   3 or 4 Sir, they appeared pretty deep.

Q43   How much of the ship was still floating when the explosions took place?

A43   The half that we went over the side was floating Sir, and just as we hit the water the stern was disappearing.

Q44   Were you wearing a life belt?

A44   No I had an oilskin all weather suit on Sir. It seemed very buoyant.

Q45   Were you wearing a piece of rope tied round you?

A45   No Sir

Q46   Were there any ships orders about wearing life belts and ropes?

A46   There was an order in the ships list Sir, and I had my life belt near at hand Sir, but when she got hit she started to list and I thought it was best to get out.

Q47   But there were no orders about pieces of rope?

A47   All men were issued with ropes Sir and were told to make them, when I was first in the ship.

Q48   But you hadn't got your ropes end on at the time?

A48   No Sir, it was with my gas mask.

Q49   Did you stay on the flotanet until you were picked up?

A49　No, we were all drifting together. There were 2 carley floats and when we got there we swam onto the Carley float, but there were still two men on the flotanet.

Q50　How many men did you see in the water?

A50　About 60 or 70 I should think Sir.

Q51　You went out of the fore mess hatch and over the port side. Do you recall anything of what happened to No 2 guns crew?

A51　No Sir

Q53　Was there much oil in the water?

A53　When we went over the side we were in clear water Sir, but when we started swimming to the float we found the oil and it kept us warm, so we tried to stick near to the oil fuel all the time.

Examination of witness terminated Witness withdrew

LEADING SEAMAN DANIEL BRANNIGAN D/SSX 23262

Witness Called and Cautioned

Q54　Are you Leading Seaman Daniel Brannigan Off No: D/SSX 23262?

A54　Yes Sir

Q55　Were you serving in HMS *Kite* on the 21st August 1944?

A55　Yes Sir

Q56　Will you tell the Board what you know of what happened that morning?

A56　I was lying on the lockers on the for'd mess deck when I heard the first explosion. I just dashed up the ladder and as I　was on the ladder there was another explosion, and I just got up and jumped over the port side. I got on the Carley Float and then I was picked up by HMS *Keppel*.

Q57　Were you wearing a life belt?

A57　No Sir. I got one out of the port whaler as I came up.

Q58　Were you wearing a ropes end secured round you?

A58　No Sir.

Q59　Were there any orders in the ship about the wearing of life belts and ropes ends?

A59   Not when you were off watch or turned in Sir.

Q60   Did you see any signs of a U-Boat?

A60   No Sir, only what Leading Seaman Bradley said to me on the float, when he told me to duck because he thought they were firing at us.

There was no Question 61 on the copy received by me.

Q62   Did you see many other people in the water?

A62   About 70 I should say Sir.

Q63   On the port side?

A63   Yes Sir

Q64   Was there any oil on the water?

A64   There was no oil fuel as we jumped into the water at the start Sir, but as we swam away we came into it Sir.

Q65   Did you notice any other explosions when you were away from the ship?

A65   As the stern was going down there was another explosion Sir.

Q66   Were there any under water explosions that you noticed?

A66   Yes Sir

Q67   Did they shake you up?

A67   There was not much of a shaking with it Sir.

Q68   How many of these explosions were there? Did you notice?

A68   About 5 I think Sir.

Q69   You did not hear any orders being given regarding abandoning ship or anything of that sort?

A69   No Sir, no orders at all came through; we were very lucky to get on top at all Sir.

Q70   What were the orders in HMS *Kite* in case of collision?

A70   It was a long ring on the bell Sir.

Q71   Was that done?

A71   No Sir, because if it had we would have all been at Action Stations in a couple of seconds.

Examination of Witness terminated

Witness withdrew

ABLE SEAMAN CHARLES BONSALL Off No: D/JX 419597

Witness Called and Cautioned

Q72 Are you Able Seaman Charles Bonsall Off No: D/JX 419597?

A72 Yes Sir

Q73 Were you serving in HMS *Kite* on the 21st August 1944?

A73 Yes Sir

Q74 Will you tell the Board what you know of what happened that morning?

A74 Well I don't know much Sir because I was in the for'd mess deck. I had
come off the middle watch and was going to sleep using my life belt for a
pillow. I heard a bump, and it threw me off the lockers. Then there was
another bump which threw me over. I got up and went up top and by this
she was over on her side, and that's about all I know Sir.

Q75 You went into the water on the port side?

A75 No Sir, on the starboard side; the same side as she was listing.

Q76 Had you got your lifebelt on by that time?

A76 No Sir. When the first bump threw me off the lockers my first thought was
to get up top.

Q77 Had you a piece of rope secured round you?

A77 No sir.

Q78 What were the Ship's Orders as regards life belts and ropes ends?

A78 If you were on the upper deck you had to wear your life belt Sir, but I don't
know about ropes ends.

Q79 But there were no definite orders that you had to wear them the whole
time?

A79 No Sir, I don't think so. It was just made clear that we always had to wear
them on the upper deck.

Q80 When you got into the water, what did you swim to to keep you up?

A80 To a flotanet Sir, but we couldn't unroll it so I swam for a fender and then saw a Carley float and swam for that, I stayed there until I was picked up.

Q81 Was there much oil about?

A81 Yes Sir, I was covered from head to foot in oil. I think that is what finished one or two of the chaps Sir, their nostrils were full with oil.

Q82 Did you see many others in the water?

A82 Yes Sir, there were quite a few floating round on wreckage but I don't know how many there were.

Q83 Did you see anything resembling a U-Boat?

A83 No Sir.

Examination of Witness terminated Witness withdrew

ABLE SEAMAN ARTHUR PRATT SHARPLES Off No: D/JX 563041

Witness Called and Cautioned

Q84 Are you Able Seaman Arthur Pratt Sharples D/JX 563041?

A84 Yes Sir

Q85 Were you serving in HMS *Kite* on the 21st August 1944?

A85 Yes Sir

Q86 Will you tell the Board all you know of what occurred that morning?

A86 I do not know very much Sir. I was asleep on the lockers. The explosion woke me up and as I was getting up the hatch another bang knocked me down again. Then I got on deck and pieces of debris were all about. I went along the port side to the port whaler, looked over the side, saw the quarter deck floating a few yards astern, and then I went to the Oerlikon gun deck, climbed up there and ran over the ships side.

Q87 What happened after you got into the water?

A87 I swam away from the ship to get away from the suction. I was floating round on my back and then got away clear from the oil that was about. There was a life buoy there with two or three of the lads on it but I couldn't get hold because of the three already on it, so I kept swimming round until I saw a Carley float. I got on to that but I went right through it and when I came up the other side again there were Bradley and Bonsall and they joined me and we got on a Carley float. Then HMS *Keppel* came along and picked us up.

Q88 Had you a life belt on?

A88 No Sir

Q89 Or a piece of rope secured round you?

A89 No Sir, I never had one of these pieces of rope. There were some on the ship and we were given rope to make them, but I never got one Sir.

Q90 Do you know what the Ship's Orders were about wearing life belts and securing ropes ends round you?

A90 As regards life belts, when we fell in of a morning the First Lieutenant used to pick us out and put us in his report for having no life belt, but he never had one himself Sir. (One law for them, one for us)

Q91 Did you see any signs of a U-Boat about?

A91 No Sir, I never noticed anything like that.

Examination of Witness terminated Witness withdrew

ABLE SEAMAN GEORGE HENRY JOHNSON Off No: D/JX 568812

Witness Called and Cautioned

Q92 Are you Able Seaman George Henry Johnson Off No: D/JX 568812?

A92 Yes Sir

Q93 Were you serving in HMS *Kite* on the 21st August 1944?

A93 Yes Sir

Q94 Will you tell the Board what happened that morning?

A94 I was sleeping in my hammock Sir, and I heard two explosions. I dashed up the ladder, through the for'd hatch, and slid down the port side with Leading Seaman Bradley. We swam round for about a quarter of an hour, saw a Carley float, and after we had been on that for about a couple of minutes I saw a submarine.

Q95 You actually saw a submarine yourself?

A95 Yes Sir

Q96 How much of it did you see?

A96 The conning tower Sir.

Q97 Were you wearing a life belt at the time?

A97 No Sir, just a vest.

Q98 Were there any Orders about wearing life belts and ropes ends?

A98 Only one about wearing life belts Sir.

Q99 But there were no definite orders that you had to wear them at all times?

A99 No Sir

Q100 Did you see any other people in the water?

A100 Yes Sir, plenty of them.

Q101 Were most of the men undressed when they turned in?

A101 Yes Sir.

Examination of Witness terminated Witness withdrew

ABLE SEAMAN LIONEL IRISH Off No: D/JX 351286

Witness Called and Cautioned

Q102 Are you Able Seaman Lionel Irish Offr No: D/JX 351286?

A102 Yes Sir

Q103 Were you serving in HMS *Kite* on the 21st August 1944?

A103 Yes Sir

Q104 Will you tell the Board what you know of what happened that morning?

A104 I was in the after mess deck in my hammock Sir, at the time, and all we knew was just two bangs. I went up the ladder through the bulk head door, starboard side, Sir and walked along aft towards the funnel. I went to assist and tried to get the port whaler away but we just could not do it; she listed over too far. Then the next thing I knew I was in the water.

Q105 You went into the water on the port side?

A105 Yes Sir

Q106 Were you wearing a life belt at the time?

A106 No Sir

Q107 Were there any Ship's Orders that you know of about wearing life belts and ropes ends secured round yourself?

A107 Well the First Lieutenant gave strict orders about life belts Sir, but I was Quartermaster and could never feel comfortable in the wheel house with one on Sir, so I never had one on.

Q108 Were there any orders to wear them at all times?

A108 Well he was very strict Sir.

Q109 As far as you know, did many of the Ship's Company sleep in their life belts?

A109 There were quite a few did Sir.

Q110 Was there any definite mention about having ropes ends secured round you?

A110 No Sir, not that I know of.

Q111 Did you see any signs of a U-Boat when you got into the water?

A111 No Sir

Q112 When you got into the water, did you notice any other under water explosions?

A112 Yes Sir, there were some.

Q113 Can you say about how many?

A113 I should imagine about three or four Sir, but I could not be sure.

Q114 But not very violent?

A114 Well, not enough to shake you up Sir, they must have been very deep.

Q115 Did they appear to be far away?

A115 It would be very difficult to say Sir. I just heard them, that is all, but I didn't feel any vibration.

Q116 What did you swim to when you got into the water?

A116 I picked up an oar Sir, then I saw a plank and transferred to that and then I went over to a sort of butcher's block Sir.

Q117 Did you have much difficulty in getting on to HMS *Keppel*?

A118 I don't really remember Sir. I was told that I went down twice and I don't remember much about being taken on board.

Examination of Witness terminated Witness withdrew

ABLE SEAMAN REGINALD HOLMES Off No: D/JX 369266

Witness Called and Cautioned

Q118 Are you Able Seaman Reginald Holmes, Off No: D/JX 369266?

A118 Yes Sir

Q119 Were you serving in HMS *Kite* on the 21st August 1944?

A119 Yes Sir

Q120 Will you tell the Board all you know of what happened that morning?

A120 I do not know very much Sir. At the time I was on watch on the bridge as telephone number, and at 0640 there was an explosion aft and then there was another two or three seconds later. Then I saw all the debris coming over, depth charge racks and all sorts of stuff and then I ducked and I saw Lieutenant Savage who was Officer of the Watch, crouched down as well and dodging out of it. I came out and the Captain came on the bridge and said "Have you sounded action stations yet?" but by that time Lieutenant Savage was over the side. Then the Captain used some foul language and then went inside again.

Q121 Do you mean that the Lieutenant had left the ship or that he had left the bridge?

A121 He had definitely left the bridge. I saw him jump off the bridge so I presume he went into the water Sir.

Q122 How far was the bridge from the water at that time?

A122 I should say about 60 degrees Sir.

Q123 What did you do then?

A123 I threw my coat off, took off my boots, and dived over the port side Sir.

Q124 Did you see any more of the Captain?

A124 No, Sir, I never saw anything more of him.

Q125 Did any more of the bridge personnel get away as far as you know?

A125 Well, I never saw any of them Sir. The messenger was sent on a message to the First Lieutenant and there was only me and Lieutenant Savage and a signaller up there at the time.

Q126 Had there, to your knowledge, been any report from the Asdic to the bridge?

A126 Nothing at all that I know of sir.

Q127 Within the last few minutes previous to the explosion?

A127 No Sir

Q128 Was the Asdic. so far as you know, operating satisfactorily?

A128 Yes Sir

Q129 No reports of breakdowns?

A129 No Sir, nothing at all.

Q130 How many Officers of the Watch were there?

A130 Two on watch, but Sub Lieutenant Strutbers went below on a message for Lieutenant Savage. I don't know what the message was Sir.

Q131 As far as you know, had any signal been received which gave you the impression that U-Boats were in the vicinity?

A131 Not that I know of Sir

Q132 What was the reaction of the signalman and the four lookouts when the two explosions occurred?

A132 Well, I never really had time to look Sir. The first thing I thought of was getting out of the way of the stuff coming over.

Q133 Did anyone follow you?

A133 No Sir. I was the last person to leave the bridge. The Officer of the Watch had gone.

Q134 You do not recall what happened to the lookouts or the signalman?

A134 No Sir.

Q135 You say that Captain used bad language and went below. What did the bad language indicate?

A135 It was something about Germans Sir.

Q136 Did you gather from his action what he intended to do by going below?

A136 No Sir.

Q137 Did you hear him give any order at all?

A137 He did not give any orders at all Sir. The first thing he said was "Have you sounded action stations yet?" then he used the bad language and went below.

Q138 Did the Officer of the Watch do anything further, apart from crouch, between the explosions and leaping over the side? Did he give any orders?

A138 No Sir.

Q139 How long would you estimate the time between the two explosions and the time Lieutenant Savage went over the side?

A139 About 50 seconds, something like that Sir.

Q140 How long do you estimate it was before you went over, say between the first explosion and the time you left the ship?

A140 About 45 or 50 seconds Sir. As soon as I got into the water I turned round and looked and the ship had turned right over and was going down at the stern.

Q141 Were you wearing a life belt at the time?

A141 Yes Sir, but I didn't have time to blow it up.

Q142 Had you got a rope end secured round you?

A142 No Sir, they were not very strict about us carrying those.

Q143 Did you succeed in time in getting your left belt blown up?

A143 No Sir, when I felt for it in the water it was broken. My hands were numb anyway, and I couldn't feel it in any case.

Q144 What did you swim to when you got into the water?

A144 It looked like a butcher's block Sir.

Q145 Did you stay there all the time until you were picked up?

A145 I got on a big plank, there were two of us Sir.

Q146 Did you see many other people in the water at that time?

A146 I should think about 80 or something Sir.

Q147 On the port side only?

A147 Yes Sir.

Q148 Did you notice any under water explosions?

A148 Yes Sir, but I don't know if they were from us or from the *Keppel.*

Q149 Was any part of the ship still floating when the explosions occurred?

A149 There might have been about 12 foot of the bows; the stern had completely gone Sir.

Q150 Have you any idea what the course and speed of the ship was at 0640?

A150 I couldn't tell you the course Sir, but we were doing about 4 knots I should think. We had slowed down to get in the foxers.

Q151 Do you know what speed you had been doing previously?

A151 I cannot say Sir, I have no idea.

Q152 Did you at any time sight anything that resembled a U-Boat?

A152 No Sir.

Q153 Can you remember what revolutions were ordered when you reduced speed?

A153 I could not tell you what revolutions they were Sir, but I remember looking on the board and it averaged 4 knots.

Q154 Are you sure about that?

A154 Certain Sir.

Q155 Did you see anything resembling torpedo tracks?

A155 No Sir.

Q156 You spoke of this debris and the depth charge racks; can you amplify that at all as to what you saw?

A156 Well it was all spars of wood and stuff that you could see.

Q157 You could see separate depth charges coming into the air?

A157 Yes Sir.

Q158 Did any of the depth charge throwers come adrift?

A158 Yes Sir, they just blew up. They all blew to bits and several splinters of the rack came on the bridge.

Examination of Witness terminated Witness withdrew

ABLE SEAMAN FRANK WEBB Off No: D/JX 418096

Witness Called and Cautioned

Q159 Are you Able Seaman Frank Webb, Off No: DJ/X 418096?

A159 Yes Sir.

Q160 Were you serving in HMS *Kite* on the 21st August 1944.

A160 Yes Sir.

Q161 Will you tell the Board all you know of what happened that morning?

A161 I had the morning watch Sir, B Guns crew doing the lookout on the starboard Oerlikon. Next thing I knew there was an explosion and we had taken a list to starboard. I just took my duffle coat off and went over the side Sir.

Q162 Which side did you go over?

A162 The starboard side, Sir.

Q163 Was there one explosion or more?

A163 Two explosions sir.

Q164 As lookout, did you observe any torpedo tracks?

A164 No Sir.

Q165 Did you at any time then or afterwards observe what might have been a U-Boat?

A165 No Sir

Q166 Had you got your life belt on?

A166 Fully inflated Sir.

Q167 Had you a ropes end on?

A167 I had it round my duffle coat Sir, but before going over I took it all off.

Q168 Did the life belt keep you afloat?

A168 Yes Sir, I couldn't have done without it.

Q169 Did you subsequently, in the water, get on to anything?

A169 I floated to a plank of wood Sir.

Q170 Was there much fuel oil where you were?

A170 Yes Sir, a lot. And the First Lieutenant jumped over the side with me Sir. I don't know whether he put his life belt on, but I saw him swim away from the ship's side and that is the last I saw of him.

Q171 What were the Ship's Orders, so far as you know, about the wearing of life belts?

A171 Very strict Sir. You had to have them half inflated when you fell in in the morning Sir.

Q172 Did you have to wear hem while you were alseep?

A172 There was nothing compulsory about that Sir.

Q173 How were you picked up by HMS *Keppel*?

A173 I don't remember being picked up at all Sir. I woke up in sick bay on the *Keppel* Sir and that is all I remember.

Q174 Did you notice any explosions after you got into the water?

A174 Yes Sir, three or four. I thought it was depth charges going off myself, but I don't know.

Q175 Have you any exact idea as to where the explosions occurred?

A175 No Sir.

Q176 You did not hear any orders given?

A176 I saw the Captain come out on the upper deck Sir and heard him use foul language, then he went back again.

Q177 That was outside his sea cabin?

A177 Yes Sir.

Q178 So the officers you saw were the First Lieutenant and the Captain and that was all?

A178 Yes Sir. Except Sub Lieutenant Strubers in the water. He was Second Officer of the Watch.

Q179 Where did the First Lieutenant normally sleep at sea?

A179 In his cabin Sir as far as I know, but I had seen him on the upper deck between 6 and 6.30. He may have been on the bridge, I am not sure.

Q180 What was he doing at the time you both went over the side?

A180 Just standing there Sir. I jumped in first and then he jumped in and got hold of me.

Q181 In fact you were supported in the water the whole time by your life belt?

A181 Yes Sir.

Q182 Did you hear either the First Lieutenant or the Captain give any orders at all?

A182 No Sir, I only heard the Captain shout some foul language and that was all I heard him say.

Examination of Witness terminated Witness withdrew

LIEUTENANT JOHN ARTHUR DOUGLAS ROYAL NAVY FIRST LIEUTENANT HMS *KEPPEL*

Witness Called and Cautioned

Q183 Are you Lieutenant John Arthur Douglas, Royal Navy, of HMS *Keppel*?

A183 Yes Sir.

Q184 Were you serving in HMS *Keppel* on 21st August 1944.

A184 Yes Sir.

Q185 Will you tell the Board all you know of the loss of HMS *Kite*?

A185 I was on the morning watch that day, HMS *Kite*, when I came on watch, was 45 degrees on the starboard bow, as far as I can remember about 5000 yards. We both had our displacers streamed, ours was tripped, and hers were not, they were in the rattling position. At about 5 o'clock I asked the Captain whether we could ask *Kite* to trip her PNM's because it was making a hell of a noise in our Asdics as we zig-zagged, and it seemed as if we could not pick anything up at all. He asked what our Asdics were like and I said "Poor", so we asked HMS *Kite* to trip her PNM's. That must have been about 5 o'clock as far as I can remember. HMS *Kite* reduced speed and dropped back on us; I think convoy speed at the time was about 6 1/2 knots. I gathered she had some difficulty with her PNM's, because she told us she was reducing speed. About 6.30 - I am not sure what the exact time was, but I think it must have been about 6.30, I was on the port side of the bridge. We have a sort of raised platform on the starboard side and I was standing on the lower portion when I heard two bangs and I picked up my glasses and looked at the convoy. I could not see anything, so I turned and look at *Kite* and all I could see then was her bow and everything else was obscured by the explosions. I could not see most of her hull at all. The Captain came on the bridge and I rang the alarm bells and we went hard to starboard and came down to 7 knots. Soon afterwards one of the lookouts reported an object in the water near HMS *Kite* and we all looked from the bridge, but we did not see anything. I got hold of the lookout afterwards and he said he thought it was a conning tower, but no one saw anything of it from the bridge. Anyway we swept over the area until the other ships came up. I think the submarine may possibly have gone under the wreck, anyway we did not pick it out. I should say HMS *Kite* sank within a minute, because by the time the Captain came on the bridge, which was within 10 seconds of my ringing the bell, she was already going and we did not see her at all. She seemed to go down in a matter of seconds. This is all I know about the actual torpedoing Sir.

Q186 What speed were you doing at the time?

A186 As far as I remember 9, 9 1/2 and 10 knots according to how we were maintaining station.

Q187 What form of zig zag were you doing?

A187 An independent zig zag Sir, 30 or 40 degrees either side.

Q188 Continuous weaving?

A188 We usually altered about every 10 minutes. There was no indication at all on our Asdics, no indication of torpedoes or anything.

Q189 Was it your impression on board that there were definitely U-Boats in the are?

A189 Yes, in the vicinity, but not in the immediate vicinity Sir, not within 30 miles anyway, which I believe was the HF/DF bearing.

Q190 Did you drop any charges after the torpedoing?

A190 No Sir, we set one, and then put it back to safe again. We did not drop any charges at all until later on.

Q191 Did you trip the PNM's as soon as you increased speed?

A191 No Sir

Q192 Did you start them rattling when you increased speed?

A192 No Sir we did not use them at al because they were not working particularly well. We had got them in the previous day, and as the Captain did not think U-Boats were in the immediate vicinity, he got displacers out. HMS *Kite* had difficulty with hers, but she eventually got them going. We could not get ours going at all. We eventually left them out altogether thinking they would work later on after they had been running for a while. It was not until we got our other displacers out that we got them to work at all.

Q193 As far as you knew yourself, what were the Asdic conditions like that morning?

A193 As far as I know, average for those waters. They were generally bad throughout the trip and it is a rather difficult question really to assess them; comparing them with the Atlantic or somewhere like that, they were bad.

Q194 Was there any temperature gradient at the time? Did you hear any standard echo?

A194 Yes I believe they had one at 500 yards.

Q195 Did you hear any unexplained explosions subsequent to HMS *Kite* being torpedoed?

A195 Yes I heard about 2 minor ones, which I assume came from HMS *Kite* breaking up.

Q196 Did they appear to HMS *Keppel* to be like depth charges going off?

A196 Yes.

Q197 When you came to pick up survivors, how many were floating in the water at that time?

A197 My estimate was 30, but I must say that differs from other people's in the ship.

Q198 Are others more or less?

A198 The Captain said less, about 20.

Q199 Did you have much difficulty in getting them out of the water?

A199 Yes. Great difficulty. The oil was particularly thick. We lowered the whaler, which was the best way of getting them in, and then the boats crew found great difficulty in getting them in, it was so slippery.

Q200 Would it have helped if they had been wearing ropes ends round themselves?

A200 Yes Sir, it would have helped very much indeed. I feel very strongly on this point Sir and have made a report on it.

Q201 Were all the survivors picked up wearing identity discs?

A201 No they were not; only with one or two exceptions.

Examination of Witness terminated Witness withdrew

SUB LIEUTENANT RAYMOND WILLIAM HALL, ROYAL NAVY VOLUNTEER
RESERVE - HMS *KEPPEL*

Witness Called and Cautioned

Q202 Are you Sub Lieutenant Raymond William Hall RNVR?

A202 Yes Sir

Q203 Were you serving in HMS *Keppel* on the 21st August 1944?

A203 Yes Sir

Q204 Will you tell the Board all you know about the loss of HMS *Kite*?

A204 I was Second Officer of the Watch and keeping a lookout all round. We
were not looking in the direction of HMS *Kite* at the time, but heard an
explosion and looked round and saw HMS *Kite* enveloped in smoke. That
is all I know about it really, Sir, because then I went down to the plot to
my action station.

Q205 What were the Asdic conditions reported to be like that morning?

A205 Rather poor Sir, we could not hear very much, most of the time, because
of HMS Kites foxers.

Q206 Were HMS *Kite*'s foxers rattling immediately before the explosion or not?

A206 We could hear them Sir, we had a signal about a quarter of an hour before
that she was reducing to 6 knots to recover her displacers.

Q207 You did not personally see anything that resembled a U-Boat?

A207 No Sir

Q208 Did you stay on the plot until you started the rescue operations?

A208 I stayed during the rescue operations as well, Sir.

Q209 Did you notice any explosion subsequent to HMS kite being torpedoed?

A209 There was an explosion Sir, about 2 or 3 minutes afterwards. It sounded
much deeper than the others; under water explosion rather than torpedo
explosion.

Q210 Only one?

A210 Well, I could not be sure about that Sir.

Examination of Witness terminated Witness withdrew

PETTY OFFICER JOHN RICHARD LEWIS PAYNE D/JX 154993

Recalled

Q211 Have you any idea what time you reduced to 6 knots?

A211 As far as I can remember, about half an hour before the explosion Sir.

Q212 Did you see much debris flying after the explosion?

A212 Yes Sir, a lot of debris went up but I could not distinguish what it was.

Q213 You did not see any depth charge equipment flying in the air?

Q214 No Sir.

Examination of Witness terminated Witness withdrew

The main purpose of the board of Inquiry seems to me, a landlubber and ex Army, that they wanted to ascertain why more sailors had not been rescued than the 14 and why were the majority of the sailors not wearing what was apparently standing order issue in the event of such an event. Whether or not they were even interested in finding out how incompetent the temporary Captain appeared to be I do not suppose I will ever know. What did he do when he retired back to his bunk, a holder of a DSC? The officers on board did little to help in the brief time they had and Lieutenant Savage, on the bridge, seemed totally "out of it" and completely lost according to Reg Holmes testimony. It was quite literally "every man for himself" from the first seconds of the torpedo hits. *Kite* being only a sloop, one torpedo would have put her down almost immediately. The firing of two can only be a "safety" feature by the U-Boat Captain, in case the first missed. Only hours before, *Keppel* and *Kite* had detected a U-Boat, gave chase, and launched depth charges - so why does the Board's witnesses from the *Keppel* say, "not in a radius of 30 miles did we expect any U-Boats" (Q192). Did these Officers really expect to have chased off what was probably U344 as easily as that! Why scale down to cruising watch on CONVOY ESCORT in a minefield of U-Boats and possible contacts that could have found them? This is the Arctic, U-Boat infested, wartime waters we are talking about here, not a lake in some suburban park! The region was notorious for U-Boat and aircraft interceptions! I certainly would not go to "cruise watch" there, especially not after having been "in contact". I also feel that *Keppel* was somewhat economical about the truth in one or two aspects. A witness mentions earlier on that they "sucked survivors under" with the turn of the screws. I am not a sailor, but having spent 17 years in the Army, I do feel that I know the "officer" mentality; but my reaction to all this is that nobody seemed to either know what they were doing nor, in the cases of some, actually cared. 217 men here lost their lives, many thousands more have lost their lives in convoys across the Atlantic and in the northern seas en route to Russia - but to lose your life to gross incompetence is actually murder, gross stupidity and should not have been overlooked by the Navy.

The board then sent out its findings:

REPORT ON THE TORPEDOING OF HMS KITE - HMS *KEPPEL*

11th September 1944. At 0640N on 21st August 1944 HMS kite was hit on the starboard side by two torpedoes. Survivors state that the ship heeled over to starboard at once and that the stern was cut off and floated clear for a few seconds before sinking. The bow floated for about a minute then sank at a steep angle. "*Kite*" was proceeding at about 6 knots, course 050 degrees at the time of the explosion. She was clearing her foxers displacers, which had become twisted round one another. Two survivors state that they sighted a conning tower off the starboard bow at close range soon after the explosions. This was not seen from *Keppel's* bridge, but one lookout reported an object in the water near *Kite*. It is thought that the U-Boat may have surfaced for a few seconds on firing and dived again at once. *Keppel* closed the wreck at once and then carried out a search, but no contact was obtained.

At 0736, with *Mermaid* and *Peacock* carrying out observant, *Keppel* stopped to pick up survivors. The oil in the water was particularly thick and difficulty was experienced in getting survivors inboard quickly. Grapnels were most useful for hoisting men inboard, but several men had little clothing on and some were without life belts. Men wearing jacket type capok life belts and cork life belts were easier to deal with. In all cases the men in the water were unable to help themselves at all. Extra moveable scrambling nets would have enabled more to be saved. There were about 30 men in the water when rescue work started but this number diminished rapidly, due to the thick oil, and it is believed, to lack of life belts. 14 men were rescued, of which 5 died within a few minutes.

The following ratings are survivors:

CT Bonsall AB D/JX 419597

A Sharples AB D/JX 563041

JR Payne PO D/JX 154993

D Brannigan L/Sea D/SSX 23262

EC Bradley L/Sea D/JX 136903

GH Johnson AB D/JX 368812

L Irish AB D/JX 351286

R Holmes AB D/JX 369266

F Webb AB D/JX 418096

The following died on board and were buried at sea:

T. Holden AB D/JX 569255

JF Savage Lieutenant RNR

N Regan

A Williscroft Acting/AB

2 unidentified ratings

Position: (D/R) 73 01 N 03 57 E

Wind: W by N Force 3

Sea and Swell: 22

A/S Conditions: Fair

James Tyson - Commander RNR

SECRET

OFFICE OF FLAG OFFICER IN CHARGE GREENOCK

13th SEPTEMBER 1944

Greenock 2010 (4 lines) Communications to be addressed to:

The Flag Officer in Charge No 0163/9716 Commander in Chief Western Approaches (copies to: Vice Admiral Commanding 10th Cruiser Squadron. Captains (D) Greenock

LOSS OF HMS KITE - BOARD OF ENQUIRY

The attached Minutes and Findings of a board of Enquiry held to investigate the loss of HMS *Kite* are forwarded in accordance with Commander in Chief Approaches' message T.O.O. 071155B/9.

2. With reference to Flag Officer in Charge, Greenock's message T.O.O. 131248B/9, the following are the remarks on the findings by Captain (D), Greenock:

Paragraph 17 (5) of the Findings of the Board of Inquiry is not concurred in. The reduction in speed to 6 knots was contrary to paragraphs 9 and 13 of Western Approaches General Order No 73, and the maintaining of a steady course for 30 minutes does not appear to have been justified by the difficulty of recovering the Foxer equipment, who could have been slipped.

With reference to paragraph 18(b), of the Findings, experience up to date has shown that the provision of a third set of Foxer gear is not necessary.

The remainder of the findings are otherwise concurred in

R HILL

REAR ADMIRAL

LOSS OF HMS KITE - BOARD OF INQUIRY (Flag Officer in Charge, Greenock's No. 0163/9716 dated 13th September 1944)

II

THE SECRETARY OF THE ADMIRALTY

Forwarded for the information of Their Lordships, concurring in the Findings of the Board as amended by the remarks of the Flag Officer in Charge, Greenock.

2. This ship was torpedoed by a U-Boat whilst steaming at 6 knots on a steady course. She had reduced to 6 knots forty minutes earlier to facilitate the tripping of the PNM Units, the recovery wire of one which was foul of the displacer towing wire. There appears to have been no adequate reason for the reduction to this low speed nor for the cessation of the zig-zag.

3. All the regrettable omissions in the ships life saving organisation pointed out by the Board are fully covered in AFO 3111/44. The attention of all Commanding Officers will again be drawn to the instructions in this order and Senior Officers directed to pay particular attention to this aspect of a "ship's organisation during inspections at sea".

SECRET

DIRECTOR OF TORPEDOES AND MINING

November 1944

Sir, We have the honour to report that in accordance with instructions a Board of Inquiry consisting of the undersigned met at 1Q00 hours to-day, 9th September, 1944, at Navy House, Clarence Street, Greenock, to investigate the circumstances attending the loss of H.M.S. KITE. We have considered the evidence given by the several witnesses and our opinion of the occurrence is as follows:-

2.   At 2230 on the 20th August, 1944, H.M.S. *KEPPEL* and H.M.S. KITE were ordered by Vice Admiral Commanding 10th Cruiser Squadron in H.M.S. VINDEX to take station in the Starboard Quarter Sector in diagram No.2. Between 2340 20th August and 0121 21st August they investigated a depth charged suspicious contact, but there was no result. H.M.S. KITE was stationed 5,000 yards on the starboard bow of H.M.S. *KEPPEL*.

3. Displacers were streamed in both ships; in the case of H.M.S. KITE "A' type were in use. H.M.S. *KEPPEL* had PNM's tripped whilst those in H.M.S. KITE were in the rattling position.

4. About 0500/21st August H.M.S. *KEPPEL* requested H.M.S. KITE to trip PNM's which were causing interference with the Asdics.

5. At some time about 0600 H.M.S. KITE reduced to 6 knots to clear port PNM unit, the towing wire of which was wound round the displacer towing wire. During this time starboard PNM unit was still in the rattling position.

6. From H.F.D.F. bearings, U-boats were known to be in the vicinity, but were not thought to be in the immediate vicinity. H.M.S. KITE had one cruising watch closed up.

7. Wind was West by North, Force 3; weather, overcast; visibility, 7' sea and swell, 22; course and speed, 050, 6 knots; Asdic conditions fair to poor. Temp Air 39 F, Sea 45 F.

8. About 0640 in position 73 01' N 03 57' E, H.M.S. KITE was struck on the starboard side by two torpedoes; there was an interval of a few seconds between each one hitting. The first struck in the region of the break of the boat deck, and the second further aft in the vicinity of the depth charge throwers. The ship broke in two, and the fore part listed heavily to starboard whilst the stern floated away.

9. From the evidence of Able Seaman Reginald Holmes, no Asdic warning of any sort was received on the Bridge prior to the explosions.

10. The actual time the ship floated cannot be accurately assessed, but it was undoubtedly only for a very short period, probably not much in excess of one to two minutes. One result of these explosions was that depth charges and throwers were hurled into the water, amongst other debris.

11. No orders were given to abandon ship, but those Officers and ratings who could get up on deck took to the water almost at once. A Petty Officer and some ratings did actually attempt to lower the port whaler, but this quickly proved impracticable. However, a certain amount of life-saving equipment, such as a Carley raft, Flotanets, timber and a life buoy floated off onto the water.

12. Shortly after abandoning ship there were four to five under-water explosions, of no great violence.

13. Leading Seaman Bradley and Able Seaman Johnson both state that after taking to the water they saw a U-boat conning tower break surface for a very short period, about 150 to 200 yards on the starboard bow of the fore portion of H.M.S. KITE. This was not corroborated by any other survivors, though H.M.S. *KEPPEL*'s look-out, at about this time, reported an object in the vicinity of H.M.S. KITE which he thought was the conning tower of a U-boat. This was not seen by anyone else in H.M.S. *KEPPELL*.

14. From all the available evidence, it seems that about 70 to 80 of the Ship's Company got out of the ship and into the water. After the explosion the following Officers were seen :

(a) The Captain, Lieutenant Commander A. N.G. Campbell, R. N He appeared on the Bridge for a short period but was not afterwards seen in the water.

(b) The First Lieutenant, Lieutenant J. A. JONES, R.N. who was seen to get into the water.

(c) Sub. Lieutenant J. C. Struthers, R.N.V.R., who was seen in the water,

(d) Lieutenant J. F. Savage, R.N.R., who was picked up and subsequently died onboard H.M.S. KEPPLE.

15. H.M.S. KEPPLE, on observing the explosions, closed H.M.S. KITE's position and carried out an A/S search, which, however, proved fruitless.

16. At 0736 H.M.S. *KEPPEL* stopped to pick up survivors whilst H.M.S. *MERMAID* and H.M.S. PEACOCK carried out operation observant round

her. Considerable difficulty was experienced in getting survivors out of the water owing to the large quantity of oil about and the fact that few were wearing life belts, and none had lengths of rope secured round them. When the rescue work commenced there were about 30 men in the water, but these rapidly diminished, and only 14 were picked up, of whom 5 died within a few minutes.

17.   We find that :-

(1) H.M.S. KITE was sunk by two torpedoes fired from a U-boat on the starboard side at short range.

(2) There is no evidence to show that the magazine exploded.

(3) Although the second torpedo hit in the vicinity of the Starboard propeller, it is not considered that either torpedo was a Gnat, as the ship' s speed of 6 knots was below the critical speed.

(4) Despite the poor Asdic conditions it is nevertheless considered that some warning should have been obtained from the Asdic Set. (Even though crewmen said it would not work at all - mk)

(5) The loss of H.M.S. KITE must, in some measure, be attributed to the unsatisfactory performance of the Foxer gear, which necessitated the ship steaming on a steady course at 6 knots. It is, at the same time, noted that the old type displacers were in use.

(6) The explosions heard and felt by survivors in the water subsequent to the ship breaking in two, are considered to have been caused by depth charges separated from the throwers by the force of the second torpedo explosion. These charges were set to safe, but due to being separated from the throwers the primer 'placer 'gear would have come into action and, in fact, the charges exploded at a considerable depth.

(7) No alarm was passed or orders given to abandon ship, but we do not consider that there was, in fact, time to do so.

(8) The large loss of life must be attributed to the amount of oil fuel about, the low temperature of the water, and the fact that few of the Ship's Company were wearing lifebelts. The orders regarding the wearing of lifebelts on deck seem to have been rigidly enforced, but the necessity for wearing them when below does not appear to have been fully brought home to the Ship's Company. Further, very few were wearing ropes ends secured round them.

RECOMMENDATIONS -

(a.) That once again attention be drawn to the necessity of wearing life-belts and ropes ends secured round the body at all times. This also applies to the wearing of identity discs, which were not being worn by all survivors.

(b) That additional spare Foxer Gear be allowed to ships, so that when operating in positions where the risk is above normal and the escorts are likely to be the main target, they can cut away their Foxers, when they run foul, in preference to reducing to a low speed for considerable periods in order to disentangle them.

As an example, this would apply to ships, stationed in the quarter positions when submerged attack is the main threat and escorts will be the principal target for U-boats which have failed to get in a shot at the convoy.

It is considered that one additional spare set above the present allowance would be a reasonable increase.

Signed by the officers of the Board.

Despite offers to be transfered to the cruiser *Jamaica*, the survivors stayed aboard the *Keppel* and endured more action when the *Keppel* participated in the sinking of U-394 on the homeward journey. Later, a Court of Enquiry found that the main cause of the *Kite*'s sinking was the German torpedoes! And a contributory factor was the straight line speed of only 4 knots. The findings above state that the orders given by the Captain were contrary to Standing Orders and that the Foxers should have been "slipped". Well, at least the Captain is obliquely blamed which is no consolation for the survivors, relatives of the dead, nor the dead themselves.

8 of the 9 survivors coming ashore L-R: Bonsall; Brannigan; Irish; Webb; Holmes; Johnson; Sharples; Bradley.

Just for the record, U344 did not get away with sinking the *Kite*; recorded fate of U344 is that it was sunk with all hands, at 0830 hrs 22 Aug 1944, the next day, in the Barents Sea, northeast of North Cape, in position 72.49N, 30.41E, by a Fairey Swordfish from HMS *Vindex*, piloted by Gordon Bennett. *Kite*, a Royal Navy sloop of 1,250 tons, was escorting the aircraft carriers *Vindex* and *Striker*, which in turn were escorting a large convoy to Northern Russia when the convoy was sighted by German aircraft. Soon a pack of U-boats attacked the convoy and one U-boat was sunk by Swordfish aircraft from one of the carriers. Two more were sunk by other destroyers.

Ray Holden's Story

I was a boy of thirteen when HMS *Kite* was sunk and I still remember how devastated I was to have lost Tom. The world might just have well come to an end. However I hid my emotions and kept them well inside until some weeks later I read the lesson for the day in the school assembly hall. I can still remember that lesson, "Give unto Caesar that which belongeth to Caesar". Something was telling me that I had to give Tom up, it wasn't any use hoping that he was going to come back and in the corridor, on my way to the classroom, all those emotions deep inside were let loose, the tears fell like rain.

In the very dark days of the Battle of the Atlantic, Tom was on leave for two or three days, he brought home with him a mate who had missed his connection to Crewe and he stayed with us overnight. His name for some reason or other was burnt into my brain. Reg Holmes, from Stoke on Trent. How I yearned to find him to find out what had happened to Tom. Reg was one of the nine men to survive, but, as a boy, I had no idea of even where to start. In early 1950, I joined the Royal Navy at the tender age of 17, hoping that my service would lead to someone who could tell me what had happened to HMS *Kite* and my brother. I spent 8 years in the service but didn't find out a thing.

And so I returned to Civvy Street, to my wife and young family, but HMS *Kite* would not go away. I felt that Tom would not rest until we knew where he was. After writing to a local newspaper in Stoke, without any success, I turned my attention to my family's history, this really was rewarding. I found centuries of farmers and landowners and a famous Barrister and a Politician. My father had worked all his life to support his family and didn't have a penny. On the 21st August 1993, the 49th anniversary of the sinking of HMS *Kite*, my wife called me to the phone. A lady was enquiring about the family. This I thought, was one of the researchers I had been using. Instead I was given the third degree! Did I live in Cherry Orchard when I was a boy? Did I have a brother who lost his life on HMS

Kite? I was able to answer a positive yes and then she told me that her husband wanted to speak to me. Straight away I told her I knew who that person was, Reg Holmes, and so it was. Reg spoke to me through his tears, telling me he hadn't lost a mate - he had lost even more. Tom had been like a brother to him.

Reg came to see me the following morning and what a meeting that was! Through Reg I was introduced to Clem Bray who was running a small HMS *Kite* Association. This man, although he served only a few months on HMS *Kite*, has done so much to keep their memories alive, he deserves a medal as big as a bloody dustbin lid! It was he who organised a 45th Remembrance Service at Liverpool's Anglican Cathedral, attended by veterans of the 2nd Escort Group and also the Swordfish pilot who sank U344, Gordon Bennett.

He also produced another Clem Bray classic - a 50th Remembrance Service at Gloucester Cathedral. It was here that I met Lionel Irish. He took me to one side and told me something he had not spoken about before. Tom, a great mate of his, had died alongside him on board HMS *Keppel*. At last ghosts could be put to rest, but I fear that the full story will never be told because crew members of HMS *Keppel* who I have spoken to do not recall any burials. The 5 men who died on board that destroyer were probably put over the side, which is what I would expect when a ship is still actively hunting U-Boats; their departed comrades would not have wanted them to risk their own lives. And yet the Admiralty insist that these men are missing, presumed dead. The log book of HMS *Keppel* would have recorded the deaths as would the Medical Officers Journal.

In 1994, at the slipway in the dockyard at Plymouth, Clem came up with another, last classic. A presentation in front of the veterans of Walkers Group, a ships crest of HMS *Kite*, presented to the Church at HMS Drake, in safe keeping and in remembrance of the 217 Johnnie Walker Pirates who died with HMS *Kite*. I formed part of the escort party with Lionel Irish. Reg could not attend because his wife was very ill. Shortly afterwards, Reg lost his beloved Betty, the angel who brought us together. The names of the men of HMS *Kite* need to be written in the sky for all to see, these were the real heroes of the Group, those who gave their lives.

My thanks in this chapter go to: Ray Holden – for introducing me to *Kite* Christine Chaplin – for the Signals, Board of Inquiry & Reports Rob and Steve Webb – Encouragement and gratitude Lionel Irish – for introducing me to Pussers, if nothing else! Braintree Council & Museum – *Kite* Memorial Capt Pat Walker RN (Retd) for his encouragement Tom Holden RIP – for having a brother who wanted to find out! Gordon Bennett - RIP Kathleen Irish – for tolerance! Alan McMillan – in Dublin's fair city Sue, my wife – a computer widow! Tony Green - HMS *Mermaid* Harry Busby – HMS *Keppel* Joe Bennett – HMS *Keppel*

Oil painting of HMS Kite signalling 'General Chase'
by Bryan Phillips of St Ives, Cornwall; commissioned by Ray Holden.
Prints no longer available (sold out).

HMS Kite.

The few HMS Kite survivors.

10. The USS *Indianapolis*

At 0014hrs on 30 July 1945 the USS *Indianapolis* was torpedoed by a Japanese submarine in the Philippine Sea. She sank in only 12 minutes. Of the 1,196 men on board approximately 300 went down with the ship. The remainder, about 900 men, were left floating in shark-infested waters with no lifeboats and most with no food or water. The ship was never missed, and by the time the survivors were spotted by accident four days later only 316 men were still alive. The ship's captain, the late Charles Butler McVay, survived and was subjected to a court-martial and convicted of "hazarding his ship by failing to zigzag" despite overwhelming evidence that the Navy itself had placed the ship in harm's way, despite testimony from the Japanese submarine commander that zigzagging would have made no difference, and despite that fact that although 700 navy ships were lost in combat in WWII Captain McVay was the only captain to be treated thus. Recently declassified material adds to the evidence that Captain McVay was a scapegoat for the mistakes of others.

In October of 2000, following years of effort by the survivors and their supporters, legislation was passed in Washington and signed by President Clinton expressing the sense of Congress, among other things, that Captain McVay's record should now reflect that he is exonerated for the loss of the *Indianapolis* and for the death of her crew who were lost. In July 2001 The Navy Department announced that Captain McVay's record has been amended to exonerate him for the loss of the *Indianapolis* and the lives of those who perished as a result of her sinking. The action was taken by the American Secretary of the Navy, Gordon England, who was persuaded to do so by Senator Bob Smith, a strong advocate of Captain McVay's innocence. The survivors are deeply grateful to Secretary England and Senator Smith and also to young Hunter Scott of Pensacola, Florida, without whom the injustice to Captain McVay would never have been brought to the attention of the media and Congress.

This action, however, does not remove the conviction from Captain McVay's record, nor would a presidential pardon. A pardon simply frees a person from punishment, but it does not clear the conviction nor the stain of guilt from that person's record. Thus, the survivors still seek a presidential order to expunge the conviction from Captain McVay's record and bring final justice to this story.

What Happened?

The world's first operational atomic bomb was delivered by the *Indianapolis*, (CA-35) to the island of Tinian on 26 July 1945. *Indianapolis* then reported to CINCPAC (Commander-In-Chief Pacific) Headquarters at Guam for further orders. She was directed to join the battleship USS Idaho (BB-42) at Leyte Gulf in the Philippines to prepare for the invasion of Japan. The *Indianapolis*, unescorted, departed Guam on a course of 262 degrees, making about 17 knots.

At 14 minutes past midnight on 30 July 1945, midway between Guam and Leyte Gulf, she was hit by two torpedoes out of six initiated by I-58, a Japanese submarine. The first blew away the bow, the second struck near midships on the starboard side, adjacent to a fuel tank and a powder magazine. The resulting explosion split the ship to the keel, knocking out all electric power. Within minutes she went down rapidly by the bow, rolling to starboard.

Of the 1,196 aboard, about 900 made it into the water in the twelve minutes before she sank. Few life rafts were released. Most survivors wore the standard kapok life jacket. Shark attacks began with sunrise of the first day and continued until the men were physically removed from the water almost five days later.

Shortly after 11am on the fourth day, the survivors were accidentally discovered by Lt (jg) Wilbur C. Gwinn, piloting his PV-1 Ventura bomber on a routine antisubmarine patrol. Radioing his base at Peleiu he alerted, "many men in the water". A PBY (seaplane) under the command of Lt R. Adrian Marks was dispatched to lend assistance and report. En route to the scene Marks overflew the destroyer USS Cecil Doyle (DD-368) and alerted her captain of the emergency. The captain of the Doyle, on his own authority, decided to divert to the scene.

The USS Indianapolis

Arriving hours ahead of the Doyle, Marks' crew began dropping rubber rafts and supplies. While so engaged they observed men being attacked by sharks. Disregarding standing orders not to land at sea, Marks landed and began taxiing to pick up the stragglers and lone swimmers who were at greatest risk of shark attack. On learning the men were the crew of the *Indianapolis*, he radioed the news, requesting immediate assistance. The Doyle responded she was en route.

As complete darkness fell, Marks waited for help to arrive, all the while continuing to seek out and pull nearly dead men from the water. When the plane's fuselage was full, survivors were tied to the wing with parachute cord. Marks and his crew rescued 56 men that day. The Cecil Doyle was the first vessel on the scene. Homing on Marks' PBY in total darkness, the Doyle halted to avoid killing or further injuring survivors, and began taking Marks' survivors aboard.

Disregarding the safety of his own vessel, the Doyle's captain pointed his largest searchlight into the night sky to serve as a beacon for other rescue vessels. This beacon was the first indication to most survivors that their prayers had been answered. Help had at last arrived. But of the 900 who made it into the water only 317 remained alive. After almost five days of constant shark attacks, starvation, terrible thirst, suffering from exposure and their wounds, the survivors of the *Indianapolis* were at last rescued from the sea.

The impact of this unexpected disaster sent shock waves of disbelief throughout Navy circles in the South Pacific. A public announcement of the loss of the *Indianapolis* was delayed for almost two weeks until August 15, thus ensuring that it would be overshadowed in the news on the day when the Japanese surrender was announced by President Truman.

The Navy, however, was rushing to gather the facts and to determine who was responsible for the greatest sea disaster in its history... on whom, in effect, to pin the blame. It was to prove a faulty rush to judgment.

It is important to note at the outset that vital information pertinent to determining responsibility for the loss of the *Indianapolis* was not made public until long after the subsequent court-martial and conviction of Captain McVay. US intelligence, using a top-secret operation labelled 'ULTRA' had broken the Japanese code and was aware that two Japanese submarines, including the I-58, were operating in the path of the *Indianapolis*. This information was classified and not made available either to the court-martial board or to Captain McVay's defence counsel. It did not become known until the early 1990s that, despite prior knowledge of the danger in its path, naval authorities at Guam had sent the *Indianapolis* into harm's way without any warning, refusing her captain's request for a destroyer escort and leading him to believe his route was safe.

Captain McVay's request for a destroyer escort was denied despite the fact that no capital ship lacking anti-submarine detection equipment, such as the *Indianapolis*, had made this transit across the Philippine Sea without an escort during the entire war.

Captain McVay was not told that shortly before his departure from Guam a Japanese submarine within range of his path had sunk a destroyer escort, the USS *Underhill*.

Shortly after the *Indianapolis* was sunk, naval intelligence decoded a message from the I-58 to its headquarters in Japan that it had sunk an American battleship along the route of the *Indianapolis*. The message was ignored.

Naval authorities then and now have maintained that the *Indianapolis* sank too quickly to send out a distress signal. A radioman aboard the *Indianapolis* testified at the September 1999 Senate hearing, however, that he watched the "needle jump" on the ship's transmitter, indicating that a distress signal was transmitted minutes before the ship sank, and sources at three separate locations have indicated that they were aware of a distress signal being received from the sinking ship. It is very likely that these distress signals were received but ignored as a Japanese trick to lure rescue vessels to the area.

Confusion on the part of Navy communications and a faulty directive caused the failure of the *Indianapolis* to arrive on schedule to go unnoticed, leaving as many as 900 men at the mercy of a shark-infested sea.[25]

A hastily convened closed-door court of inquiry had been convened in Guam on August 13 with the Judge Advocate (prosecutor), Captain William Hilbert, stating that they were "starting the proceedings without having available all the necessary data." Little was done to add to such data prior to the court's decision. As the first witness, Captain McVay was asked, among other things, whether he had been zigzagging the night the ship was sunk. His answer was simply, "No, sir," but apparently little weight was given to the fact that he was under orders to zigzag at his discretion. Testimony by survivors that visibility was severely limited the night of the attack, thus explaining Captain McVay's orders to cease zigzagging, was heard but never considered again (either then or at the subsequent court-martial). The Surface Operations officer at Guam who had sent the *Indianapolis* across the Philippine Sea without a destroyer escort and who was responsible for advising Captain McVay of any perils in his path testified that the danger was "practically negligible."

No one seemed to consider why his intelligence was so inadequate, and those aware of the ULTRA intelligence and who should have warned Captain McVay remained silent, very possibly con-

---

[25] The faulty directive, which required only reporting the arrival of non-combatant ships, was corrected days after the *Indianapolis* survivors were discovered to require reporting the arrival of combatant ships as well.

scious of their own culpability. The court of inquiry ultimately recommended that Captain McVay be court-martialed on two vague
charges: (1) culpable inefficiency in the performance of his duties
and (2) negligently endangering the lives of others.

Over 350 Navy warships had been lost in combat during World
War II, but none of their captains had been court-martialed. Both
Fleet Admiral Chester Nimitz and Vice Admiral Raymond Spruance
for whom the *Indianapolis* served as Fifth Fleet flagship opposed
court-martialing Captain McVay and never had an officer been
court-martialed over the objection of his superiors, much less such
prominent flag officers.

With the war ended, the scene then shifted to Washington. When
orders were given to proceed with the court-martial of Captain
McVay only days before the court-martial actually began on December 3 at Washington Navy Yard, he and his defence counsel learned
for the first time of the charges against him. The Navy finally had
decided on two charges against Captain McVay. There was no evidence to substantiate the first charge, which was failure to issue
timely orders to abandon ship. The fact that it was even lodged
against him was curious. Well before the trial began, the Navy was
aware that the torpedo attack had knocked out the ship's electrical
system and that orders to abandon ship could only be shouted by
word of mouth in the din and confusion about the sinking ship.

The second charge against Captain McVay was that he had hazarded his ship by failing to zigzag in good visibility. Here are the facts
that made this charge shamefully unjust:

1. The orders which Captain McVay received in Guam directed
   him to zigzag at his discretion.

2. No Navy directive in existence then or now requires zigzagging
   at night in limited visibility.

3. The charge against Captain McVay stated that the visibility was
   good on the night of the sinking (a fact never contested by the
   inexperienced defence counsel who was assigned to Captain
   McVay).

4. When Captain McVay issued orders to cease zigzagging shortly
   before midnight, the visibility, according to all eyewitnesses

aboard the ship, was and remained very poor up to the time of the torpedoes struck, so bad that crew members could not identify their shipmates several yards away.

5. Statements taken by survivors immediately after rescue that the visibility was severely limited were not made available as evidence at the court-martial. And only recently surfaced as the result of research into old Navy records.

6. The commander of the Japanese submarine which sank the *Indianapolis* and who testified at the court-martial said that he could have sunk the ship whether it had been zigzagging or not.

7. A decorated US submarine commander testified at the court-martial that, given the identical circumstances which faced the Japanese submarine that night, he could have sunk the *Indianapolis* whether it had been zigzagging or not.

Nevertheless the Navy court-martial found Captain Charles Butler McVay III guilty of hazarding his ship by failure to zigzag in good visibility, thus diverting attention from so many others whose negligence and misjudgements were the real cause of this tragedy, humiliating Captain McVay, and damaging his promising naval career beyond repair.

In early 2000, only months before his death at the age of 91 in Kyoto, Japan, the commander of the Japanese submarine which sank the *Indianapolis* gave an interview and, referring to Captain McVay's court-martial, said, "I had a feeling it was contrived from the beginning." A trial is most often contrived to find a scapegoat. That is the story. It remains a tarnish on the reputation of the United States Navy more than a half a century later. And it will remain a stain on the conscience of the Navy until the conviction is expunged from Captain McVay's official record.

A 1920 graduate of the US Naval Academy, Charles Butler McVay III was a career naval officer with an exemplary record whose father, Admiral Charles Butler McVay II, had once commanded the Navy's Asiatic Fleet in the early 1900s. Before taking command of the *Indianapolis* in November 1944, Captain McVay was chairman of the Joint Intelligence Committee of the combined chiefs of staff in Washington, the Allies' highest intelligence unit. Captain McVay led

the ship through the invasion of Iwo Jima, then the bombardment of
Okinawa in the spring of 1945 during which *Indianapolis* antiaircraft
guns shot down seven enemy planes before the ship was struck by a
kamikaze on March 31, inflicting heavy casualties, including 13 dead,
and penetrating the ship's hull. McVay returned the ship safely to
Mare Island in California for repairs.

On July 16, 1945, the *Indianapolis* sailed from California with a top
secret cargo to Hawaii for refuelling, then to Tanian where it
unloaded its cargo, the uranium and major components of the
atomic bomb to be dropped on Hiroshima by the Enola Gay on August 6. The *Indianapolis* was then routed to Guam enroute to Leyte in
the Philippines. It was at Guam that the seeds for the destruction of
the *Indianapolis* were laid. Hostilities in this part of the Pacific had
long since ceased. The Japanese surfaced fleet no longer existed as a
threat, and 1,000 miles to the north preparations were underway for
the invasion of the Japanese mainland. These conditions resulted in a
relaxed state of alert on the part of those who were to route the *Indianapolis* across the Philippine Sea.

Here is the evidence:

- Although naval authorities at Guam knew that on July 24, four
  days before the *Indianapolis* departed for Leyte, the destroyer escort USS Underhill had been sunk by a Japanese submarine
  within range of his path, McVay was not told.

- Although a code-breaking system called ULTRA had alerted naval intelligence that a Japanese submarine (the I-58 by name
  which ultimately sank the *Indianapolis*) was operating in his path,
  McVay was not told. (Classified as top secret until the early
  1990s, this intelligence – and the fact it was withheld from
  McVay before he sailed from Guam – was not disclosed during
  his subsequent court-martial.)

- Although no capital ship (unequipped with antisubmarine detection devices such as the *Indianapolis*) had made the transit
  between Guam and the Philippines without a destroyer escort
  throughout World War II, McVay's request for such an escort
  was denied.

- Although the routing officer at Guam was aware of the ULTRA
  intelligence report, he said a destroyer escort for the *Indianapolis*

was "not necessary" (and, unbelievably, testified at McVay's subsequent court-martial that the risk of submarine attack along the
Indianapolis's route "was very slight").

- Although McVay was told of "submarine sightings" along his
  path, none had been confirmed. Such sightings were commonplace throughout the war and were generally ignored by navy
  commanders unless confirmed.

Thus, the *Indianapolis* set sail for Leyte on July 26, 1945, sent into
harm's way with its captain unaware of dangers which shore-based
naval personnel knew were in his path. Captain McVay's orders were
to "zigzag at his discretion." Zigzagging is a naval manoeuvre used to
avoid torpedo attack, generally considered most effective once the
torpedoes have been launched. No Navy directives in force at that
time or since recommended, much less ordered zigzagging at night
in poor visibility. At about 11pm on Sunday night, July 29, the *Indianapolis* travelling alone was about halfway across the Philippine Sea.
There was heavy cloud cover with visibility severely limited. Captain
McVay gave orders to cease zigzagging and retired to his cabin. Minutes later the ship was spotted as an indistinct blur by Japanese
submarine commander Mochitura Hasimoto of the I-58. It was
coming directly toward him from the east. Shortly after midnight the
ship was struck by two torpedoes and sank in about twelve minutes.
An estimated 300 men went down with the ship, leaving almost nine
hundred men floating in the sea, including Captain McVay. Their
ordeal lasted four days without lifeboats, food or water. Some of the
men were in the water five days. McVay's ordeal was to last 23 years.

When the ship failed to arrive at Leyte on Tuesday morning, a series of blunders ensued. First, there was confusion as to which area
the *Indianapolis* was to report when it arrived. Second, there was no
directive to report the non-arrival of a combatant ship. And, third,
there was no request to retransmit a garbled message which would
have clarified the *Indianapolis*' arrival time. As a result, the surviving
crew of the *Indianapolis* was still floating in shark-infested waters until 11am on Thursday, August 2, when Lt. Wilbur C. Gwinn, the
pilot of a Ventura scout-bomber, lost the weight from his naviga-
tional antenna trailing behind the plane, a loss which was to save the

lives of 316 men. While crawling back through the fuselage of his plane to repair the thrashing antenna, Gwinn happened to glance down at the sea and noticed a long oil slick. Back in the cockpit, Gwinn dropped down to investigate, spotted men floating in the sea, and radioed for help. At 3:30 that afternoon Lt. R. Adrian Marks, flying a PBY Catalina, was the first to arrive on the scene. Horrified at the sight of sharks attacking men below him, Marks landed his flying boat in the sea, and, pulling a survivor aboard, he was the first to learn of the *Indianapolis* disaster.

Rescue

Upon their rescue by different vessels the *Indianapolis* survivors were scattered at various Pacific bases. Captain McVay was taken to Guam where he faced a board of inquiry ordered by Fleet Admiral Chester Nimitz (CINCPAC), which convened on August 13, one day before the sinking of the ship was announced to the public, simultaneously with the announcement that the Japanese had surrendered, thus insuring minimum press coverage for the story of the *Indianapolis'* loss. Conceding that they "were starting the proceedings without having available all the necessary data," the board nonetheless recommended a general court-martial for McVay. Admiral Nimitz, however, did not agree and on September 6, six weeks after the disaster, wrote to the Navy's Judge Advocate General opposing a court-martial and stating that, at worst, McVay was guilty of an error in judgment, but not gross negligence. Nimitz recommended a letter of reprimand, which constituted a slap on the wrist but was far from being a career-ending punishment. In a CINCPAC report, Nimitz pointed out that the rule requiring zigzagging would not have applied in any event, since McVay's orders gave him discretion on that matter and thus took precedence over all other orders (a point which, unbelievably, was never made by McVay's defence counsel during the subsequent court-martial).

Overriding the opposition of both Nimitz and Admiral Raymond Spruance (for whom the *Indianapolis* had served as Fifth Fleet flagship), naval authorities in Washington, specifically Secretary of the Navy James Forrestal and Admiral Ernest King, Chief of Naval Operations, directed that court-martial proceedings be held against McVay, and the trial was scheduled to begin on December 3, 1945, at the Washington Navy Yard. Captain McVay was notified but not told what specific charges would be brought against him. The reason was simple. The Navy had not yet decided what to charge him with. Four days before the trial began they did decide on two charges. One, failing to issue orders to abandon ship in a timely fashion. And, two, hazarding his vessel by failing to zigzag during good visibility.

Captain McVay was denied his first choice of defence counsel, and a Captain John P. Cady was selected for him. McVay was also denied a delay to develop his defence, and thus Cady, a line officer with no trial experience, had only four days to prepare his case. It is difficult to understand why the Navy brought the first charge against McVay. Explosions from the torpedo attacks had knocked out the ship's communications system, making it impossible to give an abandon ship order to the crew except by work of mouth which McVay had done. He was ultimately found not guilty on this count. That left the second charge of failing to zigzag. Incredibly, the Navy brought the commander of the Japanese submarine, Mochitura Hashimoto, to testify at the court-martial, which was held at the Washington Navy Yard. Hashimoto implied in pre-trial statements that zigzagging would not have saved the *Indianapolis* but was not pressed on this point during the trial itself. One prosecution witness which they wished they had never called was a veteran Navy submariner named Glynn Donaho. A four-time Navy Cross winner during the way, Donaho was asked by McVay's defence counsel whether "it would have been more or less difficult for you to attain the proper firing position" if the *Indianapolis* had been zigzagging under the conditions which existed that night. His answer was, "No, not as long as I could see the target." It was either deliberately ignored by (or passed over the heads of) the court-martial board, and it was not pursued by McVay's defence.

There was also information withheld from McVay's defence counsel. It involved the testimony of a Captain Oliver Naquin who had been in charge of the routing instructions for the *Indianapolis* from Guam to Leyte. When asked about the risk of enemy submarine activity in the ship's path, Naquin replied "it was a low order" and "the risk was very slight." Being responsible for sending the *Indianapolis* across the Philippine Sea without a destroyer escort, Naquin's response served him well. Later it was learned that Naquin was aware of the ULTRA report indicating that the I-58 was operating in McVay's path and had not told him. Perhaps the most egregious aspect of McVay's ultimate conviction for failing to zigzag, however, was in the phrasing of the charge itself. The phrase was "during good visibility." According to all accounts of the survivors, including eye-witness accounts of survivors only recently declassified and not made available to McVay's defence at the trial, the visibility that night was severely limited with heavy cloud cover. This is pertinent for two reasons. First, as stated in an earlier section, no Navy directives in force at that time suggested, much less ordered, zigzagging at night with visibility limited. Second, McVay's orders were "to zigzag at his discretion." Thus, when he stopped zigzagging, he was simply following procedures set forth by Navy directives.

It is reasonable to assume from the evidence that a decision to convict McVay was made before his court-martial began. The survivors of the *Indianapolis* are convinced that he was made a scapegoat to hide the mistakes of others, mistakes which included sending him into harm's way without warning and failing to notice when the *Indianapolis* failed to arrive on schedule, thus costing hundreds of lives unnecessarily and creating the greatest sea disaster in the history o the United States Navy. McVay was found guilty on the charge of failing to zigzag. The court sentenced him to lose 100 numbers in his temporary rank of Captain and 100 numbers in his permanent rank of Commander, thus ruining his Navy career. In 1946, at the behest of Admiral Nimitz who had become Chief of Naval Operations, Secretary Forrestal remitted McVay's sentence and restored him to duty. McVay served out his time in the New Orleans Naval District and retired in 1949 with the rank of Rear Admiral. He took his own life in 1968.

Mochitsura Hashimoto was the commander of the Japanese submarine I-58 which sank the USS *Indianapolis*. He died on October 25, 2000, at the age of 91, having spent the last years of his life as a Shinto priest in Kyoto, Japan. For reasons which will be explained, his death saddened many *Indianapolis* survivors. His path was to cross theirs again in years to come. When the decision was made in November of 1945 to court-martial Captain McVay, a decision was also made to bring Hashimoto to the trial as a witness, and a military plane was dispatched to Japan with an armed escort to bring him to Washington. Public animosity toward the Japanese was still very high, and using Hashimoto, so recently an enemy, as a witness against a decorated American officer created a storm of controversy both in the media and in the halls of Congress. Dan Kurzman interviewed Hashimoto for his 1990 book *Fatal Voyage*, however, and wrote

> *"Commander Hashimoto was amazed by the Americans. While penned up in his dormitory during the trial, he was treated more like an honoured guest than an enemy officer who had caused the deaths of so many American boys."*

His treatment by the Navy undoubtedly stemmed from the fact that he was to be one of their witnesses in the prosecution of Captain McVay. The charge against Captain McVay was that he had hazarded his ship by failing to zigzag at the time Hashimoto's torpedoes struck, and Hashimoto confounded the prosecution by stating that he would have been able to sink the *Indianapolis* whether it had been zigzagging or not, testimony which appeared to have no impact at all on the court-martial board which found McVay guilty anyway, and Hashimoto was returned to Japan.

On December 7, 1990, with the war's bitterness faded, survivors of the *Indianapolis*, including Giles McCoy, met Hashimoto in Pearl Harbor on the 49th anniversary of that attack. Speaking through a translator, Hashimoto told McCoy, "I came here to pray with you for your shipmates whose deaths I caused," to which McCoy, apprehensive about encountering the man who had caused him so much pain and sorrow but touched by Hashimoto's comment, replied, "I forgive you." Nine years later Hashimoto responded to this forgiveness by volunteering support to the survivors in their efforts to clear Captain McVay's name.

In 1999, when a Japanese journalist was interviewing the elderly Shinto priest about his life and about the sinking of the *Indianapolis*, she informed him that an effort was being made in the United States

Congress to exonerate Captain McVay. Hashimoto told her he would like to help, an offer which was relayed by e-mail to young Hunter Scott in Pensacola, Florida, who suggested that Hashimoto write a letter to Senator John Warner, chairman of the Senate Armed Services Committee, and passed on Warner's address. The text of that letter follows:

November 24, 1999
Attn: The Honourable John W. Warner
Chairman, Senate Armed Services Committee
Russell Office Building, Washington, D.C. 20510

I hear that your legislature is considering resolutions which would clear the name of the late Charles Butler McVay III, captain of the USS Indianapolis which was sunk on July 30, 1945, by torpedoes fired from the submarine which was under my command." I do not understand why Captain McVay was court-martialed. I do not understand why he was convicted on the charge of hazarding his ship by failing to zigzag because I would have been able to launch a successful torpedo attack against his ship whether it had been zigzagging or not. I have met may of your brave men who survived the sinking of the Indianapolis. I would like to join them in urging that your national legislature clear their captain's name. Our peoples have forgiven each other for that terrible war and its consequences. Perhaps it is time your peoples forgave Captain McVay for the humiliation of his unjust conviction."
Mochitsura Hashimoto
former captain of I-58 Japanese Navy at WWII
Umenomiya Taisha
30 Fukeno Kawa Machi,
Umezu Ukyo-ku,
Kyoto 615-0921, Japan

Hashimoto's letter received press attention during the effort to clear Captain McVay's name, and, as a result, it no doubt helped in getting Congress to exonerate him. For some reason, however, it was not included in the Senate Armed Services Committee report. Meanwhile, some very interesting comments by Hashimoto were revealed in an English translation of his interview with the same journalist who acted as the go-between in arranging his letter to Senator Warner. Here are some excerpts from that interview in which Hashimoto speaks about his involvement in the court-martial of Captain McVay:

"I understand English a little bit even then, so I could see at the time I testified that the translator did not tell fully what I said. I mean it was not because of the capacity of the translator. I would say the Navy side did not accept some testimony that was inconvenient to them ... I was then an officer of the beaten country, you know, and alone, how could I complain strong enough?"

When asked how he would feel to have his views known about the court-martial, here was his response:

"I would feel great. It will be pleasant. No matter what the occasion would be. Because at the time of the court-martial I had a feeling that it was contrived from the beginning [and] I wonder the outcome of that court-martial was set from the beginning."

The stigma of Captain McVay's conviction, however, has remained to this day.

Japanese submarine I-58

Credits & References

My thanks **to Ian Sharpe**, a Coventry lorry driver, for "throwing out the bait" on this project. "Why don't you put it into a book?" he said!

Ray Holden for hundreds of hours of passing information and research into HMS *Kite*; the sloop on which his brother Tom lost the battle.

Christine Chaplin for the Board of Inquiry and classified signals relating to HMS *Kite*.

Frank Allen of the HMS Hood Association for the permission to access the Assn's web site for detailed information.

MacKenzie J Gregory for permission to use information on his superb website.

Captain Patrick Walker RN, the grandson of Captain Johnnie Walker, for writing the forward.

SS Athenia references:

I got the information in this book from many sources, some more accurate than others. Some were wildly inaccurate; such as a Liverpool Museum site that states that the U-110 sank the Athenia. NOT, I might add, the one listed below. However, the main sites that I can suggest you read are:
1. http://www.greatships.net/athenia.html
2. http://uboat.net/history/athenia.html
3. http://www.naval-history.net.
The photograph of the Halifax Herald is on display in HQ Western Approaches, Rumford Street, Liverpool that has its own web site at:
4. http://www.liverpoolwarmuseum.co.uk
5. http://smmlonline.com/articles/athenia/athenia.html

6. http://www.onthenet.com.au/~biss/athenia.htm

Battle of the Atlantic references:

Convoy. The Greatest U-Boat Battle of the War by Martin Middlebrook. Cassell Books. 1976. The story of the attacks on convoys HX229, 229a and SC122.

The Internet. Many sites now exist, all good, all informative, far too many to attempt to list here.

HMS Hood References:

I had to read through, and scribble notes, bits here, bits there, from many sources, web sites and books. I lost a lot of web site addresses due to a computer crash.
The main HMS Hood Site, however, is http://hmshood.com

Bismarck references:

http://www.faasig.org/colors/bismarckattack.htm
http://www.kbismarck.com
http://www.faasig.org/colors/bismarckattack.htm - The Account of the Attacks from HMS Victorious & Ark Royal. At the time of preparing this I could not find the site again. Hopefully it is not in a cyberspacial "black hole". However, I did have pre-permission from the author.
http://battleshipbismarck.hypermart.net/friends.htm
http://www.bletchleypark.org.uk

Books:

Battleship Bismarck, A Survivors Story – Baron Burkard von Mullenheim-Rechberg
Enigma, The Battle For The Code – Hugo Sebag-Montfiorre

Scharnhorst references

The Battle of the Narrow Seas – Peter Scott

My thanks to the person, sadly unknown, who sent me the old photo of the torpedo boat

Exercise Tiger references
The Internet
Emails from relatives
The Forgotten Dead – Ken Small

U-Boats references
http://www.uboat.net
Walker RN by Terence Robertson

Wilhelm Gustloff references:
http://www.feldgrau.com/wilhelmgustloff.html
http://members.iinet.net.au/~gduncan/maritime-1b.html#maritime_disasters_1945

HMS *Kite* references:
Ray Holden – for introducing me to the *Kite*
Christine Chaplin – for the Signals, Board of Inquiry & Reports
Rob and Steve Webb – Encouragement and gratitude
Lionel Irish – for introducing me to Pussers, if for nothing else!
Kathleen Irish – for tolerance eternal!
Braintree Council & Museum – *Kite* Memorial & Museum pieces
Capt Patrick Walker RN (Retd) for his encouragement & Forward
Tom Holden RIP – for having a brother who wanted to find out!
Gordon Bennett, Fleet Air Arm – RIP – avenged the *Kite*
Chris Burgess – for the account of AB John MacKay (his grandfather) HMS *Keppel*
Alan McMillan – in Dublin's fair city
Tony Green - HMS *Mermaid*
Harry Busby – HMS *Keppel*
Joe Bennett – HMS *Keppel*

Last but not least:

There were at least a hundred web sites where, over the last 3 years I have gleaned bits of information from, some later proved inaccurate. A lot of these sites have vanished and others probably replaced some, not others. Due to a computer crash about a year ago, I lost all my references and had to attempt a rebuild from scratch. For those of you who have read thus far and would like to chase up on a particular aspect on the internet I recommend a "freebie" internet program known as Web Ferret. I use it every day to search out details. http://www.ferretsoft.com is the home site for this program; how long it remains there is in the lap of the gods as with all internet sites. Items that I read about on one site are not necessarily the same on the next. It's an information minefield. A lot of my information is backed up with eye witness accounts. Those, to my mind, give me the edge. My thanks to the senders of hundreds of emails received over a long period of time, many asking for information which I tried to provide, many thanking me for providing information they thought they would never see or find out about and one or two critical of a particular piece of information. Special thanks to those who sent me information and anecdotes and for the accounts of eye witnesses, usually their fathers, now sadly passed on. My thanks to Mark E Horan for the Swordfish attack on *Bismarck*.